Stephen F. Flehartx

Our Regiment

A History of the Illinois Infantry Volunteers

Stephen F. Flehartx

Our Regiment
A History of the Illinois Infantry Volunteers

ISBN/EAN: 9783744692168

Printed in Europe, USA, Canada, Australia, Japan

Cover: Foto ©ninafisch / pixelio.de

More available books at **www.hansebooks.com**

OUR REGIMENT.

A HISTORY

OF THE

102d ILLINOIS INFANTRY VOLUNTEERS

WITH

SKETCHES OF THE ATLANTA CAMPAIGN,
THE GEORGIA RAID, AND THE
CAMPAIGN OF THE CAROLINAS.

By S. F. FLEHARTY.

BREWSTER & HANSCOM, PRINTERS,
184 DEARBORN STREET, CHICAGO, ILLINOIS.
1865.

DEDICATION.

OFFICERS, NON-COM. OFFICERS & PRIVATES

OF THE

102d ILLINOIS INFANTRY VOLUNTEERS,

To you, one and all, as a testimonial of enduring regard for the *Generous* and the *Brave*, this volume is respectfully dedicated.

PREFACE.

In presenting this book to the public, it is not claimed that "Our Regiment" was in any special way distinguished above more than a hundred organizations of the kind, sent into the field by our noble State.

The field of active service was one of common suffering and common danger, and all the regiments that participated in the work of suppressing the rebellion, will be honored according to their deeds, by the people whom they served.

In preparing the manuscript I have had frequent occasions to refer to the diaries of Capt. J. Y. Merritt, Lt. Byron Jordan and Sergt. T. M. Bell. Their kindness in permitting me to use them is gratefully acknowledged.

Numerous extracts have been made from productions of my own pen; published in the form of newspaper correspondence, at intervals while in the service.

For many expressions of good will, and for material aid in the enterprise of publishing the "History," the officers and soldiers of the regiment have my sincere thanks.

S. F. F.

GALESBURG, ILL., Aug. 11th, 1865.

OUR REGIMENT.

A HISTORY OF THE 102D ILLINOIS INFANTRY VOLUNTEERS.

CHAPTER I.

The "war feeling" in 1862. Call for 600,000 Volunteers. The Response. Organization of the 102d Ill. Regiment. The Camp at Knoxville—Peoria—and the ride to Jeffersonville.

During the summer of 1862—the second year of the war for the suppression of the rebellion—in response to the call for "six hundred thousand more," the question came home to the hearts of loyal men everywhere, "is it my duty to go?" and the conviction became universal that the Government would need the services of all. To hesitate then, was to connive at treason. The loyal people answered, "we will go," and catching the popular refrain:

"We are coming, Father Abraham, six hundred thousand more,
From Mississippi's winding stream, and from New England's shore.
 *   *   *   *
If you look across the hilltops that meet the Northern sky,
Long moving lines of rising dust your vision may descry,"

—they marched to fields of glory and of death.

In response to this call the 102d Ill. Reg't was organized. Political issues had been dropped. The language of the lamented Douglas was apparently verified—there were "only patriots" on the one hand, "and traitors" on the other. The "War Democracy" was developed, and our first commander, Col. Wm. McMurtry, was universally considered a proper man to organize and direct this element. He had been known as the "Old War-Horse" of the Democracy; and when he announced his intention to raise a regiment, his fellow-citizens—Democrats and Republicans—quickly rallied to his standard.

The companies of the 102d were raised in the counties of Knox, Mercer, Warren and Rock Island, during the month of August, 1862, and were brought together at Knoxville, Ill., during the last week of the same month. Companies A, F, D, I, H and B were made up almost exclusively in Knox County. Companies C, E, K, and G were organized in Mercer. In the companies of Knox County, there were a few men from Warren, and in those from Mercer, there were a number from Rock Island County.

The Regiment was composed of men who had associated together as friends and neighbors, and had labored together in the workshop and the field, during the quiet years of peace. Almost every branch of industry, and most of the leading professions were represented, the farmer, the mechanic, the tradesman, the teacher, the lawyer and the minister fell into ranks, shoulder to shoulder.

The transition from the pursuits of peace—from the quiet home life to the noisy camp of recruits was a severe trial to many of the amateur warriors. From beds of down, to beds of straw! From mahogany tables to tables of rude boards! From the light and excellent bread that "mother made," to the army substitute—"hard-tack. O, yes! those were days of trial to the raw recruit.

Days of labor, too—for the embryo officers prosecuted the work of drilling and instructing the men with the energy of those who believed the perpetuity of the Government depended upon their individual exertions. And with what supreme awe we looked upon a veteran officer —and there were several of this class in camp; perchance the heroes of one battle, and a three month's term of service. *Their* word was law. Who then would have dared to question their decision of any mooted point in tactics?

And those were days of turmoil. All were patriotic, of course; but the patriotism of many was of such a character that it led them to believe they could best serve their country in some exalted position. Hence there was much wire-pulling, and many who had expected to wear what the boys called "pumpkin rinds," were compelled to march by the side of those who were lured into the service by pure patriotism, and thirteen dollars a month, with allowances.

The wonder with us was, that amid so much contention, so many good and faithful men received commissions. There were some who afterwards proved failures. I need not mention their names here. They are fixed in the minds of the men of the regiment, indelibly.

I will not, by any personal allusions, resurrect the bitter feelings of jealousy that existed for a time at Knoxville; doubtless the experience of the 102d was the experience of all other regiments, in this respect. Suffice it to say that the extreme desire for official preferment had a very demoralizing tendency. Men of little or no capacity aspired to the highest positions in the regiment. An incident illustrating this recklessly ambitious spirit was subsequently related to me as having occurred when the regiment was at Knoxville. One of the newly promoted captains was but half satisfied with his responsible position, and learning that the Adjutancy was vacant, a bright idea struck him. Forthwith he went to wire-pulling, and approaching Lieut. ——— explained to him that he *desired to be promoted to Adjutant of the regiment*, and asked his support!

The regiment was mustered into the service on the 2d of Sept., 1862—921 strong. So at least says the morning report of that date.

The field and staff officers were: Colonel, Wm. McMurtry; Lieut. Col., F. C. Smith, Major; J. M. Mannon; Asst. Surg., Wm. Hamilton; Adjt., J. W. Pitman; Chaplain, M. K. Tullis; Quartermaster, F. H. Rugar.

The companies were commanded as follows: Co. A, Capt. R. R. Harding; Co. B, Capt. E. C. Atchison; Co. C, Capt. F, Shedd; Co. D, Capt. H. H. Wilsie; Co. E, Capt. Thomas Likely. Co. F, Capt. C. H. Jackson; Co. G, Capt. J. P. Wykoff; Co. H, Capt. L. D. Shinn; Co. I, Capt. Geo. H. King; Co. K, Capt. S. H. Rodgers.

The soldiers were soon all clothed in the army blue, and were fast becoming initiated into the mysteries of their profession. With surprising dignity they paced to and fro when on duty with the old mud-filled, broken-locked muskets in their hands! All were anxious to leave Knoxville; willing to go anywhere; willing to do anything rather than remain imprisoned there. At length the order came, and on the 22d of Sept., a bright and beautiful day, the right wing was marched on board a train of cars, and there receiving the loving adieus of dear friends,

"With hearts too full for utterance—with but a silent tear,"

they glided away from their homes and hearthstones—away to a new encampment at Peoria. The left wing was transferred to the new rendezvous, on the following day.

The camp was about two hundred yards from Peoria Lake, and was beatifully located. The scene from the bluff in the rear of the encampment was very fine. In the foreground were the regimental barracks—long, sharp-roofed board quarters, and near these, groups of cloth tents; beyond was the placid lake and away in the back ground, a dense body of timber crowning the opposite bluffs.

Our stay at Peoria was brief, but while there the regiment was drilled every day, and we participated once in a brigade drill under Col. Bryner.

Few would have regreted a longer stay at Peoria. We had but learned the first rudiments of drill and discipline, when the order came to be ready by the 29th of the month to go to Louisville, Ky.

Government needed men in the field. Bragg was overrunning Kentucky and pressing Buell back to Louisville. Our Colonel had reported the regiment ready for the field, and declared his anxiety to lead us at once "to glory or to death!"

Consequently on the 30th of October we marched to the depot of the Peoria, Burlington and Logansport R.

R., and there in the midst of a drizzling rain, which soon increased to a steady "pour," awaited the departure of the train. A "speck of war," however, delayed our departure. There were not passenger coaches enough for all. As the only alternative, freight cars were substituted. "What!" said the unlucky men who failed to obtain cushioned-seats—"make us ride in cattle cars!—we can't see it!"—and why should they? They did not enlist to be treated like animals; huddled together like so many cattle on their way to the slaughter-pen! The comparison suggested was not pleasant! Here let me anticipate somewhat by stating that long months after that time, away down beneath the burning sun of Georgia, I heard the men of the 102d make the soldiers' comment upon this little episode. Hungry, weary, footsore, one would say, "Partner would you like to ride in a cattle car?" "Yes, indeed I would, still I am able to *hoof it!*" and in perfect good humor, with spirits that nothing could dampen, they would trudge wearily on.

The difficulty at Peoria was settled by a promise from the conductor that the unlucky ones should all be transferred to express cars at some point not far distant on the road.

And then we had a glorious ride over the broad prairies east of the Illinois river. The eye grew weary scanning the wide expanse. The broad, billowy, green prairie sea. As mile after mile our train sped along, the sun sinking low in the west, lighted up the horizon with a golden lustre—not unlike what we had often dreamed of the magnificent sunsets at sea. What a moment for reflection! How like heaven, or the gateway to heaven, seemed the glowing, gorgeous West, and beneath that golden, purple and orange hued sky were our homes. Then the soldier breathed a long farewell to his "prairie-land" and turned to welcome the dark and stormy future. As the shadows of night closed around, occasional lights from quiet cottage homes caused his mind to revert to his own loved circle, now far away.

Late in the evening we crossed the State line, and early next morning reached Logansport, Ind. Thence through immense forests, anon flitting by little log huts and small "clearings,"—on through a number of beautiful villages including Lafayette and Delphi, the train dashed away to Indianapolis. We witnessed there some indications of war—rifled cannon, piles of ammunition, and a large number of paroled Federal prisoners, fresh from the lost battle-field of Mumfordsville.

On the morning of October 2d, the regiment reached Jeffersonville, opposite Louisville, Ky. Shortly after our arrival the camp was filled with rumors of fighting across the river. That night we received our guns—French muskets—and "*slept upon our arms.*"

CHAPTER II.

Crossing the Ohio. Louisville. The first march. Great privations. Arrival at Frankfort. Dissatisfaction in the Regiment. Lieut. Col. Smith assumes command. Chase after John Morgan.

At one o'clock, on the morning of October 3d, the "long roll" sounded, three day's rations were issued, and at daybreak we marched across the Ohio river, on a pontoon bridge, made of flat-boats; passed through Louisville, and halted for a time in the suburbs of the city, near Cave Hill Cemetery.

At Louisville the regiment was brigaded with the 79th Ohio and 105th Illinois regiments, under the command of Brig. Gen. W. T. Ward. Subsequently the 70th Ind. and 129th Ill. regiments were attached to the brigade, and thenceforward until the close of the war the brigade retained the same organization. Never were regiments more harmoniously associated.

Louisville was then a gloomy city. For many days the citizens had been expecting the arrival of the rebel army. Business was at a stand-still. Soldiers were pouring in from the North, monopolizing all the routes of travel. All was bustle and busy preparation, but the note of preparation was for war.

The regiment remained at Louisville but a few hours. Late in the afternoon of the 3d, the memorable "Frankfort march" commenced.

The "first march," is a time of trial with all new troops. Our first was one of peculiar trials. The day was excessively warm; so warm, indeed, that as we waited orders, every available shade was sought by the panting soldiers. When the order came to fall in, it would have amused a veteran to witness the men take their places with their huge burdens upon their backs. Almost every man carried a well-filled knapsack. Each one had been supplied with forty rounds of ammunition and three days rations. Add to this a heavy musket, and you have a load that might well strike terror to the heart of a raw recruit.

For a time the men kept their places very well, but at length they commenced dropping out, one by one, then in squads, until finally the roadside was lined with exhausted soldiers. Water was extremely scarce. Relentlessly our commanders kept on their way. Why, no one could tell; no one could detect the wisdom of a movement which if continued would precipitate a disordered column of worn out and exhausted men upon the enemy. Far into the night the march was continued. At midnight probably three-fourths of the regiment had turned in by the wayside, to rest at will until morning. A few continued on, scarcely enough to keep up the organization of the regiment. Scattered like flocks of quails, they would call to each other in the darkness, thus; "Here's the 102d." "Co. D," "Co. B." "Right this way to Co. K." The head of the column camped at length fifteen miles from Louisville. By ten o'clock the next day, a majority of the men came up, and at eleven o'clock the march was resumed. The regiment reached the vicinity of Shelbyville at a late hour that night, Oct. 4th. The camp at Shelbyville was in every respect uncomfortable; water was scarce; rations were not to be had; we had no tents; were exposed to the rays of a very warm October sun, and obliged to make our beds on the plowed surface of a yellow, Kentucky hill.

Monday evening, October 6th, the *forward trot* was resumed. We were ordered to proceed two miles east of Shelbyville and encamp for the night,—and went almost "on the double quick." There were many pretty and patriotic young ladies in the beautiful village of Shelbyville, but we could not halt to talk with the fair creatures. There is in our minds at this time a dim recollection of a panoramic scene like this: A lovely collection of houses, crowded awnings; waving flags; wavy tresses, blue eyes, pearly teeth and rosy cheeks, and that was all they would let us see of Shelbyville.

Wednesday morning, the 8th, we continued on towards Frankfort. Soon there were rumors of fighting in advance, and presently an order came to give way to the right and left, and permit a body of cavalry to pass.

There was a dense cloud of dust in the rear which increased and enveloped everything as the horsemen passed by. Late in the evening we entered a narrow defile where the dust in the road was deep, and light as flour. At that moment a battery was ordered up from the rear, and it came thundering by—the horses in a sweeping trot, raising a cloud of dust that filled the atmosphere from hill-top to hill-top and veiled the face of the rising moon. The terrible machinery of war seemed about to be let loose. At length the column filed off into a plowed field; we slept a couple of hours, were aroused by the unwelcome notes of the bugle sounding "forward," and were quickly on the road again. Continuing down the narrow pass we debouched at length near the city of Frankfort. There had been a short skirmish at the bridge across the Kentucky river, but when we came up it was all over. The rebels had attempted to burn the bridge, but our cavalry was too quick for them.

As we marched over the bridge and into the city, the moon shone brightly and all things were hushed in deep repose. There was little, save the marching columns, to indicate the existence of war. The faithful cavalry boys were resting at the roadside near the bridge. Some sleeping on their horses—some on the ground. We filed through the quiet streets, then up, up, up a hill that seemed as if it would reach the sky—found a comparatively level surface, formed in line of battle, stacked arms and slept, the sweet sleep that is seldom enjoyed save by weary soldiers.

At daylight the right wing of the regiment was ordered to a new position in support of a masked battery. It will be recollected that here, on the slope of a hill that made an angle of at least forty-five degrees with the plane of the horizon, Acting Adjutant Ogden endeavored to have battallion drill. Among other lessons he attempted "firing by file" and "by platoon." The men were quite awkward, as they had never been taught these things. Ogden became impatient, declared we ought to have understood those exercises, thought we "never would learn anything," and marched us in a short time to camp. We changed camp twice while at Frankfort. During the last week of our stay there the regiment was encamped two miles east of the city. The men were there supplied with bell tents—which were but a slight improvement upon the cedar houses they had learned to construct. In the bell tents we were crowded so closely, that comfortable sleeping was out of the question—to escape being "overlaid" was as much as could be hoped for under such circumstances.

The practice of "standing at arms" was observed, for a time, at Frankfort. This ceremony consisted in forming a line of battle an hour or two before daylight, and remaining in line until sunrise,—so at least it was ordered, but the letter of the law was not obeyed and the troops were usually dismissed at dawn of day. The design was a good one—namely, to guard against surprise. But the men were aroused at an earlier hour than was necessary;—the mornings were very cold, and coming out from their warm beds they stood shivering as with an ague. Many became sick in consequence of the exposure, and the obnoxious practice was abandoned.

The first scouting party from the regiment went out at Frankfort. It was commanded by Acting Adjutant Ogden, who manifested a commendable thirst for glory. Some miles away from camp the party captured a fine large rebel flag, at the house of an old citizen. This then was a grand achievement. The rebel flag was borne proudly into camp—the old citizen accompanying the squad as a prisoner. An officer who had remained in camp proposed "three cheers for our brave boys," and the commanding officer of the scouts in due time made a formal and dignified report of the capture. Glory was comparatively cheap then.

During our sojourn at Frankfort the celebrated Lawrenceburg march took place. While at dress parade on Saturday evening, Oct. 18th, news reached us that John Morgan had captured Lexington. Shortly afterwards a body of Federal cavalry, eight hundred strong, went dashing by from the direction of Frankfort; next came a battery, and finally a large force of infantry, in wagons—some drawn by four mules, some by six—all making the best possible time, and making an appearance that was well calculated to awaken a sense of the ludicrous.

We rolled ourselves into our blankets that night with the full expectation of hearing the "long roll" ere morning—and were not disappointed. About midnight it was sounded and in an incredibly short time we were up, dressed, equipped and on the march. Contrary to our expectations we moved in the direction of Frankfort. The movement was then inexplicable to us. We learned afterwards that Morgan having heard of the cavalry and mule-wagon-mounted-infantry movement against him, evacuated that city and set out for Lawrenceburg. Our business was to intercept him at that point—distant sixteen miles from camp. For some reason unknown to us there was an hour's halt in the road a short distance south of Frankfort. Probably it was feared that Morgan, would diverge from his course, dash in and capture Frankfort. However, the march was resumed, and as if to make up for lost time the men were kept almost on a run. Gen. Ward led the brigade, and when near Lawrenceburg, in the grey light of dawning day, he halted the column and with the usual Kentucky accent gave the command "*prepah to load*—LOAD!" The leaden balls were quickly sent home. The men were just then in a fighting mood. They would have faced Beelzebub and all his angels and would never have thought of running.

We continued on to Lawrenceburg, but the bird had flown. Morgan had passed through the town an hour and a half previous to our arrival. The pursuit was continued by other troops. We rested a few hours— some of the men sleeping—with stones for pillows— others munching hard crackers and raw pork.

The return march was made in slower time. Many of the men were completely worn down and they marched into camp at a snail's pace—literally dragging themselves along. We reached camp at 7 o'clock in the evening, having marched thirty-two miles.

If our brigade had been mounted John Morgan would doubtless have been headed-off, but the anti-cavalry theory was popular at that time, and the brilliant combination against the guerrilla chief was an entire failure.

While at Frankfort the officers of the regiment endeavored to convince Colonel McMurtry that it would be well for him to transfer the command to some other person. The Colonel refused to be convinced. There was much dissatisfaction, and not a little unwarranted murmuring. The old Colonel meant well. Beneath a rough exterior he had a kind heart, and at this distant day his men would not tarnish the honors of age by any harsh criticisms. Col. McMurtry was in poor health, and finally became seriously sick, went to the hospital for treatment and eventually to his home.

The command then devolved upon Lieut. Col. F. C. Smith, an untried man. Col. Smith very modestly assumed command; acknowledging his inexperience, but declaring his willingness to learn, and to do the best he could by the men. For a long time there was much dissatisfaction in the regiment. Many were clamorous for a commander who "had seen service."

On the evening of the 25th of October, an order came to be in readiness to march the following day—destination, Bowling Green. That night snow fell to the depth of three inches. It was a cheerless morning that dawned Oct. 26th, 1862. But there could be no postponement of the march,

The army under Rosecrans was on the move, and the work before it was to defeat and hurl back the rebel hordes that had marched so triumphantly from the Tennessee to the Ohio. At the appointed hour the regiment struck tents and marched cheerfully away to face new trials and unknown dangers.

The brigade marched twenty miles that day and camped at Salt River. The men spread their blankets on the snow and slept very uncomfortably.*

*The accompanying abridged account of the march to Bowling Green is principally taken from brief notes furnished by Lieut. D. W. Sheahan and Corp. J. E. Gilmore. Being sick at the commencement of the march, I was absent from the regiment from Oct. 26th until Nov. 4th.   S. F. F.

Passed through the romantic little town of "Dog-walk" on the 27th. The town is a miserable old dilapidated place, located in a deep hollow. Some of the men foraged quite extensively there, and among other articles secured a quantity of whisky. The column marched ten miles during the day over a very bad road, and went into camp at a place which the soldiers called Hell's Point. The camp was boisterous that evening;—the whisky obtained at "Dog-walk" had been freely imbibed, and the usual consequences followed.

The brigade moved at 8 o'clock A. M., on the 28th, and marched 17 miles, passing through Johnsonville and Chaplin Hill. Camped at Sugar Grove.

Passed through Bloomfield and Bardstown on the 29th. Marched thirteen miles, and camped one mile from the last named place.

On the 30th of October, the column marched thirteen miles, reached New Haven, and went into camp near the town. At that place the first regimental muster and pay rolls were made out.

Marched eighteen miles on the 31st, and near Hodgkinsville passed by the birth-place of Abraham Lincoln. The log building in which he first breathed the breath of life, had been torn down, re-erected and used as a stable. Camped that night near Nolen's Run, in Larue County.

On the first day of November the brigade marched twelve miles and reached Bacon Creek Station. There the sick and worn out soldiers were placed on board the cars and sent forward.

During the 2d, the column passed through Mumfordsville and crossed Green River. Marched fifteen miles and camped at Horse Cave. Many of the men visited the cave.

Marched eighteen miles on the 3d, passed within a few miles of the celebrated Mammoth Cave, and went into camp fifteen miles from Bowling Green, in a plowed field.

Passed through Bowling Green on the 4th, and camped at Lost River, three miles southwest of the city.

The march from Frankfort to the camp at Lost River, near Bowling Green, was accomplished in ten days—distance one hundred and fifty-four miles;—average march per day, a fraction over fifteen miles. During the latter part of the march the roads were dry and dusty. Great clouds of dust constantly filled the atmosphere. The soldiers were literally coated with dust, and comrades marching together could scarcely recognize each other.

Many of the men were foot-sore when they reached Lost River, but in other respects they endured the march like veterans.

The brigade remained at Lost River from the 4th until the 11th of November.

Lost River is a small stream which, apparently rising out of the ground, flows a few hundred yards and disappears in the mouth of a yawning cavern—hence its name. The stream makes no approach in size to the dignity of a river.

Being determined, notwithstanding the retiring disposition of the little river, to seek a further acquaintance, a number of us explored the underground channel.

Lighting our candles we wandered over detached rocks, far into the interior, where the solemn stillness of the place was broken only by the murmuring stream, and the sound of our own voices. The ceiling of the cavernous passage reaches in some places almost to the bed of the stream, and in other parts rises in a dome-like form, so high that the outlines were rendered but dimly visible by the aid of our imperfect lights. Our voices resounded with startling effect through the rugged aisles, and the report of a pistol was as deafening as the ordinary sound of a cannon.

While underground we were almost directly beneath the camp of our brigade. We occupied over an hour picking our way over the rocks and through the sinuous aisles, and at the end of that time were contented to live in the "upper world" again.

Col. Bryner of the 49th Ill. Regiment, visited the 102d at Bowling Green, and an effort was made to elect him Colonel of the regiment. But the election resulted in the choice of Lieut. Col. F. C. Smith for that place.

As Col. McMurtry had not yet resigned, Col. Smith could not then be commissioned, but by the action of the officers at that time the mooted question was effectually settled.

On the 9th of Nov. our division was reviewed by Maj. Gen. Rosecrans. Riding to the right of the division and then guiding his horse slowly along the front towards the left he received the salute of each regiment as he passed, and to each addressed a few well-timed words. Approaching the 105th he said: "Men of the 105th when you go into battle fire deliberately and aim low. Remember that if each one of you hits a man you will kill and cripple a great many. It is a short lesson and I hope you will remember it." Then riding on he said; "These are tall men—very tall; they must have been raised where they grow such tall corn." In passing, he paid the 102d a handsome compliment. He carefully observed the condition of the soldier's equipments, noticing the least deficiencies. "Where is your canteen," said he, addressing a soldier who had none. "Lost." "Well, tell your Captain to get you another." Gen. Rosecrans makes a fine appearance on horseback. He has a genial countenance which at once enlists the good will of the soldiers.

The camp at Lost River was so pleasant, that we received marching orders with strong feelings of regret. The weather was much of the time very fine, and during leisure hours we enjoyed rare sport rambling through the woods, gathering hickory nuts, walnuts and persimmons.

CHAPTER III.

The march to Scottsville. Brief Rest. Yankee tricks. An unsophisticated maiden. The march to Gallatin. Permanent encampment. Morgan Alarms. A gloomy period. Regimental changes. Reminiscence of Gallatin.

At an early hour, Nov. 11th, the camp at Bowling Green was abandoned, and we marched by an unfrequented road, over high hills and through deep valleys in the direction of Scottsville. The hills were in many places so steep that the wagon train moved with great difficulty. The wild appearance of the region and the anti-progressive character of the people attracted the attention of all observers. The majority of the dwellings were rude log cabins—with but one redeeming feature—the old-fashioned fire-place, which always suggests a picture of primeval happiness. Looking at those well worn hearthstones the mind of the native or pioneer western man went back to the time, long ago, when as one of a happy family circle he was accustomed to sit before a brightly blazing fire made of hickory logs. Oh! there is not in the wide world another such place to dream day dreams and build air castles!

During the first day's march we passed a school house —the best that had been seen in the journey through the State. The children came out enmasse, to look at the soldiers. A Yankee soldier was something of a novelty in that region. Butternut colored clothing was almost universally worn. Many of the whites used the genuine negro brogue in conversation.

That there should be so much difference in dress, habits and manners between Kentuckians and Illinoisans, seemed very strange. No Western man could be induced to live in that portion of Kentucky. The soil had the appearance of having been blasted by a thousand years of furnace heat.

What enterprising Yankee even, could resist the enervating influence of a Kentucky Indian Summer day—with its hazy atmosphere, and the great red sun glowing upon a forest of red and yellow leaves, and a deep red soil!

Tobacco was the staple article—cultivated by all, and used by men, women and children. The soldiers gave it the name of "Kentucky scrip," and it seemed to be the only kind of currency on which there was no discount. An incident, by the way, will illustrate how popular the weed is in that part of Kentucky:

Sergt. Gregg, of Co. C, feeling weary and very hungry, halted at a house by the roadside and asked for something to eat. "O, yes, you shall have something to eat as soon as I can bake some biscuits," said the lady of the house. George took his seat, but while patiently waiting the supper which the woman was busily preparing, his nerves received a violent shock as she turned to him with the question: "Mister will you please to let me have a chaw of tubbacker?" He gave her a plug and was astonished to see her bite off a huge piece and commence munching it with all the eagerness of a veteran chewer. Cooking supper, and at the same time spitting tobacco juice here and there, did not comport with George's idea of decency, yet he was hungry, and that was no time to entertain squeamish misgivings about what was placed on the table before him. He sat down and ate with the resolution of a soldier.

We camped at Sulphur Springs the night of the 11th: Reached Scottsville on the evening of the 12th of Nov. and went into camp on the sunny side of a long hill, near a stream of excellent water.

Scottsville is the county seat of Allen County, and at the time of our visit probably contained a hundred and fifty inhabitants. The people appeared to be generally loyal. They carried on a lively trade with the soldiers, which was not always very profitable to them. They brought in corn-meal, dried apples, dried peaches, bread, pies, etc. Money was scarce among the soldiers, and some of the more unscrupulous resorted to strategy to obtain what they wanted, and in some cases imposed most

shamefully upon the credulity of the people. One
men repeatedly deceived them in this way:—he s
a small quantity of corn, placed it in a sack, told tl
was coffee, and traded it for pies and other lux
Another removed the pole straps from a citizen's
carried the straps around to the driver and exch
them for something to eat. One-cent labels from b
of "Painkiller" were passed readily for one-dollar

Two other incidents that occurred at Scottsvill
fully illustrate the unsophisticated nature of the p

An old gentleman who was dealing in apples and
thought he was too sharp for the Yankees, and r
to receive postage stamps for his edibles. Presentl
of the boys brought out some stamps which h
taken from some old letters. Offering them to the
zen they were eagerly accepted with the remark—
yes! I'll take those; I know they are good for t
been used!"

The other case was one in which our friend Lie
H. Trego figured. The Lieutenant was purchasing
pies of an interesting young lady and, no doubt, wi
to prolong the interview, commenced a convers
with her, and in the course of the colloquy aske
distance to the Tennessee line. Noticing that she l
at him enquiringly, without immediately replying
question was repeated: "What!" said she, "To
see Line!" no such folks live around here,—I've
here all *my* time and there's nobody of that name
here *I'm shore!*" The conversation here ended.]
T. asked no more questions about the Tennessee
but struck a bee-line for his quarters.

The routine of duty at Scottsville was quite h
At five o'clock every morning the camp was arouse
the discharge of a cannon. Then followed the r
the drums, and then roll call. At eight o'clock g
mounting. In those days we had camp guards as
as pickets. Company and squad drill from ten to
past eleven o'clock. Battallion drill from half-past
until four o'clock p. m. Dress parade at four.

On the morning of the 25th of Nov. we resumed
march southward in the direction of Gallatin.
marching a few hours, and while passing through a

valley, loud cheers were borne to our ears from the head of the column. We had found the "Tennessee line."

At a late hour that evening, when expecting every moment to be halted for the night, the column commenced descending a narrow valley—down, down, down; deeper and darker, and only room enough at the bottom for the road! Where would an encampment be found? The question was soon answered. A halt was ordered. The men stacked arms. The wagon train halted in the road. A fence on the hillside near by, afforded fuel. Owing to the lateness of the hour and the inequalities of the ground we were unable to pitch our tents, and slept in Indian style by the brightly blazing camp fires.

We continued on at an early hour next morning and passed through what appeared to be the nucleus of a town. The only thing we saw there worth commenting upon, was a satirical representation of Bragg and Buell, rudely charcoaled on the door of a blacksmith shop,— one smoking a pipe, the other a cigar, and apparently chatting in a jovial, hail-fellow-well-met style. It was thought that the soldiers of both armies could appreciate the caricatures. The town or neighborhood was called Rock House Valley.

We reached Gallatin in the evening—Nov. 26th—little thinking then that we would remain there six long months. But such was to be our destiny.

Gallatin is a pleasant village of about two thousand inhabitants; has some neat residences, and the people had exhibited taste and refinement in decorating their grounds and ornamenting their buildings. The pretty groves of evergreens in which neatly painted white cottages were cosily nestled, presented a pleasant picture during those cool December days.

The weather became excessively cold a few days after our arrival. Considerable snow fell. Rude chimneys were hastily constructed in our tents, but with all his labor the soldier was only comfortable when snugly stowed away in his bed. When the weather became more moderate the Brigade commenced work on Fort Thomas. Finally the 102d was ordered to finish the fort and garrison it until further orders.

In the meantime there were many of "war's alarms." The first occurred at the time of the Hartsville disaster. The startling news came one quiet Sabbath evening that the enemy,—six thousand strong—had surprised our forces at that place; fifteen miles distant—killing and capturing the entire garrison, save a few stragglers. Their captures included part of Nicklin's Battery, and the wagon train and stores belonging to the command. Our forces were commanded by Col. Moore, and consisted of a brigade of infantry, three hundred cavalry, and a section of Nicklin's Battery. The rebel victory was complete. This was one of the minor lessons of the war which taught our officers the necessity of eternal vigilance.

The morning after the disaster we were aroused at an early hour and ordered to be in readiness to move at a moment's notice. But no move was made. The next night we were ordered to hold ourselves in readiness to meet the advancing enemy; every preparation was made for a fight; we "slept upon our arms" and were up ere the "first faint streaks of dawn" appeared in the East, but the enemy did not come. Again, on the next night, the "long roll" sounded; the men tumbled out of bed; flew to arms, and were rapidly formed in line of battle. After shivering awhile in the cold they learned that they were the victims of another false alarm.

But those days were not altogether gloomy. While in our first camp at Gallatin an installment of luxuries from home was received by several companies of the regiment. Cans of preserves, piles of cakes, green apples, dried apples, cheese and choice butter! What a princely bill of fare for soldiers! Many were the delighted recipients of warm mittens, gloves, stockings, and a host of minor articles, such as pins, needles, thread, ink, pens, writing paper and postage stamps. The lucky ones liberally shared their luxuries with those who unfortunately received none. For many days there was a heavy discount on "fat pork and hard crackers." After a bountiful meal of the good things had been dispatched it was common for the men to gather about their camp-fires, and smoke their fragrant cigars with all the gravity becoming gentlemen of leisure.

The articles were contributed by friends at home. The soldiers were much indebted to Capt. J. A. Jordan for his zeal and perseverance in taking charge of the goods, shipping them to their destination and delivering them in person to the men.

About the first of December the command of the Post at Gallatin was given to Brig. Gen. E. A. Paine. Gen. Dumont, our Division commander, had resigned, and all the troops at the Post were ordered to report to General Paine. The General made a speech to us shortly after our arrival. He referred to the anomalous position of the amateur soldier;—characterized the strict discipline necessary to the proper discharge of the soldier's duties as repulsive to the feelings of Americans, yet urged its absolute necessity, and asked us to preserve untarnished the brilliant name Illinois had already won in the annals of the war. He was followed by Gen. Ward, who is a very fluent speaker. He paid a glowing tribute to Illinois soldiers, and his speech was of course well received.

Our Brigade was ordered into winter quarters about the 10th of December. The 70th Ind. Regt. camped near the race-course, northeast of the town—a detachment from that regiment was stationed at Sandersville.

The 105th Ill's. Reg't went into camp about a half mile east of town, and the 79th Ohio Reg't camped about the same distance north.

The 102d went into winter quarters at Fort Thomas on the 12th of December. Companies I, K and G were detailed the following day as Provost Guards, and were assigned comfortable quarters in houses around the Public Square. Co. C was sent to Station Creek—three miles south of town—to guard a railroad bridge, and was there soon established in good quarters. The company had a splendid position,—the men led a free and easy life; foraging extensively and conseqently living like princes. The companies that remained at Fort Thomas constructed underground chimnies, or fire-places in their tents, and thus all were prepared for inclement weather. Thus divided, the regiment passed the gloomiest period of its term of service. Lieut. Col. Smith and Major Mannon were in poor health, and were much of the time absent. Many of the men were sick. Our numbers were rapidly diminishing on account of resignations, deaths and discharges. The effect of dividing the regiment was unfavorable to advancement in our profession as soldiers.

The military situation, East and West, was unsatisfactory, and the startling reports of disaffection in the North added to the general gloom. Although there was but little transpiring in our immediate vicinity, we could almost hear the rush and the roar of the distant storm, and the creaking timbers of the Ship of State,—buffeting the waves. Two long years had passed since the setting of the sun of peace, and as we looked back through the shadows of increasing night, the glory of those halcyon days seemed ever more enchanting. Could they ever return to us?

The battle of Murfreesboro afforded but slight relief. Within hearing of the guns we awaited the issue of the contest with intense solicitude. As the smoke cleared away it became evident that the advantages gained were secured at a terrible cost. How different the result might have been if our army had been in fighting qualities, up to the standard it reached a year later. And here the secession sympathizers and the croakers in the North might have detected some of the fruits of their work. Many of our soldiers were discouraged and did not engage in the battle with the enthusiasm which bore down all opposition at Lookout Mountain, Mission Ridge Resaca and Atlanta. Bravery was not wanting. No braver men ever breathed than those who restored the fortunes of the day and held in check the surging masses of rebels on the ever memorable 31st of December,—they wanted the prestige of success.

During the dark days of our sojourn in Gallatin, the mortality on account of disease in the different regiments was absolutely frightful. Daily, almost hourly, the sound of the muffled drum and the plaintive dirge fell upon our ears.

In addition to all this, the weather was for a long time very inclement. Cold rains were frequent, and occasionally snow fell.

The only class of people that seemed contented amid so much misery was the colored community. They enjoyed their usual festivities, cotillon parties, etc. My mind reverts to one or two sleek, sable lasses who were accustomed to dance on the pavement with every manifestation of ecstatic delight when the martial bands would play, on their return from the burial of a soldier. A funeral was evidently a treat to these miserable creatures.

At the opening of Spring the regiment had dwindled away from nine hundred and twenty-one to a small fraction over seven hundred men. But a brighter day was at hand. The regiment had passed through the ordeal of purification. Much of the useless material, rank and file, had been thrown off as an effete encumbrance.

Lieut. Col. Smith commenced the work of introducing some ideas of discipline into the minds of the men. He conducted battalion drill every day and ordered company and squad drill. Harmony was in a measure secured among the officers. A strong prejudice existed against the Colonel, but the soldiers were treated by him as friends and as fellow citizens—temporarily subservient to the military powers. He thus won their confidence and in a measure overcame their prejudice. Under his command the highest possible degree of personal liberty, consistent with the good of the service, was enjoyed by the men.

During the winter months of 1862–3 there were several of the "Morgan-alarms" which had caused so much excitement about the time of our arrival.

Most frequently these alarms were created by exaggerated stories of excited contrabands. The magnifying powers of a negro's imagination under certain conditions are wonderful. Having seen a few guerillas a short distance from town, they would come in, exhausted from running, and with distended eyes, report "*John Mawgan comin' right down dar with all his foce!*" Quickly the order to get ready for a "brush," would fly from camp to camp. With wonderful energy the Post Quartermaster would have his wagons wheeled into line and interlocked across the streets, presenting a formidable barrier to the progress of the chivalry.

So frequent were these alarms that a sarcastic Tennessee poetess referring to them was constrained to point her sarcasm in a parody on "Maryland, my Maryland," which ran thus:

> "The Yankees they get scared at night :
> Blockade the streets with all their might ;
> Would'st know the cause—old S—— is "tight."
> Gallatin! My Gallatin!

But John never came to see us. A small affair occurred up the railroad, however, which I will briefly notice.

On the 28th of April an order came to the regiment about nine o'clock A. M., directing the Colonel to have two hundred of his men supplied with two days rations, and to report with them immediately for a scout—Col. B. J. Sweet to be chief in command. The men were soon ready. We marched to the depot and took the morning train in the direction of Louisville. It was a lovely morning. Spring had come, and the birds were singing amid the foliage of the trees. Could it be that an enemy lurked in the depths of those dark green woods?

Fifty of our detachment had been left at Gallatin on account of insufficient means of transportation. Fifty more were left at Franklin—twenty-seven miles from Gallatin. Three miles north of Franklin, as we were nearing a thick wood, the whistle screamed, the train suddenly halted, and a volley of balls was thrown into and around the cars. Quick as lightning, there was a blaze of musketry from the windows of the cars. The rebels instantly ran. Our men started enmasse right after them but were checked by Col. Sweet. Skirmishers were sent out. Capt. Wilson followed them with his Co. (K,)—accompanied by Col. Smith. The pursuit was kept up for a short distance, but was ineffectual.

The rebels had displaced a rail and evidently intended to make short work with the train. They were handsomely checkmated. There were not more than twenty-five of the villains. They lost two men killed outright and several wounded and captured. Five of our regiment were wounded—two mortally. A little drummer-boy of some other regiment, who had been furloughed and was on his way home, had one of his legs shattered by a ball. This was our first "brush" with the enemy.

RESIGNATIONS AND PROMOTIONS. 31

Col. McMurtry visited the regiment during the month of March and tendered his resignation, which was accepted. Lieut. Col. Smith who had been chosen to succeed him by a vote of the officers, when the regiment was at Bowling Green, was then commissioned and mustered as Colonel. By this change, Major J. M. Mannon became Lieut. Colonel, and Capt. L. D. Shinn succeeded him as Major.

While at Gallatin, the following additional changes occurred: Dr. D. B. Rice joined the regiment as Surgeon in charge, and Dr. T. S. Stanway joined as Asst. Surgeon. Sergt. J. E. Huston, of Co. K, became Chaplain, *vice* Rev. M. K. Tullis, resigned. Sergt. Major J. H. Snyder was commissioned Adjutant; *vice* J. W. Pitman resigned. By the resignation of Capt. Harding and Lieut. Gentry, Lieut Callaghan became Captain of Co. A, and Sergt. T. H. Andrews was promoted to 1st Lieutenant.

In Co. F, by the resignation of 1st Lieut. Orlando Sullivan, 2d Lieut. G. W. Woolley became 1st Lieutenant, and 1st Sergt. Robert S. Peebles succeeded him as 2d Lieutenant.

In Co. D, by the resignation of Capt. Wilsie, 1st Lieut. H. Clay became Captain; 2d Lieut. J. B. Nixon was promoted to 1st Lieutenant, and 1st Sergt. O. B. Matteson was promoted to 2d Lieutenant.

In Co. C, by the resignation of Capt. F. Shedd, 1st Lieut. Almond Shaw became Captain, and 2d Lieut. A. H. Trego was promoted to 1st Lieutenant; 1st Sergt. Byron Jordan succeeded him as 2d Lieutenant.

1st. Lieut. Dan W. Sedwick was promoted to Captain of Co. E, *vice* Capt. Thos. Likely resigned. 2d Lieut. T. G. Brown became 1st Lieutenant, and Sergt. John Allison succeeded the latter as 2d Lieutenant.

1st Lieut. Wm. A. Wilson became Capt. of Co. K, *vice* Capt. S. H. Rodgers resigned. 2d Lieut. J. Y. Merrit was promoted to 1st Lieutenant, and Sergt. S. E. Willits succeeded the latter as 2d Lieutenant.

In Co. G, 1st Lieut. Isaac McManus was promoted to Captain—*vice* Capt. J. P. Wycoff resigned. 2d Lieut. Wm. H. Bridgford was promoted to 1st Lieutenant, and 1st Sergt. L. P. Blackburn became 2d Lieutenant. He soon resigned and Sergt. Aaron G. Henry was promoted to 2d Lieutenant.

1st Lieut. Wm. M. Armstrong became Captain of Co. B, *vice* Capt. E. C. Atchison resigned 2d Lieutenant. J. C. Beswick was promoted to 1st Lieutenant, and Sergt. Ambrose Stegall succeeded him as 2d Lieutenant.

On the 1st day of June, 1863, the regiment received marching orders. Before proceeding with an account of the forward movement I will give a

REMINISCENCE OF GALLATIN.

A Union man had been killed in Wilson Co., Tenn., under circumstances of peculiar barbarity. After killing him the bushwhackers cut out his tongue. Gen. Paine secured a number of guerillas against whom there was convincing proof of complicity in the brutal murder. One of these men was in the hands of the Provost Marshal, Major S. In company with Lieut. Trego, I called on the Major, and we requested permission to see the prisoner. The Major granted our request and accompanied us to the jail—which was an ordinary building of the kind—gloomy and forbidding in its external appearance. The guard gave way to admit us at the bidding of the Major. Passing along an alley we halted at a side door—a huge iron door—which grated dismally as it swung upon its hinges. Through the doorway we passed into a dark and dingy apartment. The darkness and dampness of the place, and the foul atmosphere reminded me of dismal dungeons that I had read of in stories of imprisonment and persecution.

The Major called for a light, and as it threw its flickering rays into the surrounding gloom we were enabled to discern a number of persons in the apartment. One of these was lying upon the ground near the wall—confined there so closely that he could only move his hands. He was lying upon his back. This was the ruffian guerrilla. Major S—— turned to the guard and said: "What do you feed this man?" The guard stated the amount and kind of rations he had been giving him. "Hereafter give him but a half cracker per day. He is not tied as tightly as he should be—tighten him down!" Then to the prisoner: "We hung two of your comrades the other day, but we can finish you in a different way—it will not take a man long to starve to death on a half cracker per day."

There was a number of black prisoners in the room; the Major turned to them and said: "I am sorry these blacks must be confined in the room with this villain—it is a burning disgrace to the 'niggers.'" [These were his words substantially—I cannot repeat them verbatim.]

The man, up to this time, had said nothing—his countenance wearing a bitter and despairing look. Turning his eyes at length towards the Major, he said:

"Major, will you allow me to say a few words to you?"

"Not a d——d word. You assisted in depriving a loyal man of his tongue, and you shall not be allowed the use of yours."

Thus the poor wretch was taunted, only with more severity than I have written.

Gladly we turned to go. The great door creaked on its hinges and closed on the doomed man, leaving him in darkness and despair. I have been informed that he was subsequently hung at Murfreesboro. Dark as his crime was, we could not approve the spirit of vindictiveness manifested in treating him with so much severity.

CHAPTER IV.

Departure from Gallatin. Arrival at Lavergne. Stewart's Creek. Railroad guarding. Pleasant soldiering. A night ride. New disposition of troops. Regimental Headquarters at Lavergne. Armed with Spencer Rifles. The Lebanon Scout. A thrilling adventure.

The brigade was transferred from Gallatin to Lavergne by railroad, on the first day of June, 1863. From that place the 102d marched on the 2d to Stewart's Creek. The regiment was there divided. Co.'s E, K and G camped near the railroad bridge across Stewart's Creek, and were under the immediate command of Lieut. Col. Mannon. Co. H, Capt. Hiram Elliott commanding, was stationed at Overall's Creek, in close proximity to the battle-ground of Murfreesboro. Co. B at Smyrna. The remaining companies were stationed about three-fourths of a mile from the railroad bridge, at Stewart's Creek, near a small fort. There Col. Smith established regimental headquarters. Thus located we remained until the 19th day of August.

The intermediate time was occupied in drilling, visiting our friends at the front—visiting the Murfreesboro battle-ground, and picking blackberries—varying the routine of exercises by an occasional scout.

Regimental and company drills were punctually observed. Lieut. Col. Mannon drilled his detachment daily, and the "left wing" under his instructions made rapid progress. The two wings (excepting Co.'s H and B) united in battallion drill each day, in an open field near the railroad.

Col. Smith by diligent application had become tactically "master of the situation" and under his direction the regiment maneuvered on battallion drill with the precision of a veteran organization.

Those battallion drills—somewhat obnoxious to us then, on account of the excessive heat—did much to prepare us for subsequent active campaigns.

Those were pleasant days in our regimental history. The citizens were generally hospitable. The young ladies of the neighborhood were pretty, and many of them accomplished. They loved to sing the "Bonny Blue Flag" and the "Home Spun Dress" to our men. In return, the singers of the regiment sometimes favored them with the "Star Spangled Banner," and the "Song of a Thousand Years" or "Rally Round the Flag, Boys."

Blackberries!—how natural the transition from pretty girls to luscious blackberries! This tempting fruit grew in unparalleled abundance in that vicinity. There were immense quantities within the picket lines, and a few miles from camp there were large fields of briars burdened with berries. Morning, noon and evening they were placed on our table, and we had stewed blackberries, blackberry pies, dumplings and blackberries with milk—the latter a substitute for cream.

Writing at that time of those pleasant days, I used the following language, which, in the light of subsequent events, has a deeper interest. I wrote of "listening to our musical Adjutant, with his guitar, singing a variety of sweet songs. Mingling with the rich notes of the instrument we heard the beautiful words:

"Weeping sad and lonely,
Hopes and fears how vain,
Yet praying—
When this cruel war is over
Praying that we meet again."

And—

"Oh! wrap the flag around me, boys,"

Or that other incomparable piece of music, commencing,

"We shall meet but we shall miss him."

And it was interesting "to observe how quickly his impromtpu concerts collected an audience in front of his quarters—the men all listening with quiet but intense interest." That sweet, sad music, echoed back through the years gone by, seems possessed of a prophetic s gnificance since the fate of the singer is now wrapped in impenetrable mystery. Of this, more anon.

Guerillas were quite bold and troublesome during the time we were at Stewart's Creek. A detachment of the 10th Ohio Cavalry, which was encamped near us, and was under the command of Col. Smith, was often sent out after the miscreants, and was occasionally reinforced by a squad of mounted men from the 102d. Often these parties would have a jolly time before returning.

On one occasion about sunset, word ran through camp that a scouting party was going out—the object being to intercept a number of rebels, who, report said were to meet at a house south of Stone River, preparatory to going south. All available horses and mules were quickly saddled, and we were soon en route for the barrens beyond the river. A number of the 10th Ohio Cavalry accompanied us. A repentant rebel who had made known the intentions of the rebels to the Colonel, was to act as guide. We rode to his house, but the guide could not be found—his lady stating that he had gone to the house of a neighbor. To the house of the neighbor we galloped. "Not there—had been there that afternoon." Thence we hurried away to Stone River, forming a long line in single file as we crossed the historic little stream. At a farm house beyond, a colored guide was procured, to pilot us to a house about two miles distant where it was thought the migratory guide could be found. "Cuffey" led off quite briskly and for miles we dashed along through the brush at a break-neck speed. At length the senseless haste of the guide was moderated, and we—six men of the 102d—discovered that we were far in advance of the main party. Reaching the house we learned that our "guide" had not been there.

Knowing that we were so far away from the main body of the detachment that they could not find us, and confident that we could not find them, we were left to our own resources.

"Take us to Jefferson" said Mike,—a mule mounted Lieutenant, addressing the guide—and for Jefferson, a small town two miles up the river, we started. Mike was full of mischief and yelled out to the guide, "*Forward! faster!*" and away we went through the brush over logs and into dense bodies of cedars. "Faster!"

yelled the Lieutenant, and over the rocks, leaping, slipping and stumbling—the horses shoes striking fire—onward we rode. At length the mad cap was induced to rein in his steed. Refording Stone River we rode into Jefferson—an antiquated little village, picturesquely located. All the inhabitants were wrapt in slumber. The moon had fairly risen and its silvery light rendered the scene really romantic.

Dispensing with our guide who did not seem to appreciate the romance or necessity of our night ride, we continued on towards camp. But another idiosyncrasy seized upon "Mike." He would have a swim in Stone River. Lieut. W. dashed off with him. The remainder of the party rode leisurely into camp, which was reached at two o'clock in the morning. The swimmers came in shortly afterwards and the entire detachment an hour or two later—having failed to accomplish the purpose for which it was sent.

At that time the Army of the Cumberland was concentrated at Murfreesboro', but there were busy preparations for a forward movement. The forces at Nashville, and at contiguous stations on the railroad were organized into a Reserve Corps and commanded by Maj. Gen. Gordon Granger. Under his direction a new disposition of troops was made between Nashville and Murfreesboro'. Our brigade, (excepting the 102d) was ordered to Nashville. Col. Smith was directed to station six companies of his regiment along the railroad at the different stockades, and march with the remaining companies to Lavergne, establishing head-quarters at that place.

This movement was effected on the 19th of August. Co. A was stationed at Stockade No. 3 on Mill Creek. Co. B, at Smyrna. Co. D, at Stockade No. 1 Mill Creek. Co. F, at Stockade No. 2, near Antioch, on Mill Creek. Co. H, at Overall's Creek. Co. K, at Stewart's Creek. Co's. I, C, E and G were stationed at Lavergne. The regiment, aided by about two hundred of the 10th Ohio Cavalry, guarded the railroad between Nashville and Murfreesboro'—a distance of thirty miles. The cavalry was subject to the orders of Col. Smith, and the Colonel facetiously remarked at the time that his command almost equaled that of Rosecrans,—his right resting near Murfreesboro,' and his left in the vicinity of Nashville! The responsible duties of Post Commandant devolved upon him, and the citizens were constantly presenting cases of grievance,—often coming to him with cases of a civil nature.

Lieut.-Col. Mannon was appointed Provost Marshal of the Post, and his office was thronged day after day with repentant rebels, who came in to take the oath of allegiance. Doubtless many of these men sincerely regretted their rebellious course. It is believed, however, that some came in to be "galvanized," in order to place themselves in a position to operate more effectually against the interests of the government.

According to their standard of *loyalty* it was an easy matter to become possessed of that virtue. Cheap loyalty was illustrated there by an incident which I will relate.

Lieut. Courtney, Acting Quarter-Master at that time, had foraged some corn, or other article of subsistence at the "plantation" of an old citizen. The old gentleman came in to have the account adjusted. Calling upon Lieut. C. he asked receipts for the forage. The Lieutenant, being a little suspicious of the old fellow, asked him if he was a loyal man.

"O! yes, sir; I'm a loyal man, sir; *got the oath right here in my pocket!*"

Our camp was upon the crest of a hill near a somewhat extensive earthwork, and a short distance in the rear of the site where Lavergne had been—through the vicissitudes of war, the village had been reduced to ashes—save two or three houses.

Our elevated encampment gave us a fine view of an immense valley, formed by the confluence of Stone River and the Cumberland. Often this lowland was enveloped in a fog for some hours in the morning. Here and there were prominent points of timber, which looked like islands in a mythical lake, the farther shore of which was marked by a line of bold bluffs—fifteen or twenty miles distant.

HEAVY DUTIES IN GARRISON.

It was said that under favorable circumstances a range of the Cumberland mountains—fifty miles away—could be seen from our fort.

While encamped at Lavergne, tents were entirely ignored. A large number of elegant log huts had been vacated by the regiments which returned to Nashville. These were removed to our encampment and placed in regular order—forming a village of about fifty houses, with three streets.

In these commodious huts, which were furnished with fire-place, bunks, tables, etc., we were well prepared for the approaching winter.

Shortly after our arrival at Lavergne, Col. Smith received an order to have the four companies at that place mounted, and by a bit of skillful diplomacy he secured for the use of these companies, two hundred and twenty-five of the celebrated Spencer Rifles—also each man was supplied with one of Colt's or Remington's revolvers. Horses were foraged from the country. Several expeditions were made to the vicinity of Duck River for this purpose. In a very brief period, the four companies were mounted.

From that time until the regiment was ordered to the front, the duties devolving upon the men, were more severe than are usually experienced by troops in garrison.

At one time the four companies at Lavergne were compelled to assist in patroling the railroad, besides furnishing details for fatigue duty, picket duty, scouting, and being engaged in the work of getting out railroad ties.

The companies at the stockades were similarly employed, save that they had no scouting to do.

It would take up more space than I have at my command to give detailed sketches of the many interesting raids that were made by detachments of the regiment during our stay at Lavergne. A sketch of one may indicate what others were.

On the 9th of Nov., 1863, Gen. Paine commenced a grand guerilla hunt, using the troops at Gallatin and at other points—as many as could be spared. A detachment of the 102d, one hundred and thirty mounted men, commanded by Col. Smith, co-operated from Lavergne.

The evening of the ninth we marched until nine o'clock through the cedar brakes in Wilson county. Halted with an old planter. Took breakfast in squads through the neighborhood. Fared sumptuously, on such luxuries as biscuits, butter and milk. Reached Lebanon on the evening of the 10th. Found things in much confusion. Citizens evidently had not expected a visit from us at that time.

Lebanon is a pretty village. Citizens refined and hospitable, but many of them bitter rebels. The ladies particularly seemed infatuated with the dream of a Southern confederacy. The fair creatures declared they *never could* live under the old Government. The Confederacy never could be overthrown until the last man had been slain. One elderly lady pointed her bony finger at the writer and said: "Mark my word, this war will never end until there is a Southern Confederacy." But the fine rhetoric of the ladies was not sufficient to save it.

They were great admirers of Gen. John H. Morgan. A citizen stated that as an expression of their admiration of his person and qualities, many of them had actually blocked his way when riding through the streets, and with their scissors clipped portions of the mane from the neck of a beautiful mare which he rode—intending to preserve the horse hair as a memento of their beloved General.

Col. Smith was appointed Post Commander, and with part of his detachment garrisoned the town, while the remainder with other troops continued the scout.

Post head-quarters were established at the Court house in the registrar's office, and for a time the quiet village of Lebanon was the scene of active military operations.

While there, General Paine came into the Colonel's office one day, and a liquor dealer was brought before him. Gen. P. was in one of his most savage moods, and gave us the following specimens of his invective style:

General. I understand that you have been selling this infernal tangle-foot, which puts the devil into the minds of peaceable citizens, and causes them to rob and murder their neighbors.

Citizen. I have been selling whiskey, but only to citizens.

General. It is just as bad to sell to citizens as to the rebel soldiers, for whisky turns out more hell-born rebels than all other causes put together. Now, I will tell you what you must do—take a hatchet, go to your doggery, burst in the head of every whisky barrel you have, and pour it upon the ground. Leave not a drop—not a spoonful about your premises. Perhaps you think I am not in earnest?

Citizen. I have no reason to think so.

General. And more—if I learn hereafter that you have been selling whisky, (and I will know it if you do) I will make a bonfire of your doggery, and I will tie you up by your thumbs and feed you on bread and water for forty-eight hours. I will dry up this infernal traffic even if compelled to use fire-brands and hempen ropes.

(Exit citizen, looking pale and troubled.)

While our forces were in Lebanon the bodies of two bushwhackers were brought into town. They had been killed by the 4th Middle Tennessee Cavalry in retaliation for the murder of four men of that regiment by guerrillas. The cavalrymen declared that the two dead bushwhackers were but "two out of forty" to be shot before the account would be settled.

General Paine, Col. Smith and other officers of rank were hospitably entertained at the house of Col. Price, during the occupation of the town. Col. Price had been a staunch Union man from the beginning of the secession movement, and at one time was compelled to leave his home on account of his principles.

On the third day of our occupation, the scouting parties came in. They had killed about a dozen bushwhackers, and captured as many as twenty rebel soldiers.

At noon, Nov. 10th, Lebanon was relieved of its Yankee garrison, and we rode through thick cedars over one of the most rocky roads in Wilson county, to our camp—distant twenty-seven miles. Reached Lavergne at 8 o'clock P. M.

During the time we were at Lavergne, Captain Wm. A. Wilson and Surgeon T. S. Stanway became the principal actors in a very exciting adventure.

They had been visiting the stockade at which Co. D was stationed—ten miles from Lavergne in the direction of Nashville. At dusk they set out for camp. It was a bright moonlight evening, and they anticipated a pleasant ride—little apprehending that more than a score of ruffians were lying in wait for them.

When nearly half way to camp, riding leisurely along, in the shade of dense cedars, and engaged in a somewhat animated conversation, they were confronted by four men on horse-back, who presented revolvers to their heads with the words:

"Surrender—you are our prisoners."

In an instant Doctor S. had his pistol to his eye, and his first shot was fired simultaneously with their first volley. Unluckily, Capt. Wilson's pistols were buckled in the holsters in such a way that valuable time was lost in getting them out. Meanwhile the bullets of the guerrillas were whistling familiarly about the ears of our officers. One clipped the handsome whiskers of the Captain; another grazed his temple. At the Doctor's first fire one of the scoundrels threw up his hands and exclaimed, "I'm hit."

The combatants were so close together that their horses' heads almost touched each other when the affray commenced. Others of the guerrillas, who had been stationed at the roadside, now closed in upon them. The Doctor was blazing away at them, and the Captain had commenced working his piece in good earnest when a desperate hand to hand fight ensued. Doctor S. met one of them at arm's length. The rebel leveled his pistol at the Doctor's head, but the latter struck down the pistol with his own an instant before it was discharged; the ball however entered his right leg and shattered it above the knee. Then for a time he endeavored to escape, but feeling that his wound was too severe, and that he was about to fall from his horse, he steadied himself to the ground and made no further resistance.

Seeing the hopelessness of continuing the struggle, the Captain, being mounted on a fleet animal, dashed away down the pike, the balls of the enemy " zipping " around him. For at least two miles the desperate race continued, the bushwhackers at the outset riding parallel with him. Repeatedly the Captain fired at them as his good steed flew along the pike. At length he began to gain upon them very perceptibly, when a shot struck his horse in the thigh, inflicting a severe flesh wound. Still, for a time he increased the distance that separated him from his pursuers, and had got beyond their view when the animal faltered, staggered and seemed ready to fall. Dismounting he plunged into the thick cedars. A peaceable citizen, who met him the moment his horse failed, went with him, and seemed equally desirous of avoiding the guerrillas. They proceeded some distance and halted in an obscure place. The rebels followed, carefully searching in their immediate vicinity—then retired. All was still. They ventured to change their position;— again the enemy approached. The Captain and companion laid low and breathed lightly. Nearer they came, circling around their would-be victim, and cursing their luck in losing the game. The Captain had given his companion one of his pistols, intending to "sell out" as dearly as possible, if discovered. Again the rebels retired, and the two fugitives again changed their position. Once more the scoundrels approached, searched diligently very near them, but finally despairing of success, returned to their horses and galloped away.

The Captain then endeavored to reach a stockade about two miles distant, but had become bewildered among the cedars, and discovering that he was utterly lost, he remained in the woods until morning, when he came into camp. Dr. Stanway was robbed of everything valuable and in a helpless condition was left upon the ground. While the guerrillas were taking from him his overcoat, vest, dress-coat and watch, they upbraided him for his stubbornness, and said he should be shot for being so fool-hardy as to fight against so many. Citizens living near, heard the firing, and repairing to the place after it was over, took charge of the Doctor.

It was many months before he could report for duty, and his wounded limb will doubtless trouble him through life.

While encamped at Stewart's Creek and Lavergne, the following changes took place in the regiment. Capt. C. H. Jackson became Major, *vice* Major L. D. Shinn, resigned. Dr. William Hamilton became Surgeon in Charge, *vice* Surgeon D. B. Rice, resigned. Citizen Hobart Hamilton became Regimental Quarter-Master, *vice* Lieut. F. H. Rugar, promoted and transferred.

In Co. A, 1st Lieut. T. H. Andrews was promoted to Captain, *vice* Capt. Callaghan resigned. Sergeant M. L. Courtney of Co. I, was transferred to Co. A and promoted to First Lieut.

In Co. F, 1st Lieut. G. W. Woolley was promoted to Captain, *vice* C. H. Jackson, who had become Major. 2d Lieut. Robert S. Peebles then became First Lieut.

In Co. I, by the resignation or dismissal of Capt. Geo. H. King, 1st Lieut. Ed. H. Conger became Captain. 1st Sergt. D. W. Sheahan was promoted to 1st Lieut. 2d Lieut. J. L. Bonnell resigned.

First Lieut. Hiram Elliott became Captain of Co. H, *vice* L. D. Shinn, who had been promoted to position of Major. 2d Lieut. John Thomas became 1st Lieut., and 1st Sergt. Samuel Tucker was promoted to 2d Lieut.

In Co. B, 2d Lieut. Ambrose Stegall was promoted to First Lieut., *vice* J. C. Beswick resigned.

CHAPTER V.

Rumors of a move to the Front. The Citizens protest —in vain. The march.

About the beginning of February, 1864, rumors became rife in camp that our brigade would soon be transferred to the front.

The regiment had remained so long at Lavergne that the thought of leaving was not unlike the thought of leaving home. The citizens had been kind to us, and our boys loved the comparatively free life they were leading, and some of them doubtless were in love with the charming Tennessee lasses who abounded in that vicinity.

But at length the order came. Immediately the citizens circulated a petition asking the military authorities to permit us to remain as a garrison for the Post. The reader will pardon the introduction of the petition here, when I assure him that it contains several important declarations which I consider true, but would not have made on my own authority! Here it is:

"MAJOR GENERAL THOMAS, Comdg. Dept. of the Cumberland:

SIR: We, the undersigned citizens of Rutherford, Davidson and Wilson counties, residing in the vicinity of Lavergne, Tenn., hereby earnestly and respectfully request that the 102d Illinois Vols. be permitted to remain in its present position, if consistent with the good of the service, for the following reasons:

They have—officers and men—ever conducted themselves as gentlemen.

The country has been rid of bushwhackers, thieves and highway robbers, by their vigilance.

Justice has been done the citizens, and the good of the service generally been promoted under their able, just and judicious commander, Col. Smith.

We feel that to retain him and his command here will insure a continuance of peace, quiet, and good will in this vicinity."

(Signed) MANY CITIZENS.

In obedience to the dictates of the weather, which was very inclement, the movement was temporarily suspended, but the military powers were inexorable, and on Thursday the 25th of Feb., positive orders were received to be in readiness to move at an early hour the following morning. The 70th Indiana, 79th Ohio, 129th and 105th Illinois regiments marched from Nashville to Lavergne on the 25th.

On Friday morning, February 26th, the 102d abandoned the pleasant little village of log huts and marched with the brigade towards the front—the men carrying shelter tents for their future homes as soldiers. Hitherto, excepting brief periods, our soldiering had been of the most agreeable character, so far as physical comfort is considered. Thenceforward we were destined to march through shadows as well as sunlight. At that time six companies of the regiment were mounted. They were permitted to retain their horses until further orders.

Co. I, then commanded by Lieut. D. W. Sheahan, was detailed as body guard for Gen. Ward, who was in command of the division.

At the risk of being monotonous, I will, for the satisfaction of the soldiers who were there, give a brief sketch of each day's march.

The brigade camped a short distance south of Murfreesboro', in the afternoon of the first day—Feb. 26th.

Resumed the march at an early hour next morning; passed through a sterile region and went into camp thirteen miles south of Murfreesboro'.

Left camp on the 28th at five o'clock A. M.; roads very dusty. By noon reached Shelbyville—a pretty little village of about one thousand inhabitants, the county seat of Bedford county. Crossed Duck river at Shelbyville and camped three miles south of the stream. Marched sixteen miles. Rain commenced falling before the camp was established, and continued to fall all night.

February 29th was a cold, cheerless, rainy day. The troops moved at sunrise; marched fourteen miles and reached Tullahoma—an insignificant railroad station. That night a small stream near the camp overflowed its banks and submerged a portion of the camping ground, filling most of the tents with water to the depth of six inches. It was a wretched night; cold and very dark. The men could build no fires as wood could not be obtained.

Moved March 1st to a new encampment a mile and a half east of the town, contiguous to an abandoned line of rebel fortifications. It rained the greater part of the day.

Resumed the march at nine o'clock A. M. March 2d. Passed through a poor, flat and thinly settled region and camped near Elk river, nine miles from Tullahoma. The night was cold, and the men made themselves comfortable by building large fires in front of their tents.

The troops moved at eight o'clock A. M., March 3d. Passed through Dechard, and went into camp at Cowan Station, ten miles from Elk river.

March 4th, passed over the Raccoon Mountains—a spur of the Cumberland range. Owing to a blunder of the officer in command of the advance guard, the troops marched some distance on the wrong road, and were compelled to retrace their steps. Reached Tantallon in the afternoon and went into camp, seven miles from Cowan Station. A heavy rain fell during the night.

The troops remained in camp on the 5th until two o'clock in the afternoon, then marched three miles. The 102d was assigned a beautiful camp on a hill that overlooked the other regiments of the brigade. The many camp fires twinkling at night in the valley and on surrounding hills rendered the scene very beautiful.

Marched fourteen miles on the 6th, and reached Stevenson, Alabama.

Passed through Stevenson on the 7th, marched eleven miles and went into camp near Bridgeport on the Tennessee river.

Remained in camp during the 8th. Marched next morning through Bridgeport and across the Tennessee, passed Shell Mound, followed up the river and passed from Alabama into Tennessee. Camped thirteen miles from Bridgeport.

Followed up Falling Water Creek on the 10th. Passed Whiteside station and Sand Mountain. Marched twelve miles; reached Wauhatchie Valley at three o'clock P. M., and the tedious march was over. There the troops were to rest preparatory to a general movement against Gen. Joe Johnston's rebel army.

While the regiment was encamped in the valley, the weather was much of the time very cold, and on the 22d of March an extraordinary fall of snow took place. It commenced about two o'clock in the morning; before noon the ground was covered to the depth of a foot. Such an immense fall of snow, in the spring season, so far down in the Sunny South must have been a novelty to the oldest inhabitant.

Snowballing became for a brief period, an all exciting pastime in camp.

A few days of alternate rain and sunshine sufficed to leave the earth bare again.

A grand review took place on the 19th. Major Gens. Howard and Hooker were the chief reviewing officers.

The men were much occupied during the last weeks of March, in constructing and beautifying their quarters. The month of April was occupied in active military exercises.

There were daily drills, company and battalion. Dress parade each day. Regimental inspection every few days. Brigade drill almost every day, and occasionally division drill. Our regiment had an officer's school, and our enterprising chaplain, as if to vary the monotonous routine, commenced a phonographic school.

Officers and men improved the opportunity while at Wauhatchie to ascend Lookout Mountain. The scene from the summit is said to be grand beyond description. The eye roams until wearied over vast plains, varied by occasional elevations which seem in their dim and shadowy outlines, to be the boundaries of some fairy land.

From the highest elevation on old Lookout, the territory of seven States come within the range of vision.

On the 14th of April there was a grand review of the Division by Maj. Gen. Thomas.

A BEAUTIFUL ENCAMPMENT. 49

An order was received on the 16th announcing that our brigade would, until further orders, be known as the 1st Brigade of the 3d Division, 20th Army Corps, the 11th and 12th Corps having been consolidated, forming the 20th—Maj. Gen. Joseph Hooker commanding,—Maj. Gen. Daniel Butterfield commanding the Division, and Brig. Gen. W. T. Ward, the Brigade.

While at Wauhatchie, the mounted companies of the regiment gave up their horses, in accordance with orders from Corps Head-Quarters. An order was also received directing the regiment to turn over the Spencer Rifles to an ordnance officer, and draw Springfield Rifled Muskets. Want of time prevented the execution of this order previous to the commencement of the Atlanta Campaign. After that time it was inexpedient to make the change.

The camp at Wauhatchie Valley will be remembered as the most beautiful and romantic that the regiment ever occupied. The scenery was grand. Old Lookout Mountain loomed up magnificently a short distance eastward, the clouds wreathing themselves around her rugged summit; her sides covered with a dense growth of cedars and pines.

As if in rivalry with nature, the different regiments of the brigade surpassed all previous ideas of taste and elegance in decorating their encampments.

The camp of the 102d was on a small table-land, just large enough for one regiment. It was laid off with great care. The houses were of a uniform size; the streets were graded and macadamized. Elegant arches, made of cedar boughs, were put up in the quarters of each company. Inwoven with the arches were various beautiful designs. One bore the names "Grant" —" Sherman "—" Thomas,"—arranged in a triangle. Another bore Masonic emblems,—the compass, square, etc. A large eagle was represented beneath one of the arches, apparently in the act of flying. Among other beautiful objects a pulpit was prominent. It was erected in open air, and was a perfect model of taste and ingenuity. The design was very similar to that of an ordinary church pulpit, with columns at each side. Between the columns was a cross. The cross and the columns were wreathed with evergreens. The flag and banner were drooped in elegant folds at each side of the cross. The back part of the pulpit was elegantly wreathed. The floor and steps were carpeted with green boughs. The pulpit was constructed for Rev. Mr. Ryder, of the First Universalist Church, Chicago. It was occupied by him on one occasion. Subsequently it was occupied by other ministers.

A chapel was also built, and services were held in it each Sabbath, and sometimes during the week. The camp was visited by Major Generals Thomas, Howard, Hooker and Butterfield; all of whom expressed their admiration of the taste and skill exhibited in decorating the quarters.

It would hardly be supposed that soldiers, who are usually considered very rough specimens of humanity, could exhibit such a fine appreciation of the beautiful, but that lovely camp, embowered among the arches seemed more like the abode of fairies than of "boys in blue."

CHAPTER VI.

The first Campaign. Distant Artillery firing—Mutterings of the Coming Storm. On a Flank Movement. Snake Creek Gap. The Enemy in front. "Among the Pines." Sharp Firing in front. The First Day at Resaca. BATTLE OF RESACA.

With the beginning of May, the grand Atlanta Campaign commenced.

It is said that some of the rebels afterwards declared, " Old Sherman ascended to the top of Lookout Mountain, gave the command, 'Attention! creation! by kingdom right wheel—march!' and

The Yankees ' came down like the wolf on the fold !' "

The brigade moved on the morning of May 2d, at half-past 6 o'clock; passed around the point of Lookout Mountain, and through Rossville, over the Chickamauga battle-ground, camping a mile beyond, near Lee's and Gordon's Mills. Continued the march on the 4th, the 102d acting as train guard. Camped a mile and a half from Ringgold at Pleasant Grove Church. Moved again on the 6th, and went into camp that night at Leed's Farm, near Nickajack Trace.

The camp was aroused May 7th, at two o'clock in the morning, and the troops moved at five. Marched seven miles, to Taylor's Ridge—a precipitous range of hills, or mountains. Crossed the ridge, and camped in a dense body of timber near Villanow. At that place we remained until the 11th. During the intermediate time there were frequent skirmishes between the two armies. Our own pickets had a brush with a number of the enemy on the 8th, and the same day a part of Geary's Division had a sharp fight, losing over two hundred men killed and wounded. There was heavy cannonading on the 9th, in the direction of Dalton.

Moved again on the 11th of May, at a quarter past 4 o'clock, A. M. Marched twelve miles and entered Snake Creek Gap, a narrow pass between lofty ranges of the Chattoogata Mountains. Pitched our tents in the valley and on the mountain side. It was a romantic locality.

The lofty mountains towered on either hand hundreds of feet above us, their summits and slopes covered with a dense growth of timber. Thousands of troops were camped in the valley, and there was a steady tramp of columns marching to the front.

The scene from an elevated position on the mountain side, the evening of the 11th, when night was settling over the earth, and the surrounding hills were dimly outlined in the gathering gloom, was strangely beautiful. The white tents of the soldiers dotted the narrow valley, and their fires gleamed through the foliage of intervening trees. Dusky forms flitted to and fro about the camp fires, and a hum of voices came to the ear, in a monotonous sound that grew less audible as the night advanced. Above the hum of voices could be heard the constant rumbling of the wagon trains moving towards the front. At length the clear notes of a bugle sounded tattoo, then others took up the strain and were quickly followed by the crashing roll of the drums.

But our feelings at that time were not all of a sublime character. The stern realities of an active campaign subjected us to privations that we had never endured before. Transportation was limited, and many of the soldiers had nothing in the world with them save one suit of clothes, a rubber blanket and a shelter tent—vulgarly termed a "purp" tent. On their rubber blanket beneath the shelter tent, they slept without removing their clothes, day after day and week after week.

Privations which at one time would have caused them to murmur, were looked upon as mere trifles, and a spirit of cheerfulness and hopefulness pervaded all minds.

While encamped there, a number of the soldiers ascended the mountain on the left of the gap. With Adjutant J. H. Snyder, the writer climbed one of the highest peaks of this mountain, and looked down into the valley of the Oostanaula River. We observed occasional "clearings" in the valley, and connected with these were dwelling houses, which appeared in the distance like small, white tents. Everything was represented in miniature.

The use of a field glass enabled us to obtain a very distinct view of the range of mountains beyond the valley, and other mountains far away southward and westward—the lofty ranges rising hill above hill in beautiful succession, and at various points culminating in solitary peaks.

Some miles away eastward a rebel wagon train was seen, in park. We felt as we looked over the broad valley that we were viewing the land of the enemy—soon, however, to be our own.

Our Brigade was detained during part of the 11th and 12th of May in the gap, to cut out and prepare a new road through the woods. During the afternoon of the 12th we marched five miles and camped near the mouth of the Gap.

There had been some fighting in the direction of Dalton, and at intervals the low and sullen "boom" of distant cannon was heard, almost due north of us.

The 20th Corps had successfully accomplished the flank movement through Snake Creek Gap, and was now well established in a strong position, threatening the left flank of the enemy.

Friday morning, May 13th, we moved in a direction to the right of Resaca, around which place the rebels had entrenched themselves, and were ready to give us battle. The cavalry which had been thrown out in advance, became engaged with the enemy's videttes at an early hour, and we soon learned that Gen. Kilpatrick had been wounded and borne to the rear. The rebels were stubborn. In the afternoon the infantry was pushed forward to "feel" the enemy, and develope his position and strength.

We advanced through groves of young pines—the most dense we had yet seen.

Among the pines, in line of battle! How indeliby the scene is fixed in memory. What soldier of Sherman's army can view, even at this day, a grove of young pines without having those days of carnage and death recalled to mind?

Slowly the enemy's skirmish line was pressed back by our skirmishers, and late in the afternoon the skirmishers in front of the 15th Corps approached, and finally charged and captured a redoubt with two guns.

Our Division had been separated from the other divisions of the Corps, and was formed on the right of the 14th Corps. The advance was continued at intervals until dusk. Halting in an open field at the base of a range of hills we rested awhile, and ate a hastily prepared supper. After dark, moved on by a circuitous route, quietly and carefully, into line of battle, on the opposite side of the hill. The position of the enemy had now been fully developed. Only a narrow valley separated their line from ours. They had been hard pressed during the day, and perceived the necessity of constructing strong defensive works. As we formed in line, the busy click, click, click of their axes could be distinctly heard, and they seemed to be working for dear life. We occupied a ravine which ran parallel with the hill, about one hundred and fifty feet above its base. Companies E and G were sent out as skirmishers during the night. Capt. McManus had command of the line, and was assisted by Capt. Sedwick. Both most excellent men—the former, daring almost to a fault, the latter, perfectly cool and collected in any position of danger. It is related of Capt. S. that on that occasion it became necessary at one time for him to pass from post to post in a very exposed position, in plain view of the enemy, and as their balls raised the dust about his feet, the only perceptible change in his manner consisted in the more rapid puffing of the smoke from his pipe.

Early in the morning a dash forward to Camp Creek was made. Being then mere novices in the art of warfare, many of the men took up positions where they were quite at the mercy of the enemy, and were compelled to remain behind stumps and trees all day—an attempt to escape being equivalent to certain death. It was an exciting day on the skirmish line; firing commenced at daylight, and was kept up until dark.

At one time the enemy endeavored to flank the line, and Capt. Sedwick discovering the movement from his position in front, recrossed the field to his reserve, and with them advanced on the left and drove the enemy back. Meanwhile there was heavier work on the left. The skirmishing had been lively in that direction all the forenoon, but at 2 o'clock P. M. the firing became terrific. There was a perpetual roll of musketry, and the deep bass of the artillery reverberated grandly through the woods, and was echoed back by the surrounding hills.

At that time we were ordered forward, and the moment we appeared on the little elevation in front of the ravine, the rebel sharpshooters sent their balls whistling around us, killing one man instantly and wounding three. Having proceeded a short distance, we were ordered to halt and lie down.

The object doubtless was to make a feint of attacking, in order to divert the attention of the enemy from the left.

No further advance was attempted, and we remained in that position until late in the evening, listening occasionally to the whizzing of bullets above our heads, but more deeply interested in the fierce conflict on our left. The sound at times would run along the line towards us, until it would seem that our Corps must soon, also, become engaged, then it would recede, and there would be a lull, like the lulling of the winds in a winter storm.

Sometimes it would seem that our men were driving the rebels, and again it appeared that the battle was going against us. O! how terrible the suspense of waiting at such a time for victory, while contemplating the possibility of disaster!

The sound of the battle at its height could only be campared in my mind to the work of a storm, breaking and crushing to the ground, ten thousand dead trees every instant, amid the roll of heaven's artillery.

A battery about fifty yards to the left of our regiment was kept busy throwing shot and shell into the rebel lines, but the guns of the enemy were engaged where the contest raged more fiercely, and they paid no attention to this battery.

Towards evening the sounds of battle died away, and finally dwindled down to the irregular firing of the skirmishers. At dusk we retired to our position in the ravine. The regiment had lost during the day three men killed, and nineteen wounded.

Late at night the camp was hushed in repose, and beneath the lovely foliage of the trees we slept sweetly—but ere we slept, we looked up through our leafy covering to the bright stars that twinkled so peacefully in the calm blue sky, and thought of other and distant skies of peace—of those far away, as dear to us as life—and *thought of the morrow.*

At 2 o'clock next morning we were aroused, and ordered to resume the advance position that had been abandoned the evening before. During the time intervening before day light, slight breast-works were thrown up—the first we ever built.

The morning of Sunday, May 15, 1864, dawned luridly upon us. The smoke of innumerable camp fires had enveloped hill and valley in a hazy mantle.

At six o'clock we were ordered to move around to the left of the 14th Army Corps.

Quietly we marched back over the hill, and through the shadowy forest, almost feeling the death-like stillness of that memorable Sabbath morning. And how like entering the valley of the shadow of death, seemed our march down through the smoky atmosphere into the deep valley, and around to our new position confronting the enemy.

Our Division had been selected for the desperate work of charging a rebel battery, which was supported by a strong force of the enemy behind entrenchments. The ulterior object was to break the enemy's line at that point, and thereby cut the rebel army in twain.

The 1st Brigade was ordered to make the assault, while the other brigades of the division were to be held in easy supporting distance. The brigade was formed in column by regiments, right in front, as follows: 70th Indiana, 102d Illinois, 79th Ohio, 129th Illinois, 105th Illinois. The men had previously unslung knapsacks and left them in charge of a guard.

There was evidently some warm work to be done. At first the real design of the movement was known only to a few, but when the column was formed, the men were ordered to fix bayonets, and as the ominous click ran along the line the nature of the task before us became apparent. Thought was busy then, and all faces seemed a shade paler.

The distance from the point where the charging column was formed to the enemy's line, was about six hundred yards. A valley lay between, and their works were upon the crest of a hill beyond. A heavy growth of young pines covered all the hills and completely masked their position.

At length about half-past eleven o'clock the command "forward" ran along the line, and the column quickly moved down the hillside. Simultaneously with the beginning of the movement the rebels opened fire. Then "forward!" was the word shouted and repeated by almost every tongue. And a wild, prolonged battle yell that swelled from all lips, arose distinct and terrific above the roar of battle, as down into the valley and across the open field—where death rode on every passing breeze—then up the hillside where the twigs and branches of the young pines were clipped by the bullets like corn blades in a hail storm—the charging columns moved—not in regular lines, but enmasse, disorganized by the inequalities of the ground and the dense growth of pines—on to the summit, towards the rebel cannons which belched forth fire, grape-shot and shell to the last instant—men dropping dead and wounded on every hand—into the earthworks surrounding the guns, and the guns were ours.

All of the regiments in the brigade were represented within the earthwork. But the position was occupied only for an instant. The rebel line had been pierced—not broken. On the right and on the left of the redoubt, which formed a salient in their position, their line was intact. They opened a withering cross fire and our men fell back to a position immediately in front of the redoubt, commanding the guns.

At that time some one yelled out that the order was to retreat, and many retired to the foot of the hill. They were there re-organized and marched to another part of the field. Most of those who remained had heard no order to retire, and were sanguine that the position could be held. Protected in a measure by the rebel redoubt, and sheltered somewhat by trees and logs, our men kept up a steady fire all the afternoon. But the rebel fire was more active. They were protected by an excellent line of works—fired low—and their balls cut close around, occasionally killing or wounding a man.

In the squad which held the position, several regiments were represented. If any fresh columns moved up the hill they did not reach the vicinity of the guns. Towards evening it was feared the battery would be retaken. One by one the men began to retire, notwithstanding the expostulations of those who remained. After dark the enemy opened a sharp fire, as if menacing a charge to retake the guns. A volley was fired in return; the boys yelled out a defiant cheer, and one shouted to the Johnnies: "Come over and take your brass field pieces!"

Help had been sent for, and at length we heard music in the valley below. Sweet as the music of heaven, soothing the soul after the harrowing, discordant day of battle.

Inwoven with our very beings, the ecstatic sensations of that moment, when the soft, plaintive, but cheering notes of a field band were borne to our ears, will live in memory forever.

We learned afterwards, however, that the music did not herald the approach of a relieving column—but relief soon came. About ten o'clock in the evening a strong force marched into position immediately in front of the earthwork. The guns—four in number—were held and brought off that night. They were handsome pieces—brass, twelve pounders. One of them was named "Minnie, the Belle of Alabama."

When the relieving column came, those of the regiment who had remained on the field marched to the rear.

The day's work was over, and we were satisfied with the record the 102d had made.

In the charge, the Regiment was gallantly led by Col. F. C. Smith, who went into the fort among the first of those who braved the storm of leaden hail that swept our ranks away at that point.

In retiring, and proceeding to another part of the field, that portion of the regiment which left, after having charged into the rebel redoubt, was actuated by the belief that the assault was a failure, and also acted in conformity to orders.

Conspicuous among the officers who remained, was Capt. Hiram Elliott, of Co. H, who lost one of two sons that went into the battle with him.

Lieut. Col. J. M. Mannon, who had exhibited much daring in the first onset, remained on the ground until after nightfall.

Capt. Dan W. Sedwick was also there; cool, collected and busy, as usual.

Adjutant J. H. Snyder and Lieut. A. H. Trego—companions always—remained together at the post of danger. The latter commanded company C, in the fight.

Among the company commanders who fought with gallantry, Capt. McManus, Capt. Wilson, Capt. Andrews and Lieut. D. W. Sheahan were conspicuous. Others whom I have not named behaved gallantly on the occasion.

But of all those whom I have mentioned above, none were braver or more worthy of mention than scores of privates who fought with courage that has never been surpassed. Without injustice to any, I wish it were possible to record the names of all who made a glorious record on that day.

A very few members of the regiment behaved badly. Two or three committed the unaccountable mistake of charging the wrong hill—a hill in the rear.

Near the commencement of the charge, our flag bearer Sergt. R. L. Carver was severely wounded. The banner bearer Corpl. P. F. Dillon was shot through the breast an instant later. When he fell, Adjutant J. H. Snyder gallantly caught up the banner and carried it into the redoubt. Subsequently it was planted by him on the parapet of the earthwork. During the action fifty balls cut the banner, and two shattered the staff.

According to the official report, the casualties in the 102d during that day were eighteen killed, seventy-six wounded, and one missing.

Our brigade commander, Brig. Gen. W. T. Ward, was quite severely wounded. It is said that when the ball struck the old General he invoked a "string of blessings" on the rebels in a style that was more forcible than elegant. He was in the thickest of the fight cheering on the men when struck. Several of our men were doubtless struck by balls from the lines that were directed to support us. At one time the 2d Brigade opened a sharp fire on us, mistaking us for rebels.

An amusing anecdote is related of a recruit who moved forward with the column but took the earliest opportunity to get behind a stump. He was reprimanded by an officer and ordered forward, but protested in this style: "I don't want to charge on that battery. I will be sure to get shot—if Gen. Hooker wants more cannon let him say so, and I will *throw in and help buy them for him.*"

Deponent did not say what regiment the recruit belonged to, but of one thing we may rest assured, he was a genuine Yankee, and had very peculiar financial "notions" of war.

During the night of the 15th the rebels evacuated their entire line of works and retreated in the direction of Atlanta.

The scene on the battle-ground the following day was sad beyond description. The day was calm—indeed the stillness was oppressive. We were permitted to wander over the field and view the effects of the fierce struggle. The dead of both armies were being buried—some singly where they fell, others in a common grave.

In a deep trench surrounded by evergreen pines, fifty-one of the slain of the 1st Brigade were buried. The scene at the grave was deeply impressive. An immense crowd of soldiers gathered around to hear the remarks of an aged chaplain, ere the forms of their comrades were forever hidden from sight.

"Many in one," said the venerable minister, "is the motto borne proudly on our nation's banner. *Many in one grave*, our fallen brothers rest. And is not the coincidence a fitting one? Will not this common grave be cherished with a sacred pride by all who love our country's flag?"

At the conclusion of his remarks the work of burial was accomplished, tenderly and carefully as the circumstances would permit, by the comrades of the slain.

But to the living, sad as the surroundings were, the day after the battle seemed like the beginning of a new life. Peace and repose, how sweet, after the withering tornado of human wrath had swept by!

The day after the battle, Major Gen. Butterfield, our Division Commander, issued the following congratulatory order:

HEAD-QUARTERS 3D DIV. 20TH ARMY CORPS,
Near Resaca, Ga., May 16th, 1864.

General Orders No. 4.

The Major General Commanding feels it a duty, as well as a pleasure, to congratulate the Division upon its achievements yesterday. The gallant assault and charge of the First Brigade, capturing four guns in the enemy's fort; the brave support of the assault by a portion of the Second Brigade on the left, with the glorious repulse it gave twice its force, proves the Division worthy a high name and fame. Let every one endeavor by attention to duty, obedience to orders, devotion and courage, to make our record in the future as in the past, such that the army and the country will ever be proud of us.

By command of Major General Butterfield.
JOHN SPEED, Capt. and A. A. G.

Gen. Sherman in his report of the operations of his army, referring to the eventful days at Resaca, says:

"Nothing saved Johnston's army at Resaca, but the impracticable nature of the country, which made the passage of troops across the valley, almost impossible. This fact enabled his army to reach Resaca from Dalton, along the comparatively good roads constructed before hand, partly from the topographical nature of the country and partly from the foresight of the rebel chief. At all events, on the 14th of May, we found the rebel army in a strong position, behind Camp Creek, occupying the forts at Resaca, and his right on some high chestnut hills to the north of the town. I at once ordered a pontoon bridge to be laid across the Oostanaula at Lay's Ferry, in the direction of Calhoun, a division of the 16th Corps, commanded by Gen. Sweeney to cross and threaten Calhoun; also, the cavalry division of General Garrard to move from its position at Villanow, down towards Rome, to cross the Oostanaula and break the railroad below Calhoun and above Kingston if possible, and with the main army I pressed against Resaca at all points. Gen. McPherson got across Camp Creek near its mouth, and made a lodgment close up to the enemy's works, on hills that commanded with short range artillery, the railroad and trestle bridges, and Gen. Thomas pressing close along Camp Creek Valley, threw Gen. Hooker's Corps across the head of the Creek, to the main Dalton road and down to it close on Resaca.

"Gen. Schofield came up on his left and a heavy battle ensued during the afternoon and evening of the 15th, during which Gen. Hooker drove the enemy from several strong hills, captured a four-gun battery and many prisoners. That night Johnston escaped, retreating south across the Oostanaula."

INCIDENTS, ETC.

Many hair-breadth escapes occurred at Resaca. One of the men was struck by a partially spent ball, which passed through the outside of his coat into his pocket, and there buried itself in a plug of tobacco! The tobacco saved him from a dangerous, and perhaps fatal wound.

The morning after the battle, numerous ball holes were visible in the clothing of the men. Hats, caps, coats and pants had been pierced. Many had been slightly scarred, and in some cases their wounds were never officially reported. One familiar ball cut through the clothing of Capt. Isaac McManus, barely drawing blood from his right leg. Capt. Wilson was prostrated and severely bruised, apparently by the concussion of an exploding shell.

A REBEL VIEW OF THE SITUATION.

Having given a somewhat detailed history of the operations of our army, it may not be improper to conclude the account of the battle, with a rebel view of the situation at that time. It appears that after the last day's fighting was over, the Captain of the rebel battery which fell into our hands, wrote the following letter, which was subsequently captured by a member of the 105th Illinois Regiment. It is given *verbatim et literatim*.

RESACA Ga may 15.

My Dear Wife
    John Thompson is going home to Cassville wounded I thought I would drop you a line by him The Yankees charged on my battery this P M and captured 2 sections of it many of our men and attendants were wounded
It was as daring an exploit as when my brothers was charged at antietam Va by a newyork Reg .
They threw themselves into the front as unconscious of danger as ducks into a pond
I tell you and will to stow away everthing of value fearing we shall have to fall back from here if we do the yankees will get every thing in reach.
We had to fight hookers command here or else the battery never would have been taken
I hear we are gaining on the yankees in Va and we would have whipped them here if it had not been for Hookers command
They all wore a star
If we hold our ground here I will see you ere long I want you to send sis and James to grand Pas and you go to uncle Johns Take all the things you can
I must close as the train will leave immediately your husband Unto Death
 P S   w w c
   our position here was very good but we have to fall back keep up good courage I hope what I have said will not prove discouraging to you   w w c

From the allusion, in the fourth paragraph, to the men of our Brigade, throwing themselves into the front, " as unconscious of danger as ducks into a pond," the term " Ward's Ducks " originated.

CHAPTER VII.

The Campaign resumed. Cassville. A short Rest. The March to the Etowah. Burnt Hickory or New Hope Church. Battles and Marches, from New Hope Church to the Chattahoochie River.

Late in the afternoon of the 16th of May, we marched from the vicinity of Resaca. The bulk of the army had already pressed forward after the enemy. We crossed the Conasauga River after dark, and marched rapidly until a late hour—passing through a region that had been devastated by both armies. It will be recollected that the woods were in many places on fire. Occasionally a dead pine tree burned magnificently, the flames creeping upwards from the base like a living serpent, and shooting out fiery tongues, from the topmost branches, over a hundred feet from the ground.

We halted at midnight near an old mill on Coosawatee River.

The march was resumed at an early hour on the 18th. In the afternoon, when a few miles from Cassville, the regiment was halted and the men were ordered to load their guns. There was some skirmishing in front. The rebels evidently desired to go into camp and were becoming stubborn. We had made a good day's march, and pressed them closely. In such cases it was often a source of gratification to our weary soldiers to hear skirmishing in advance, which usually indicated the close of the day's march.

On the occasion referred to, our Brigade made but little progress after the first halt. Late in the afternoon, the rebels brought their artillery into play to check our skirmishers. Our Brigade went into bivouac in column by regiments, about three miles from Cassville. Moved next morning, May 19th, at half-past five o'clock. After proceeding a short distance, the brigade was formed in order of battle. In front of our regiment, Companies G and B were deployed as skirmishers, and then we advanced "by the right of companies to the front," anticipating an immediate encounter with the enemy. We halted at length in a small grove of timber. There was an open field in front, and across this about a half mile distant, the rebel skirmish line could be seen. Farther to the left in the edge of a wood, rebel horsemen rode to and fro, observing our movements.

While halted in the woods, the enemy opened upon us with artillery. A small field piece, that made a hollow, sepulchral sound, devoted its attention to our part of the line. It was fired with considerable accuracy, and as the shells came, "flutter, flutter, flutter-ing" towards us like prairie chickens on the wing, our sensations were not of the most agreeable character. It is extremely unpleasant to be subjected, in an exposed position, to the artillery fire of an enemy, when there is no reply from our own guns.

A fragment from one of the shells, wounded a member of Co. G so severely that he died during the day. No other casualties occurred.

At length we very quietly moved out of the woods, around to a new position, about two and a half miles to the right. Then, working as if for life, we made a barricade of rails. A battery near us on the right, shelled the woods in front for some time, and at two o'clock P. M. a forward movement was ordered.

At first we were fearful that our brigade was being pushed forward into a perilous position without support. But as we debouched from the woods, into an open field that extended a mile or two to the right and left, an unexpected but cheering sight met our eyes. In each direction, as far as the eye could reach, there were moving columns of troops; all with flags and banners unfurled—advancing with as much regularity as if on drill. It was a magnificent military pageant—a realization of the pride and pomp of "glorious" war.

Near the center of the open field, a halt was ordered. The enemy could be distinctly seen maneuvering in mass, in the edge of the woods, a few hundred yards in front. The 129th Ill. Regiment was deployed as skirmishers in front of our Brigade. A battery was brought up, and the moment it commenced playing upon the rebels, they disappeared in the thick woods.

With characteristic coolness Gen. Hooker rode forward with the skirmishers, to see what was there. He was accompanied by a single orderly. While awaiting further developments, two "Johnnies" came into view, advancing among the brush in front. Doubtless it was imagined by some that these men were among the advance of a charging column; for a number of guns were instantly leveled at them, but they threw up their hands with frantic energy, and then it was apparent that they were voluntarily coming into our lines.

After a time we waded a small creek, moved to the right, advanced through thick woods in line of battle; then moved off again to the right and rear—meantime there was heavy skirmishing in front, and some artillery firing. The days work ended with a return to the open field above referred to, where we went into camp for the night.

It had been an exciting day of skirmishing and maneuvering. The movements of the two armies were not unlike the movements of a *thunder cloud in a dry season* — angry, threatening, portentous — flying messengers moving hither and thither—yet without other result than a few big drops of rain, and much thunder.

Referring to the operations of our Division on the 18th and 19th of May, Gen. Butterfield, in a complimentary order says: "On the 18th the Division marched twenty miles—much of it in the heat of the sun; partially making its own roads; moving five miles in line of battle, and driving the enemy before them. On the 19th the Division again moved to the enemy's extreme right. The advance of the First Brigade unsupported, driving the enemy to within one and a half miles of Cassville, by the Adairsville road; the reconnoissance of the 3d Brigade to the railroad between Kingston and Cassville, unsupported, and in the presence of five times its number of the enemy, the defiant attitude of the Division, alone and unsupported, when threatened by thrice its number; the assault and capture of Cassville, by the 2d Brigade; the daring and boldness of the artillery, especially the section of Battery C, 1st Ohio, Lieut. King commanding; their fine practice at the enemy's retreating columns, and the conduct and bearing of the whole Division throughout the two days, especially while in the presence of the main army of the enemy, are worthy of the highest commendation. Resaca and Cassville are proud names for our banners."

It may interest the reader to know what were the designs of the rebel general at that time. I quote from the official report of General Joseph E. Johnson, commencing with the account of his plan of conducting the defensive campaign. He says:

"The fact that a part of Polk's troops were still in the rear, and the great numerical superiority of the Federal Army made it expedient to risk battle only when position or some blunder of the enemy might give us counterbalancing advantages. I therefore determined to fall back slowly until circumstances should put the chances of battle in our favor, keeping so near the United States Army as to prevent its sending reinforcements to Grant; and hoping, by taking advantage of positions and opportunities, to reduce the odds against us, by partial engagements. I also expected it to be materially reduced before the end of June, by the expiration of the terms of service of many of the regiments which had not re-enlisted. In this way we fell back to Cassville in two marches. At Adairsville, about mid-day, on the 17th, Polk's cavalry, under Brigadier-General Jackson, met the enemy, and Hardee, after severe skirmishing, checked them. At this point, on the 18th, Polk's and Hood's corps took the direct road to Cassville; Hardee's that by Kingston. About half the Federal Army took each road.

"French's division having joined Polk's corps on the 18th, on the morning of the 19th, when half the Federal Army was near Kingston, the two corps at Cassville were ordered to advance against the troops that had followed them from Adairsville, Hood leading on the right.

When this corps had advanced some two miles, one of his staff officers reported to Lieutenant-General Hood, that the enemy were approaching on the Canton road, in rear of the right of our original position. He drew back his troops and formed them across that road. When it was discovered that the officer was mistaken, the opportunity had passed, by the near approach of the Federal Army. Expecting to be attacked, I drew up the troops in what seemed to me an excellent position—a bold ridge immediately in rear of Cassville, with the open valley before it. The fire of the enemy's artillery commenced soon after the troops were formed, and continued until night.

" Soon after dark, Lieutenant-Generals Polk and Hood, together, expressed to me decidedly, the opinion formed upon the observation of the afternoon, that the Union artillery would render their positions untenable the next day, and urged me to abandon the ground immediately and cross the Etowah. Lieutenant-General Hardee, whose position I thought weakest, was confident that he could hold it. The other two officers, however, were so earnest and unwilling to depend on the ability of their corps to defend the ground, that I yielded, and the Army crossed the Etowah on the 20th, a step which I have regretted ever since."

During the 20th, 21st and 22d of May, the troops were permitted to rest in the vicinity of Cassville.

On the 23d we moved on towards the Etowah river. Crossed the river during the afternoon—slight skirmishing in front and cannonading off to the left. Camped a mile south of the stream. There is some beautiful country in the vicinity of the Etowah and many elegant residences.

The farmers had been busily at work during the spring. Fine crops were growing but were annihilated as fast as the army moved. The wheat was used for forage, and the corn was trodden down by the invading army. Fences were used for fuel.

The citizens had almost universally forsaken their homes. Many of them on our approach, had joined the rebel army. The ladies, who in some cases remained at home, and braved the Yankee invaders, were very indignant because the Yankees did not, in their opinion, fight in a fair way. Said they: "You'ns don't fight we'ns fair; as soon as our boys choose a position and get ready to meet you, Captain Hooker, with his *Rigiment*, makes a flank movement and comes round on their eends, and then they must retreat again."

It is said that some of the unsophisticated creatures actually believed the instruments of the brass bands were parts of a huge machine which General Sherman carried along for flanking purposes!

During the 24th, and until the afternoon of the 25th, we advanced in the direction of Dallas. We were in a rough mountainous region, south of Pumpkin Vine Creek, when, about 3 o'clock P. M., May 25th, the 2d Division of our corps found the enemy in force near a place called "Burnt Hickory,"—more commonly known as New Hope Church. A battle soon commenced. The roll of musketry was incessant and terific. The 3d Division immediately moved to take up a position on the right of the 2d, and with it General Butterfield was ordered to make a "vigorous attack" on the enemy's left.

Some difficulty was experienced in getting into position. The brigades were not in proper communication with each other, and owing to a multiplicity of orders, the Regiments of our Brigade became in a measure separated. Night was coming on apace. The conflict raged fiercely on the left, and the enemy in our front were making the air musical with cannon shot, shells, grapeshot and musket balls.

Some who were there will recollect how our line, with one involuntary movement, was swayed for an instant towards the earth—like a field of wheat in a storm—as the screeching shells swept over head.

Finally an irregular advance was made. The 70th Indiana and the 102d Illinois regiments were at first ordered to remain in reserve. In a short time General Butterfield rode along, evidently somewhat excited, and ordered our Colonel to advance at once with his regiment and make a "vigorous attack." We moved forward, over four lines of our troops, who were prone upon the ground, but were halted to await the 70th Indiana. Again we moved forward. It was growing dark; a drizzling rain set in. The rebel guns flashed fire not more than two hundred yards ahead, and the grape shot rattled around.

At that point we were ordered to halt and lie down. No further advance was attempted. The rebels gave a prolonged cheer of victory, and we felt that we had been slightly worsted.

The rain increased as darkness set in, and the night was most dismal. In the thick woods—the darkness rendered more impenetrable by the smoke of battle which hung around the earth—regiments and parts of regiments were moved to and fro in the vain endeavor to reorganize the columns. Pitilessly the rain came down, saturating our clothes through and through. Supperless, at length we went to bed, with our blankets only for a covering.

During the night Cos. A and F were detailed to build breastworks on a line which had been established for the purpose.

Before daylight the other companies of the regiment moved to this line and commenced building works. A heavy fog enveloped the earth when morning came, but the fog did not prevent the rebels from annoying those at work on the fortifications. They opened a galling fire, and Captain D. W. Sedwick was ordered to deploy Co. E and protect the working parties.

The Captain was the man for the occasion, and he did his work well. He had received orders to advance his men 150 yards in front of our line, but had not proceeded more than half that distance when he perceived through the fog that he was but two or three rods from the enemy's works. The enemy succeeded in wounding several of his men before he could withdraw them to a proper distance. Finally they were posted behind trees and logs, and they "let fly" with their Spencers in such an effective manner, that the rebels were compelled to retire, temporarily abandoning two field pieces which they had placed in an advanced position. The artillery horses were killed. Co. E had seven men wounded that morning.

Early in the morning a number of guns were placed in position along our line, and for two or three hours they threw shot and shell into the rebel lines with scarcely a moment's interruption. The rebel sharpshooters endeavored to silence them, but the Spencer rifles were too much for the Johnnies. During the forenoon, Generals Sherman and Hooker came along the line, quite reckless of the rebel bullets, which semi-occasionally whistled through the air.

The rebel field pieces were held in tow during all that day, and until the evening of the day following by different "reliefs" from the Regiment. It was a warm place, and there was some of the sharpest of sharpshooting done on both sides. At one time a column of rebels was seen moving towards our right, in point blank range, and the skirmishers quickly emptied the magazines of their Spencer guns, as they poured volley after volley into the moving column of gray.

The regiment lost, while in that position, one man killed and fourteen wounded.

At three o'clock in the afternoon of the 27th, we were relieved by other troops, and at dusk marched to a new position a half mile to the right, in line with the other regiments of the brigade, and on the right of the 70th Ind. The opposing lines at that place were farther apart, yet the rebel sharp-shooters were able to pick off our men who exposed themselves too recklessly. During the morning, heavy cannonading was heard in the direction of Dallas—supposed to be the guns of McPherson.

Before noon of the 28th, we were again ordered to a position in reserve, a short distace from the position first held on the line. One man had been wounded during the morning. While being relieved preparatory to moving to the rear, the rebel skirmishers opened a rapid fire. They evidently observed the change that was being made. The regiment which relieved ours had one man hurt. Ours retired without further loss.

A few moments after reaching our new position, sharp firing commenced in front. Although we were held in reserve, the rebels were so close that their balls dropped several hundred yards in the rear of us. Several rounds of grape shot were fired by them and the little *iron crab-apples*, barked the trees and rattled around so thickly, it was marvelous that no one was hurt.

In the afternoon we moved two hundred yards to the rear. Remained in that position until midnight of the 29th. In the meantime, there was constant skirmishing on some part of the line and occasional heavy cannonading.

At midnight of the 29th, an attack was made on the left of our front. The firing was terrific. There is something fearfully grand, yet terrible, in a night attack. Perhaps a little extra picket firing has caused the soldier to rest uneasily in his sleep, and perchance he dreams of being on the eve of battle. Presently the skirmishing grows more lively, then follows a roll of musketry, and then a roar that bursts upon the still night air like the sound of a hurricane. Instantly the soldier is on his feet, instinctively grasping his faithful musket. Finally the big dogs of war commence barking, as if to quell the tumult, and thus night is rendered hideous for an hour or two, and sleep is driven from all eyes, not only at the point of attack, but miles away right and left along the line.

Thus we were aroused at midnight of the 29th. Shortly afterwards we marched to a new position a half mile further to the right. Remained there until the 31st. We were then relieved by the 129th Ill. and returned to the old position in reserve line. Next day, June 1st, the corps was relieved by the 15th Corps. We then marched to the left three miles, and went into camp. Moved at one o'clock P. M., June 2d, continuing towards the left. A little deluge of rain came down, a few moments after the march commenced. Col. Coburn's brigade was in advance and it met with strong opposition. After proceeding two and a half miles, our brigade was formed in order of battle, and ordered to move forward in support of Col. Coburn. The enemy shelled us quite actively. Several of the regiments in our brigade were in an open field, and were much exposed to the enemy's fire. A number of casualties occurred in the 79th Ohio Regiment. Our Brigade

Surgeon, Dr. Potter, of the 105th Illinois Regiment, was killed by a shell. He was an excellent man and a good Surgeon. No casualties occurred that day in the 102d. Chilled and wet we bivouaced that night, without having more than a mouthful of supper. Rations were "played out."

Friday, the 3d,—marched three miles northeast— camped in an open field; cavalry on the left. Next day moved a short distance to breastworks that had been occupied by Col. Coburn's brigade. A number of bales of cotton in a building near camp, afforded excellent bedding, and some of the men slept on soft beds that night. The weather continued rainy and disagreeable. Moved again on the 6th about five miles. Halted in the afternoon, formed in line of battle, and were ordered to build breastworks in double-quick time.

There we remained until the 15th of June. Neither army seemed very belligerent, and we passed several days in perfect quiet. Rain fell almost every day. It will be remembered that the two wings of the regiment occupied separate camps at that time. The left wing was camped near a large rock that cropped out from the earth. The right wing occupied a part of the line an eighth of a mile farther to the left. The camp was ever after known in the regiment as the *Wet Tortugas!*

The temporary suspension of active military operations was followed by a general movement on the 15th of the month.

The advance commenced early in the afternoon. It did not require a long march to stir up the rebels. A mile and a half from our abandoned encampment they were found in force, at a place that is known as Golgotha Church—by some called Pine Mountain.

There had been considerable artillery firing during the day, and as we advanced, the picket firing became more animated.

Having approached sufficiently near the enemy to comprehend his position, the brigade was deployed in line of battle and the 102d was ordered to deploy as skirmishers in front of the brigade. We advanced quickly across an open field and into the edge of a wood where the enemy disputed our further progress. Companies G, I, E and part of F were deployed; the other companies were held in reserve. For hours our men plied their Spencers from behind trees, and the enemy replied with equal energy. At length an advance was made and our skirmishers drove the enemy from their first line of skirmish pits.

During the skirmish, Capt. Isaac McManus, of Co. G, was shot through the left arm, above the elbow—the ball in its course breaking the bone.

The Captain had ever exhibited a degree of bravery, that almost amounted to rashness, and his loss was severely felt during the remainder of the arduous campaign.

Several others were wounded. Lieut. A. H. Trego received a slight wound from a spent ball. It was a position of great danger, yet the skirmishers executed their task well.

Farther to the right a severe fight took place, and the 70th Indiana, 79th Ohio and 129th Illinois regiments lost quite heavily. The 105th lost several men during the day.

Late at night we were ordered to retire, but had not proceeded far before the order was countermanded. We returned to the abandoned rebel skirmish line, and constructed strong works,—the brigade being then formed on that line. The troops secured a short sleep before daylight.

Soon after daylight, Colonel Smith went out to the skirmish line to make a personal reconnoissance of the enemy's position. While there he was singled out by a rebel sharpshooter, who must have discovered his rank. The ball struck above the knee and passed through the limb, barely missing the bone.

The Colonel came in leaning upon the arm of one of his men. The men gathered around and anxiously inquired how badly he was hurt. He was unwilling to admit the serious nature of his wound, and replied: "I am only scratched a little boys." It was difficult to convince him that it was necessary for him to be taken to the rear.

The loss of Colonel Smith at that juncture, was deeply felt by the regiment. The command then devolved upon Lieut. Col. J. M. Mannon.

During the forenoon of the 16th, artillery was placed in position along our works. At one o'clock the guns opened upon the enemy, and kept up a lively cannonade until late in the afternoon. The rebel skirmishers continued actively at work, but their fire did not interrupt the serving of the guns. The woods between our works and theirs were so heavy that the effect of our shot could not be ascertained. In one case, however, a ball was seen to strike a log that lay upon the top of their works. The rebels ran in confusion from the locality, and our sharpshooters took advantage of the occasion, to throw a volley of balls into their midst.

All was quiet along the line at sunset. The men had generally finished their suppers,—some were at the small creek in the rear, washing; numbers were off some distance from the breastworks—when, "*whiz*" came a rebel shell and exploded immediately in rear of the works— then another, and another, and then,—*bang, bang, bang,* —three or four almost simultaneously, scattering fire and fragments all around. This lasted perhaps twenty minutes. In the meantime we lay close up to the breastworks, thinking the exhibition of fireworks, rather interesting, but willing to have it end at any time.

The rebel guns had been well aimed, yet, as far as we could learn, they did no damage whatever.

A short time after the shelling ceased we were relieved by another regiment, and were ordered to fall back a hundred yards.

The men could not see the justice of being relieved at that juncture from works they had built themselves.

Fortunately the rebels did not renew the bombardment. Ere morning they evacuated their line, and fell back to a new position three miles distant.

After removing to the rear on the evening of the 16th, as above stated, a large mail was received, and distributed. The moon shone brightly, and many of the soldiers read their letters by moonlight.

Next morning we visited the vacated rebel works. They were very substantial. The first line was sufficiently strong to resist heavy artillery, and in front of it the enemy had driven stakes, leaving sharpened points for the Yankees to impale themselves upon in making a charge. A battery had been stationed where it could deliver a raking fire upon an approaching column. There were three lines of works. The place could not have been taken by direct assault without terrible loss. But the rebels were compelled by a flank movement to retire.

At eleven o'clock, on the 17th, there was another general forward movement. The 20th and 23d corps, forming the right of a long line of battle, swung round and pressed closely upon the enemy, about five miles southwest of Kenesaw Mountain. The advance was made in excellent order. To cover our real strength and designs, the 3d Division marched by a circuitous route through thick timber. Through the thickest underbrush the troops moved by the right of companies to the front, and then by the left flank, debouching in an open field, where they were massed under cover of a hill. While the movement was being made there was heavy firing a short distance in advance. The cannon balls, cutting through the air, kept up for some moments a constant screeching howl, and for a time we were uncertain whether they were fired by our men or by the enemy. Reaching the open field the position became intelligible. From the summit of a hill in our front there was a fine view of the situation. Three-fourths of a mile in front the rebels had chosen a good position on a heavily wooded hill, beyond a small creek. The valley through which the creek ran had been "cleared" and cultivated. On a bare hill overlooking this valley, a mile and a half to the right of us, one of Gen. Schofield's batteries had audaciously taken up an advanced position a few hundred yards from the enemy. For some time the men worked the guns with savage energy. Firing by volley, a sheet of fire would burst forth from the battery, and then among the tree tops over the rebels, white puffs of smoke could be seen where the shells exploded, and after this, in quick succession, would come the roar of the discharge and the sounds of the exploding shells. Directly in our front one of our division batteries was actively served, and away to the left still others were at work. The guns of the enemy replied only at intervals. The skirmishing was active all along the line, and at one time far away to the left there was a heavy roll of musketry.

The cannonading on the evening of the 17th, and during the 18th, exceeded all previous exhibitions in that line—so far as our experience had extended. The picture was a magnificent one. The artillerymen working grimly amid the smoke of their guns; the hills and valleys enveloped in a hazy battle cloud, and the great dead pine trees, lifting their ghostly arms heavenward, made up a scene that reminded us of descriptions we had read of some of Napoleon's Prussian battle-fields.

It rained all day the 18th, and we were very uncomfortable in our little shelter-tents. But a ration of whisky was issued in the afternoon, and of course the situation was at once vastly improved.

During the night of the 18th, the enemy fell back to a position around Kenesaw Mountain, covering Marietta; and on the 19th our right wing made another swing to press back their left.

We crossed the little creek previously referred to, and found it much swollen by the recent rain. The bridge which the pioneers had made, was swept away, and we were compelled to wade the stream. A mile beyond we were massed on the slope of a hill, and were told that we were about to "go for them" again.

At length the brigade was deployed in line of battle— the 102d being on the extreme right of the corps was "refused," that is, formed at a right angle with the advancing line, to protect the right flank. Co. C was deployed as skirmishers.

Marching as usual through dense pines, and under a variety of conflicting orders, there was much confusion in the movement. First to the right, then to the left, then forward, then rearward the columns moved—receiving a few shots from the enemy, which did no damage. Meantime on the left there was heavy firing without any marked result.

Finally a line of works was thrown up. The evening of the next day, another demonstration was made similar to the first. The men protested very strongly against such vexatious "battallion drills."

Co. C remained on the skirmish line during the 20th. A large oak tree near the reserve post was used as an observatory and afforded an excellent view of the ground in front. Gen. Hooker climbed into the top of the tree, and Major Gens. Thomas, Howard, Schofield, McCook and Butterfield, besides one or two Brigadiers, visited that part of the field during the day, to make observations. Several of the leading Generals held a council of war in a log hut near by.

After dark the regiment was moved forward a short distance and ordered to build a new line of works. The works were completed at midnight. Remained in that position during the 21st. Co. B was that day sent out on the skirmish line, and was deployed in front of the 136th New York Regiment. The Colonel of that regiment advanced then into a position which he seemed afraid to occupy himself, or with men of his own regiment. The enemy opened a sharp cross fire upon them, and they returned the fire as best they could from behind stumps, trees, and a rail fence. Some of them were so much exposed, that the slightest movement of their bodies brought a volley of bullets around them. In that position they lost one man killed, and one wounded.

On the 22d of June the right wing of the army again advanced. There was more or less fighting all along the line. Gen. William's division of our corps was assaulted by the enemy in the afternoon. The men had commenced building breastworks when the rebels advanced in heavy columns against them. A number of batteries had been placed in position to sweep an open field through which they advanced. As they appeared in the open field they were subjected to a terrific fire of musketry and artillery. Finally they were beaten back with terrible loss.

Our division was on the left of the division engaged. The cannonading was very heavy.

In the meantime there had been much activity on our part of the line. We seemed to hover all day on the verge of battle.

The general advance was made just before noon. The brigade advanced in the following order: 102d Illinois and 79th Ohio, in the first line; the 70th Indiana, 105th and 129th Illinois in the second.

The column moved to the edge of an open field and halted for a time under fire. Several men were there wounded and others narrowly escaped being struck. A tin-cup attached to Capt. Ed. H. Conger's haversack, which was suspended at his side, was perforated by a musket ball.

Presently the word "forward" ran along the line, and we moved "at double-quick" into the open field. As the column emerged from the woods we observed that it was connected with a long line of blue that was sweeping across the field on the right. Our advance was accelerated by the inspiring scene, and we ran at the top of our speed to the edge of the woods in front. There we were ordered to halt and lie down, and many no doubt felt inclined to "grab a root."

Strange as it may appear, no one was hit in crossing the field. When we halted, the rebels poured in their balls thick and fast. One or two men were there wounded.

Light breastworks were thrown up, but had scarcely been finished when we were ordered to the right a quarter of a mile. Moved under fire to the new position. In passing over a hill were in plain view of the rebel sharpshooters. Near the summit of the hill one of the men fell, severely wounded.

Again we were ordered to fortify, and during that evening and the following night finished another line of works.

Next morning we marched to the position where Gen. William's division repulsed the enemy near the Kulp House. Some of the dead were yet unburied. We camped in line of battle—reserve line—in a hollow where many of them had fallen. A small strip of timber at the bottom of the ravine had been fairly riddled by shot and shell from William's division. Pools of blood here and there indicated where the brave but misguided rebels fell. It was one of Hood's slaughter pens.

In our position as reserves at that place, we were as much exposed to the enemy's balls as we would have been on the front line. They sometimes passed far beyond us to the rear. At other times dropped uncomfortably near. There we remained until the night of the 26th when we moved up to the front line.

During the time we were in reserve the Brigade furnished pickets every evening—as was customary when in the front. The men were thus often brought into close contact with the enemy, for the skirmishers were seldom idle, day or night.

Our position in the line was about five miles southwest of Kenesaw Mountain, and commanded a view of the Mountain, and much of the intervening country. Kenesaw Mountain proper is the highest peak of a double mountain, and rises " eighteen hundred and twenty-eight feet above the sea level."* The summit is nearly bare. A live tree, which stands on the highest point, may be seen as far as the Mountain itself is visible.

Kenesaw was in included within the rebel lines. Upon its summit they had planted heavy artillery.

The morning of the 27th the troops were ordered to remain near the breastworks—ready to take arms at a moment's notice. The programme was that there should be a demonstration all along the line, and at eight o'clock an assault at some point on the left. At an early hour the artillery commenced work, and the firing was constant until eight A. M.

At that time the cannonading in a measure ceased. Those who were in eligible positions saw dense columns of blue, far away to the left, advancing across an open field towards the enemy. Soon they disappeared in thick woods, and there was a crashing roll of musketry, which increased every moment and held all observers spellbound. From our batteries in the open field referred to,

* Lippincott's Geographical Dictionary.

the white smoke leaped; at times from each gun in succession, and then from all together, and the bursting shells left other white puffs of smoke, away over in the woods near the rebel line. And the rebel guns were not idle. Volumes of smoke arising at different points in the thick woods, indicated their position. Occasionally their balls would make the dust fly on the hillside near our batteries.

Far away beyond the immediate scene of action volumes of white smoke rolled away from the guns on Kenesaw Mountain, as they threw shot and shell into our lines. And above the mountain top, or near its summit, the smoke of bursting shells from union guns, was occasionally seen.

It was a magnificent battle scene, without a realization of all the attending horrors. Alas! amid that storm of human passion many true hearts ceased to beat forever.

The assault was made by parts of the 4th and 14th Corps. The enemy's works were impregnable, and the assault was a sad failure. The troops fought with desperate courage. The 27th Ill's regiment, planted its colors on the rebel works, but could not hold the position.

The assaulting column finally threw up breastworks within a stone's throw of the enemy.

In reference to the preliminary operations, and the subsequent battles about Kenesaw, the following interesting paragraphs occur in Gen. Sherman's report:

"Kenesaw, the bold and striking twin mountain, lay before us, with a high range of chestnut hills trending off to the northeast, terminating to our view in another peak, called Brushy Mountain. To our right was the smaller hill called Pine Mountain, and beyond it in the distance, Lost Mountain. All these, though links in a continuous chain, present a sharp, conical appearance, prominent in the vast landscape that presents itself from any of the hills that abound in that region. Kenesaw, Pine Mountain and Lost Mountain form a triangle; Pine Mountain the apex, and Kenesaw and Lost Mountains the base, covering perfectly the town of Marietta and the railroad back to the Chattahoochie."

* * * * * * *

"The scene was enchanting; too beautiful to be disturbed by the harsh clamors of war, but the Chattahoochie lay beyond, and I had to reach it."

* * * * * * *

"During our operations about Kenesaw the weather was villainously bad, and the rain fell almost continuously for three weeks, rendering our narrow wooded roads mere mud gullies, so that a general movement would have been impossible, but our men daily worked closer and closer to their entrenched foe, and kept up an incessant picket firing, galling to him."

After referring to the terrible repulse of Hood's corps at the Kulp House, he continues:

"Although inviting the enemy at all times to commit such mistakes, I could not hope for him to repeat them, after the example of Dallas and the 'Kulp House,' and upon studying the ground, I had no alternative, in my turn, but to assault his lines or turn his position. Either course had its difficulties and dangers. And I perceived that the enemy and our own officers had settled down into the conviction that I would not assault fortified lines."

"All looked to me to 'outflank.' An army to be efficient must not settle down to one single mode of offense, but must be prepared to execute any plan which promises success."

General Sherman therefore resolved to assault the enemy's fortified lines, at a point "where success would give the largest fruits of victory." Consequently, the assault of June 27th was made. After reviewing the disastrous result, he says: "Failure as it was, and for which I assume the entire responsibility, I yet claim it produced good fruits, as it demonstrated to Gen. Johnston that I would assault and that boldly, and we also gained and held ground so close to the enemy's parapets that he could not show a head above them."

During the time we were in the front line at the Kulp House, the rebel sharpshooters made frequent attempts to pick off men who exposed themselves before certain openings in the woods. They fired low and their balls often grazed the breastworks. One man had his lip cut by a ball, and another who was seated upon the ground a short distance in the rear of the works, and was about to drink a cup of coffee, had his arm barked, and his coffee upset by a ball.

An explosive ball struck a shelter tent and exploded, leaving a number of holes in the tent.

We were sometimes amused by the music of the musket balls. One would come along with the "*meow*" of a kitten, and the men would declare the rebels were throwing kittens at them. Another would come with an angry howl as if seeking its Yankee victim. And we listened to others that had the wailing sound of a winter's wind. All these sounds were more musical than the "zip" of the bullet at short range.

The brigade was relieved on the 29th, and we marched to the rear for a brief rest. Major Gen. Butterfield having been relieved, Brig. Gen. W. T. Ward—more generally known as "Pap Ward," assumed command of the division, and Col. Benj. Harrison of the 70th Indiana, succeeded him in command of the brigade.

The evening of the first of July the regiment returned to the second line of works. During the next day there was heavy cannonading, and picket firing as usual. At night we were ordered to be in readiness to move at a moment's notice. Before morning the rebels left, and shortly after daylight July 3d, the troops were in pursuit.

Our division moved out on the Marietta road; the brigade in advance of the division, and the 102d in advance of the brigade.

The regiment moved forward, first by the flank, and finally in line of battle with Cos. E, G, F and B in advance as skirmishers. The four companies were under the command of Capt. Sedwick, who first deployed Co. E, and afterwards others as they were needed.

After marching about two miles, the skirmishers became engaged with the rear guard of the enemy, which was a force of three hundred cavalry.

Capt. Sedwick managed the affair with admirable skill. The rebels slowly retired, firing irregularly. Several times they halted, and commenced forming a line to charge upon our skirmish line. But Capt. S. pressed forward with his men, and by keeping up a steady fire, gave them no time to form. After each attempt they retreated in confusion.

In the meantime the companies in reserve were kept up in supporting distance. It was a lively scene. There were stately residences at the roadside, with neatly ornamented grounds, enclosed by picket fences. In advancing it became necessary to pass through these enclosures and it was surprising to see the boards fly as the men dashed forward.

In the affair, one man had the skin peeled from his cheek, by a passing ball. There were no other casualties. Capt. Sedwick, with his detachment, finally drove the enemy's rear guard out of Marietta, occupying the town nearly an hour before any other troops.

During the morning a great many rebels came in as voluntary prisoners.

About noon there was a movement to the right, an advance in line of battle; then by the right flank, into an open field, from which the enemy could be seen busily throwing dirt—constructing works—on a range of hills a mile distant. Then there was another movement to the right into a secluded and romantic locality. The troops were massed on the slope of a hill. At that place Col. H. Case, 129th Illinois, enunciated the famous command: "*Attention*, BATTALLION! *Order* ARMS! Five men from each company take the canteens and go for water, *stack!* ARMS."

Camped near that locality in thick woods. It had been a wearisome day—weather excessively warm.

The Fourth of July was a quiet day. There was some cannonading off to the left. We celebrated the day as best we could on "hard tack," salt pork and coffee. Late in the afternoon moved southward three-fourths of a mile; camped in an apple orchard where we obtained plenty of green apples. The army seemed perfectly happy that evening. The bands were all playing, and the soldiers were singing, laughing, joking and shouting in a manner that would have astonished people in civil life.

Moved again on the 5th, in the direction of the Chattahoochie river.

In the meantime the rebels continued to fall back. There was heavy skirmishing in front. We crossed Nickajack creek and camped on the hill beyond. Advanced on the 6th to the "Chattahoochie heights," where, from tree-tops, we first beheld the spires and domes of the city of Atlanta. Yankee eyes were there fixed on the coveted prize, and Atlanta was doomed. We were at that time ten miles from the city.

It was a proud day for Sherman's men. Day after day, and week after week, they had pressed forward—worn and weary from marching, fighting and building breastworks,—and at length they seemed about to realize the triumph for which they had struggled so long.

The difficulties encountered in prosecuting such a campaign into the heart of the enemy's country could hardly be appreciated by those at a distance from the scene of operations.

The country is rugged and heavily timbered. Vegetation was very luxuriant, and all the hills were covered with a dense growth of underbrush.

It required consummate generalship to move forward a line of battle fifteen or twenty miles in length through such a wild region. Often it seemed, in advancing, that the only way was to "go it blind." A frail line of communication, extending hundreds of miles through an enemy's country, was the only dependence for supplies.

On the other hand, the enemy were thoroughly acquainted with the ground over which they fought and retreated, and they only fought in chosen positions. Whenever they halted they built breastworks of the strongest kind. Take the following description as an example. First a line of rifle-pits for their skirmishers—not difficult to capture. Then in rear of the skirmish pits—from one hundred to three hundred yards—a line of breastworks; so constructed that but little more than the eyes of the rebels were exposed—a head-log being placed upon the works. In front of the line *chevaux-de-frise*, or, as the men termed them, "horse rakes," were placed. Also sharpened stakes. The underbrush, which grew everywhere in that region, was usually cut or hacked and lopped over, between the main line and the skirmish line. The tops were so intermingled that a person could barely pick his way through when there was no enemy to oppose. Often there were two or three lines of works, and usually a deep ditch in front of the first. Military men of less genius than Gen. Sherman, would have broken the army into fragments on these impregnable works. His fertile mind suggested other expedients for defeating the enemy.

In the face of such opposition the rebel army had been pressed back from the vicinity of Chattanooga to the Chattahoochie.

It is said that after Gen. Johnston had followed his retreating policy several weeks, the rebels declared that their army was commanded by "Old Billy Sherman,"— that they invariably moved when Sherman gave the command and Johnston only superintended the details of the movement."

By the 10th of the month the entire rebel army was across the river. Our own army remained quiet a number of days, enjoying a much needed rest.

CHAPTER VIII.

In Camp on the Chattahoochie Heights. Friendly intercourse with the Rebel Pickets. Offensive Movements Resumed. GREAT BATTLE AT PEACH TREE CREEK. SIEGE OF ATLANTA.

While encamped on the Chattahoochie heights, there was a cessation of hostilities between the pickets of our division and the rebel pickets confronting them.

Friendly interviews were occasionally held, which sometimes terminated in an arrangement for the Johnnies to come over and abandon their sinking cause.

One day while the corps commanded by Hardee was still north of the river, Lyman B. Straw, of Co. B, 102d, opened communication with a rebel picket and offered to exchange papers. The Reb. agreed to exchange, but in a few moments announced that he could not obtain a paper.

"Then meet me half way and I will give you one," said 'Beecher.'

"Agreed," said the other.

The pickets on both sides were cautioned to refrain from firing. The parties met and shook hands, when the following conversation took place:

Yankee. How are you, Johnnie?

Rebel. How are you, Jimmie—and now tell me why you call us "Johnnies."

Yankee. Because you live on Johnnie-cakes.

Rebel. Well, for a nickname, we must call you Jimmies. When are you going into Atlanta?

Yankee. When will you cross the river?

[At this a squad of rebels a short distance from them laughed heartily, saying it was a genuine Yankee reply.]

Rebel. Who commands your corps now?

Yankee. Joe. Hooker.

Rebel. I thought Joe. Hooker was dead. We have been informed officially, three or four times, that he had been killed or wounded. I believe the old fellow will live forever.

Yankee. I think he will live to see the rebellion put down. By the way, are you not sick of the war?

Rebel. Yes. So much so that there are thirteen of us here who intend to go over to your lines the first opportunity we have.

Yankee. Come over to-night, then; we will not fire upon you.

Rebel. All right; we will come. After a few additional remarks the parties shook hands and separated.

During the interview hundreds of the enemy came out of their breastworks to witness the scene. A large number of our men were also spectators of the interview. When the parties separated, the spectators on both sides quietly disappeared.

According to the arrangement, the rebels attempted to come in that night. Unfortunately, however, they made the attempt some distance to the left of the picket post near which the interview had been held. The rebel pickets detected the movement and fired upon them, and our pickets, supposing the enemy were about to attack, returned the fire. Only three of the thirteen succeeded in reaching our lines.

After Hardee's corps crossed the river, the pickets of the opposing armies confronted each other on opposite sides of the stream. A lively traffic in tobacco, coffee and other articles sprang up between them. The rebels would swim across with plugs of tobacco tied about their necks, and return with a small sack of coffee. There was very little personal hostility between the soldiers of the two armies. They respected each other as brave men.

The troops marched from the heights on the 17th of July, late in the afternoon. At dusk crossed the Chattahoochie on a pontoon bridge at Paice's Ferry. Marched three miles beyond the river eastward, and camped on an elevated, stony ridge. Moved next day two and a half miles southward, towards Atlanta. Camped in heavy timber. Were aroused the morning of the 19th, at three o'clock, to build breastworks. While the work was progressing a sad accident occurred. A tree, cut near the line of works, fell across the ground occupied by Co. H, mortally wounding S. Kite, who was sound asleep at the time. He died during the day.

At seven o'clock A. M., July 20th, we were again in motion, under orders to occupy a range of hills south of Peach Tree Creek. There had been considerable artillery firing during the two previous days, and it was apparent, by all the movements, that the enemy were in strong force a short distance ahead.

As we neared the creek, skirmishing became active in front, and we were soon in range of the balls. Crossing the stream we halted for a time in a corn-field at the base of a hill. The day was intolerably warm—scarcely a breath of air stirring. At length we moved a half mile to the right. While marching by the flank through a corn-field in the valley, an advance was made by our skirmishers, up the hillside a few hundred yards to the left, or front. The rebels fired briskly and their balls whisked spitefully through the young corn. No one in the regiment was struck. We halted again at the base of the range of hills south of the creek.

The rebel sharpshooters were busily at work. Several men were struck while we were in that position. A battery which our artillerymen endeavored to plant on a bare hill a short distance in rear of our line, was subjected to such a scathing fire that it was taken away as quick as the horses could remove it under whip and spur. Nevertheless, we did not anticipate any very serious work—nothing more than a slight skirmish, when we should advance to construct works at the crest of the hill.

Our division had been formed in an irregular line of battle, on the right of the 4th Corps. The second division rested on our right—some of the regiments closed in mass, drawing rations, cooking, &c. The intention was to deploy the division in line of battle on the right of ours, connecting with the left of the 14th Corps. The movement was finally accelerated somewhat by the enemy.

The 1st Division was in reserve. About four o'clock P. M., word ran along the line that the rebels were charging. At the same moment an order was given to advance to the crest of the hill. Quickly the men sprang into line and moved forward. Reaching the summit, they immediately became engaged with the enemy.

The First Brigade had been formed on the right of the division, and the 102d was on the right of the brigade—next on the left was the 79th Ohio, and on the left of that regiment was the 129th Illinois. The 70th Indiana and 105th Illinois regiments were at first held in reserve, but they moved forward when the battle was at its height, and engaged the enemy in a hand to hand fight.

On the right of our regiment, a battery had been planted. Near this battery the left of the 2d Division rested, when the battle commenced.

The 102d occupied a knoll, in front of which was a clump of timber and a small creek. Farther to the left this stream curved northward, and across it the left of the brigade was formed.

The rebels advanced in heavy masses down the slope of a hill in front of the 2d and 3d Brigades, and the left of our brigade. The inequalities of the ground prevented them from advancing in force in our immediate front.

On the left of the 20th Corps they struck Newton's Division of the 4th Corps, and on the right engaged a brigade of the 14th Corps. Between the 14th Corps and our position on the line, they hurled a heavy column on the 2d division of the 20th Corps.

Our position on the knoll commanded a fine view of the open field through which the enemy advanced on the left. Sheets of fire blazed along the line of muskets in their front. Yet without faltering or wavering they pressed forward, their advance actually piercing the center of our division—the body of gray intermingling with the line of blue.

They were subjected to a terrible enfilading fire from the 79th Ohio and the 102d Illinois. A perpetual sheet of flame blazed from the Spencer rifles in the hands of our men. And the battery on our right with wonderful energy poured shot and shell into their ranks. Still for a time they persisted firing as they moved forward. Rebel flags waved defiantly in their front line, and were shot down—but quickly taken up and carried forward to the line where waved the stars and stripes. A hand to hand contest ensued at that point, the combattants half hidden by fire and smoke and dust.

Will the enemy never give back? With intense solicitude we mark the ebb and flow of battle. At last they waver; numbers drop to the rear, others quickly follow, and finally the entire body is rolled back in utter rout and confusion by our advancing lines. And then the suppressed feelings of the victors find utterance in a shout that rises high above the roar of battle—a wild, thrilling, prolonged shout of victory.

In the meantime, unknown to most of us, Gen. Geary's Division had been pressed back in confusion. The enemy followed up their advantage with the utmost impetuosity, and their columns surged around on our right until they had nearly reached the rear of our regiment. A battery which temporarily fell into their hands, was turned upon us, the guns enfilading the line formed by our brigade.

At that critical moment an Aid rode up to our regimental commander, Capt. Wm. A. Wilson, and told him that unless he withdrew the regiment it would be captured in less than five minutes. The Captain "didn't see it." The battery on his right was being served with unexampled skill and bravery, and he had determined to stand by it to the last.

It was a critical situation. Victory was almost within the grasp of the impetuous enemy, but at this juncture the 1st Division, which had been held in reserve, rushed forward and restored the fortunes of the day.

Defeated at all points, the rebels abandoned the field leaving the most of their dead and wounded in our hands, besides a large number of prisoners.

Sharp skirmishing and heavy cannonading continued however, until dark. As darkness came on, the smoke of battle settled down over the field, and still, through the deepening gloom the blaze of our cannons could be seen on the right and left, and the flash of picket guns at intervals along the line.

The night was calm, and as the full moon approached the zenith, it shone brightly over a quiet field, illuminating the pale features of the dead. The living had sought repose, save the watchful sentinels, and here and there a wakeful soldier, whose eyes perchance wandered to the gauzy clouds, floating before the moon, flecked with a thousand delicate hues, and faintly veiling the distant stars. In the midst of such loveliness how strange that men should enact the savage scenes of war.

The following day was occupied in burying the dead. The slope of the hill on the left, down which the enemy had moved so bravely the day before, was thickly strewn with their dead.

In the report of the Atlanta campaign, Gen. Sherman states that at the battle of Peach Tree Creek; "the enemy left on the field five hundred dead, three thousand wounded severely, seven stands of colors, and many prisoners. His loss could not have fallen short of five thousand, whereas ours was covered by fifteen hundred killed, wounded and missing." Gen. Hooker estimated the enemy's loss at six thousand. Our brigade captured three stands of colors.

Owing to the favorable position our regiment occupied we lost lightly—two men killed and nine wounded. The loss of the brigade was about one hundred and seventy killed and wounded.

Although the 102d escaped with so little loss, the regiment inflicted immense damage on the enemy. It was estimated at the time, that five thousand rounds of cartridges were fired from the Spencer rifles 'alone.

Capt. Wm. A. Wilson commanded the regiment during the action. He was ably assisted by Capt. Dan W. Sedwick. Lieut. Col. Mannon was too unwell to command, yet he remained with the regiment during the battle.

The men needed no encouragement to induce them to do their duty. They fought with the enthusiasm of patriots and the coolness of veterans.

The officers were all at their posts. Capt. Andrews, on the right, no doubt made up his mind during the crisis of the fight, that he would in accordance with his usual obstinacy *die right there* rather than give back an inch. Capt. Woolley, it is presumed, made an application of his celebrated axiom in philosophy, namely— "*Well, it is just like this, everything has a beginning and an ending—except a ring, and that had before it was welded.*" And thus fortified he endured to the end, and received due credit for his good conduct.

Capt. Clay's black eye-flashed fire as he maneuvered Co. D.

Capt. Conger, ever at his post in the hour of danger, coolly and judiciously directed the operations of Co. I.

Lieut. Trego with the light of battle in his eye told Co. C where to fire.

Co. H, commanded by Capt. Elliott—one of the bravest among the brave—did gallant work.

Co. E warmed up the Spencer guns as the hearts of the men became warmed with patriotic enthusiasm. The company was commanded by Lieut. Brown, who seemed as cool in battle as on battallion drill.

Lieut. Willets commanded Co. K, and under his guidance that company added fresh laurels to its fame.

The men of "G," were bravely led by Lieut. Bridgeford. The company was much exposed, but did its duty well.

Co B, under Orderly Terpening, moved forward where the balls flew thickest, and fought nobly.

Adjutant J. H. Snyder was conspicuous along the line, aiding the commanding officers.

Capt. J. Y. Merritt, was in the fight as Brig. Provost Marshal. Lieut. Peebles commanded the sharpshooters.

Lieut. Sheahan and Lieut. Jordan, efficiently aided their respective company commanders.

The brigade commander, Col. Ben. Harrison *alias* "Little Ben," moved from point to point along the line, utterly reckless of flying balls.

General Ward had established his headquarters in the valley, near the creek, and at a point that commanded a view of the field where his Division fought. It is said the old General was in ecstacies when the 1st Brigade went into action. "See my old Iron Brigade," said he, striking his fists together. "See my old Iron Brigade—see them go in—the best d—d brigade in the service!"

Throughout the fight the 1st Brigade preserved an unbroken line, giving back not an inch, and never wavering for a moment.

The entire corps was elated with the victory. It had been an open field fight, in which the advantages were with the enemy. The morning after the battle General Hooker rode along the lines and received the tumultuous cheers of the soldiers. Subsequently he issued a congratulatory order.

An extensive budget of incidents could be made up in giving an account of each battle. These were sometimes amusing and sometimes painful. The conduct of some of the men while under fire at Peach Tree Creek was particularly amusing. An excentric member of Company C was in his element. Wild with enthusiasm, he committed all kinds of antics, firing his gun and waving his hat alternately, and yelling occasionally like a Comanche Indian.

An instance of unsurpassed courage is related of a rebel Captain, whose maneuvres were observed by an officer in the 129th Illinois regiment. The rebel officer was a tall, fine looking man. With drawn sword he walked along the rear of his company and urged the men forward to our line of battle, manifesting not the slightest regard for the bullets that were thinning the ranks about him. As the rebel line commenced giving away he vainly endeavored to rally his men, and when they fled in utter confusion, he walked away as coolly as if promenading for pleasure. It was an extraordinary exhibition of cool courage. Among the rebel wounded there was a young girl only nineteen years of age. A ball had struck her ankle and she was obliged to have her foot amputated. She bore her suffering heroically. Stated that she had been twenty-eight months in the rebel service, and was not sorry that she had enlisted, but would willingly suffer twice as much for her country.

The night after the battle, a member of the 129th Illinois Regiment, being posted as a vidette, heard men talking in a ravine about fifty yards from him. He hailed them and threatened to fire, and they replied that they would surrender. They immediately marched up, fourteen in number, and surrendered to the astonished vidette. A commissioned officer was with them. During the battle they had advanced into a position from which they could not retire without great peril. When hailed by the vidette they were making preparations to return to their own lines.

It is said that General Hood told his men, when about to advance, that they were "going out to gather acorns;" alluding to the men of the 14th corps, who wore a badge representing an acorn. Their intention was to break through the line on the left of that corps, as we subsequently learned. They did not suppose they would encounter anything more than a mere skirmish line in their front, but were wofully disappointed, for in their course they met the ubiquitous "stars.".

The advance was resumed July 22d, the enemy having fallen back from the position occupied the previous day. We advanced some distance without opposition—marching in line of battle through dense underbrush, where the briars were thick, and loaded with luscious blackberries, which we were compelled to leave for the "bummers."

Many thought we would march into the city without further opposition. Gen. Sherman, in his report referring to the evacuation of the rebel line in front of Peach Tree Creek, says: "On the morning of the 22d, somewhat to my surprise, this whole line was found abandoned, and I confess I thought the enemy had resolved to give us Atlanta without further contest."

But the enemy was soon developed, and by noon the great battle in which the lamented McPherson fell, commenced on the extreme left of the army.

The 20th corps pressed up close to the enemy's forts around Atlanta, and erected breastworks, our Brigade occupying a position on the line three-fourths of a mile east of the Chattanooga and Atlanta railroad.

In that position the enemy shelled us very actively during the evening of the 22d, also on the 23d, 24th and 25th. Two men in the regiment were wounded.

The shelling at night was really interesting. The flash of rebel guns at different points along the horizon resembling the blaze of lightning from a rising cloud; but the occasional bursting of shells in close proximity to our works, detracted immensely from the romance of the situation. While in that position the pickets had several sharp encounters with the enemy. The Brigade picket line was driven in by a superior force on the 24th of July. By a special order from the Brigade Commander, Captain Sedwick, with Co. E, was directed to reinforce the line and recover the lost ground. After a sharp skirmish the rebels were compelled to retire.

The picket line in front of our Brigade was considerably in advance of the line on the right and on the left. A deep ravine running from the rebel line traversed the left of our line and passed in rear of the reserve post. By following this ravine the rebels might have flanked the line at any time. The knowledge of this fact rendered the men constantly uneasy when on duty in that advanced position. On the night of the 24th, about 11 o'clock, the enemy made a heavy demonstration on that part of the line. The stillness of the night was suddenly broken by a terrific fire of musketry. Lieut. A. H. Trego commanded the outposts at that time. A few of his men became panic-stricken and fled to the rear, but the Lieutenant gallantly rallied the remainder, and, amid a shower of rebel bullets, urged them to stand firm. And they did, for there were a number of dauntless spirits under his command. Among others "Booth" Abbott, of Co. A, handled his Spencer magnificently on that occasion. At length the rebels were repulsed. Lieut. Trego then learned that the reserve post had been abandoned by all save Lieut. Willard Scott of the 105th, and a handful of men. It appears that there were two heavy lines of rebels. This force was repelled by a weak skirmish line, which had been ingloriously deserted by a majority of the reserve or supporting force.

The night of the 25th we moved to a new line of works a hundred yards in advance. At that place we remained under fire until the evening of the 26th. While there a member of Co. I was severely wounded. Just as we were preparing to go to bed, the evening of the 26th, the regiment was relieved and ordered to another part of the field. We then moved to the rear and right, occupying a portion of the second line of works in good shelling range of the enemy. And while there they improved the opportunity to shell us day and night—occasionally throwing some huge missiles that had the appearance of old-fashioned wagon hubs.

At that place, on the 29th, General Hooker assembled the officers of the 3d Division and bade them adieu, stating that he had been misused and could not consistently retain the command of the 20th corps. The old General had become very popular among the officers and men of his corps during the campaign, and all regretted his departure.

Many who had looked upon him with distrust and prejudice, before serving under him, became convinced, after a few months campaigning, that he could handle his troops with masterly skill, and when assuming a hazardous position in presence of the enemy, they only asked to know that old "Uncle Joe" was around.

During the afternoon of the 28th, the battle of Ezra's Church took place. The fight was several miles away towards the right. The 3d Division was ordered around to support the troops engaged but had not proceeded far before the order was countermanded. Our assistance was not needed, and we returned to the camp on the left of the railroad.

Next morning the Division moved to the extreme right flank of the army, where it was formed in line of battle at a right angle with the main line, thus covering and protecting the flank and rear.

Nothing of special interest occurred while in that position. On the 2d day of August the 23d Corps moved around to the right flank. Our Division was relieved and we marched towards the left. Halted late in the evening in an open field in rear of the 14th Corps. Moved next morning at sunrise into a position on the left of the 14th Corps, occupying a beautiful plat of ground in rear of strong works, west of, and very near the railroad.

Colonel Smith, having recovered from his wound, rejoined the Regiment on the 10th.

We remained in that vicinity until the 25th of the month, occasionally advancing the lines. The work of advancing the lines was usually accomplished in the following manner. A new general line was selected from 50 to 100 yards in advance, shortening a part of the curved line formed by the besieging army. The brigade or brigades in rear of the new line furnished fatigue parties from each regiment, which parties finished substantial works in a day or two, and under cover of night the troops took possession of them. We moved thus into a new line on the night of the 5th of August, and again on the 13th of the month.

A sketch of one day's experience at that time would be almost a counterpart of the history of each day passed before Atlanta.

There were occasional exciting moments when the pickets became engaged far away on the right, on the left, or in front. Sometimes these affairs occurred in the daytime, but more frequently at night. One quiet afternoon, when the men were variously employed about the quarters—reading, writing, playing cards, etc., an alarm of this kind occurred. The rebels made a dash on the picket line in front, and for a time we thought they were *coming for us*. Quickly every man was at the breastworks with gun in hand. The balls of the enemy flew around very lively for awhile. But it was only a demonstration on the picket line, and soon all was quiet again.

SIEGE OF ATLANTA.

During all those days picket firing and cannonading scarcely ceased for a moment. It is true that on some parts of the line the pickets of the opposing armies occasionally agreed to an informal truce, but at other points the firing was perpetual.

Many guns had been placed in position along our works. One 4½ inch rifled piece on the left of the railroad, sent a huge shell into the city every five minutes regularly, day and night. Far in the night we listened to its heavy "boom," followed by the fluttering of the shell, and then a dull, hollow, unearthly roar away over in the city, as if the bursting shell had crashed through huge buildings.

The rebels sometimes opened vehemently with their guns, but they were usually silenced by our batteries.

The practice of standing at arms was strictly observed at that time, or, at least, strict orders were issued requiring the men to be in the trenches with their guns by four o'clock each morning. It was sometimes a little difficult to enforce the order as the men had been overtasked for many weeks in succession.

An amusing incident illustrating this phase of our experience occurred on the morning of August 18th. At four o'clock, as usual, the orderly sergeants commenced the task of arousing the men. But the men were drowsy; some yawned and rolled over, while a few reluctantly threw their blankets from them and got up. The orderlies were making unusually slow progress in their work, when the sound of a rebel cannon broke on the still morning air, and a shell burst with a deafening sound near our breast-works, scattering fragments promiscuously through the quarters. Others followed, passing close to the works, and in less time than it requires to write this sentence every man was at his post in the trenches.

Several mornings the enemy commenced firing about daylight, but a converging fire was brought to bear upon their forts from batteries along our line, and they were soon willing to let us alone.

A battery on our right which was called the Dutch Battery "talked" to them in a way that was amusing. Whenever the rebel guns commenced, the Dutch

Battery opened—"firing by file"—"bang," "bang," "bang," one gun after another quickly dropping a shell in the rebel line. It was evident the enemy got the worst of it whenever they stirred up the Dutch Battery.

The opposing picket lines were in some places very close together. The post on the extreme left of the line was established for a time on the railroad in an old wood shed, and was not more than fifty yards from the rebel picket line. The men were compelled in that position to remain closely under cover, as the least exposure of the person attracted a rebel ball. Several men were wounded in that vicinity, and a Lieutenant from the 105th was killed there.

The left of the brigade being on higher and more open ground, was more exposed to the enemy's fire than the right. The 105th suffered most severely. Men were struck by stray balls while lying in their bunks in rear of the works. The 102d had but three men wounded while there. It is strange that the casualties were so few as the men were exposed to the enemy's fire, day after day, and week after week, on the picket line and in camp, and had almost reached the conclusion that lead was a primary element in the Georgia atmosphere.

Some of the most imposing scenes of the war are associated with our recollections of the siege of Atlanta. Sherman's grand army formed a line of battle at least fifteen miles in length. Let us look at the picture: First we observe the irregular line of breast-works winding mile after mile, over hill and valley. In rear of these were the small white shelter tents, pitched in regular order, and a little farther to the rear were long lines of red earth, indicating the positions from which the army had advanced. From several points the city was plainly visible, and through openings in the forest the rebel forts and line of earthworks could be seen; at times thronged with men in gray. From a high range of hills in the rear of our position we had a fine view of the situation. Farther to the rear the immense wagon trains were grouped. Here and there were clusters of neat hospital tents. All the roads were thronged with footmen and horsemen, teamsters, orderlies, Generals and staff officers. In the front the scene was no less active. The inevitable picket firing, as regular as the "droppings" of a slow rain, reached the ear from the picket line. Men in blue, as busy as ants, were constantly moving hither and thither, in the rear of the main line. Light wreaths of smoke were visible where our cannons were at work, and little white "puffs" were occasionally suspended in mid air by exploding rebel shells. The deep, dull roar of artillery, far away, right and left, was heard.

If a single element was needed to render the impression intensely vivid, it was supplied by the glorious music of the field bands, playing those noble campaign pieces, which will never be heard in these days of peace without bringing a tear to the soldier's eye.

The long delay before Atlanta tested the moral courage of the army. What would be done next? The enemy's position seemed impregnable in front. Was Sherman at last brought to a dead lock? Had his flanking machine entirely played out?

Thus we queried, watched and waited. "Grape-vine" —that is, army news received through unofficial sources, —was for a time very scarce, and commanded a premium. At length the prolongation of the line to the right commenced, and every individual in the vast army evinced almost as much interest in the result as Gen. Sherman himself. Finally it appeared that the rebel line of communication could not be reached in that manner, and there were rumors of a grand movement of the whole army to the right.

The character of this movement was fully developed on the 25th of August. We received orders that day to march the following night to the Chattahoochie—the 20th Corps having been assigned the duty of guarding the supplies and the railroad bridge at that point. Portions of the main army at the same time commenced the grand movement to the right on the West Point and Macon railroads. Every arrangement was made during the day for the contemplated movement, and the utmost care was taken to prevent the enemy from suspecting that anything unusual was transpiring. The wheels of the artillery wagons were carefully wrapped with cloths, and in the order directing the details of the movement it was announced that the signal for the movement to commence would be communicated in the following manner: The field bands playing as usual after night-fall, were to cease precisely at eight o'clock, concluding with a piece previously agreed upon, and at that instant the columns were to move.

Night came; all was quiet; the bands assembled, gave us several inspiring strains, and finished up with Yankee Doodle, at precisely eight o'clock, then quietly the troops retired, leaving the skirmish line intact.

It was almost daylight before we got into position at the Chattahoochie. The pickets did not abandon the line confronting the rebels until two or three o'clock in the morning, and failing to get the order to retire, the pickets of the 105th Ill. remained until about daylight. The movement was effected without any loss, and the enemy was surprised and sadly puzzled, when, as daylight dawned they found the whole line in their front abandoned.

The 1st Brigade was finally moved across the Chattahoochie to a position on the railroad a mile north of the bridge, occupying a line of old rebel works, which effectually commanded all approaches from the North.

In the meantime the main army swept down upon the rebel lines of communication south of Atlanta; compelling the evacuation of the city, which took place on the night of the 1st of Sept., and early on the morning of the 2d, Gen. Ward, with a part of the 3d Division occupied the place.

Thus at last the object for which we had marched, fought, and suffered so many months, had been attained. When the regiment left Wauhatchie, four months previous, to a day, it reported four hundred and fifty enlisted men for duty. When it left the front line before Atlanta, August 25th, it numbered two hundred and eighty of that class. Disease and rebel bullets had thinned our ranks. Two hundred and eighty men in line of battle out of about nine hundred non-commissioned officers and privates who put on the blue uniform at Knoxville!

The reader is referred to the concluding chapter for a full and very interesting "Report of operations of the 102d during the Atlanta campaign," by Col. F. C. Smith.

CHAPTER IX.

*Railroad guarding at the Chattahoochie. A long rest. Mysterious rumors. "Grape-vine" played out. Diary of "*THE MARCH TO THE SEA.*"*

From the fall of Atlanta to the commencement of the great Georgia raid, the 102d was principally occupied in guarding the railroad. There were several changes of position and a short sojourn at Atlanta. We marched to that city on the 16th of Sept., and camped in the rear of the vacated line of rebel forts and earthworks southeast of the town.

While encamped near Atlanta, Col. Benj. Harrison went home on a leave of absence and Col. Smith succeeded him in the command of the brigade. The Colonel remained in command during the subsequent long march through Georgia.

Lieut. Col. Mannon had resigned a short time previous on account of physical disability, and the command of the regiment devolved upon Capt. Wm. A. Wilson.

Every preparation was there made for a permanent encampment. Vacated buildings in the city had been set apart for each regiment. These were torn down, "toted," and hauled into camp, and transformed into neat little camp huts. Day after day, from morning till night, the sound of the hammer was heard, and by the 1st of October, the little village of huts was almost finished. Some of the men were still at work, however, when just after dinner on that day an order was received to pack up and return immediately to the Chattahoochie river.

The soldiers declared it was "rough"—swore a little —marched until after night, part of the time through a heavy rain, and most of them next day were pleased with the change.

The occasion of the sudden march was the beginning of Hood's celebrated flank movement. Soon the whole army, excepting the 20th Corps, was on the move northward, and during the 3d and 4th of Oct., heavy columns of infantry and cavalry with artillery, constantly crowded the road leading northward, near our camp.

Our camp had been established on an elevation north of the river a short distance from the railroad bridge. While there a freshet carried away the central sections of the bridge. The afternoon of the 4th we re-crossed the river and with the 79th Ohio and 129th Illinois regiments, took up a position behind a strong line of works, covering the main approaches to the bridge from the south and southwest. The 70th Indiana was then stationed at Sandtown. The 105th was in camp north of the river, where it had been subsequent to the time the other regiments of the brigade moved to Atlanta on the 16th of Sept.

Thus we were left during many monotonous days. Still it was a pleasant encampment. The weather was much of the time beautiful. During those calm, delicious autumn days, it was a pleasure to wander along the bank of the dark and rapid Chattahoochie, and into the groves, gorgeous with the many hues of autumn. The forests of the South, at that season of the year excel our own in beauty. The variety of colors, and shades of colors, is wonderful. There is a general sombre hue, but this is varied by deep scarlet, purple, and bright yellow foliage, and intermingled with these, the deep green of the pines.

Instead of being suddenly browned as our woods are by early frosts, the forests of the South are changed from the green of Summer to the hues of Autumn more naturally. The leaves die of old age and seem crowned with its honors.

But we were not altogether inactive in that position. Several foraging expeditions were made by detachments from the regiment, and those who participated had some hard marching mixed in with a little fun, and a very little fighting.

While encamped there, several casualties occurred to members of the regiment who were absent on furlough. A train going northward, about the first of Nov., was attacked near Vinings, by Guerrillas. 1st Sergt. Thomas Merrick, Co. F, was severely wounded by them. The wound subsequently proved fatal. Abner T. Morford, of Co. E, was captured. A brief account of his captivity will be found in the final chapter of this work.

About the same time one man was killed and two were severely wounded by a railroad collision near Lafayette, Indiana.

The circumstances attending these casualties were of such a peculiar nature that it will be a pardonable digression to sketch them here. The men from the 102d on board the train, were Sergt. Geo. P. Cumming, Co. H, 1st Sergt. Geo. W. Gregg, Co. C, and "Booth" Abbott, Co. A. They had taken seats in the car next in rear of the baggage car, but at the moment of the collision, Sergt. Gregg was standing on the forward platform of the car with about a half dozen other soldiers. By the force of the collision, the baggage car was driven back through the one in rear of it, the passenger car encasing it like a shell. Within the passenger car, crushed beneath the baggage car, there was a bleeding mass of humanity, but Sergt. Gregg, as if by a miracle, was forced through the car without having any bones broken. His injuries were nevertheless serious, and unfitted him for duty for some time. Sergt. Cumming was instantly killed. How easily our destinies may be changed, apparently at least, by trifling circumstances. The case of Sergt. Cumming is one in point.

One day while we were on the front line before Atlanta, it occurred to him that it would be pleasant to take a walk a short distance along the line of works. In doing so he passed into a somewhat exposed position and was struck by a rebel bullet which wounded him quite severely. In consequence of the wound, he received a furlough and started home just in time to meet death on the ill-fated train.

Our friend "Booth" of course came out all right, yet he came out through great tribulation. He was caught and held fast in the car in such a situation that he was, for about an hour, at the point of suffocating. When relieved, he came forth black as an Etheopian, sweating profusely, and puffing like a porpoise.

Booth's adventures while on furlough would alone make quite a volume. In Kentucky he fell into the hands of guerrillas, and at some place enroute for the Regiment, fell into the hands of some drunken Irish soldiers. It is said, however, that in the latter case he gained a decided victory.

On the 26th day of October, Capt. Wilson having resigned, Capt. H. H. Clay, of Co. D, took command of the Regiment. He was subsequently commissioned and mustered as Major.

About the first of November mysterious rumors reached us in regard to a contemplated movement in which the 20th Corps would participate. By the 5th of the month all surplus baggage was packed up, and, as fast as transportation could be furnished, it was sent to Chattanooga. But the order to move was for a time suspended.

For once the army was completely nonplussed. The impending campaign, or march, was an inexplicable riddle. In what direction would we move? Some persons said after Hood, others on Mobile, and the most knowing suggested Charleston or Savannah. "Grape-vine" was utterly at fault; all the reports through that channel tending only to confuse the judgment.

But the conviction was universal that the army was in safe hands while directed by Sherman, and with it he could go where he pleased. Preparations for the campaign went rapidly forward from day to day, and on the 12th of November the last train of cars went Northward. That afternoon the work of destroying the railroad commenced. For an account of the subsequent march, the reader is referred to the following diary, which is given substantially as it was furnished by myself for the *Galesburg Free Press:*

DIARY OF THE GREAT GEORGIA RAID.

[The original notes from which the following diary has been transcribed, were written "in season and out of season," in camp and on the march, in daytime and at night, and were intended to be a true record of events as the days rolled by. The original diary is repeated here, with but slight alterations. A few items have been omitted, and a few paragraphs have been added by way of amplification. Where stars have been inserted, the reader may usually understand that a march intervened between the time of writing the paragraphs which are thereby separated.]

MONDAY, Nov. 14, 1864.

Marched from the bridge at Chattahoochie River, by a circuitous route, to Atlanta. Camped on our old camping ground near the city. All very tired.

Before leaving camp at the bridge, everything that could be of use to the rebels was destroyed. They will hardly have the road repaired between Alatoona Mountains and Atlanta a year from this time. The process of destroying the bridge was very interesting. The evening before we marched we witnessed a large portion of the structure fall with a terrible crash. The moon was in the eastern sky, and we took up a position that placed the bridge directly between us and that luminary. A cable was attached to some part of the bridge. A regiment pulled at the cable, giving the work a swaying motion that increased to a pendulum-like swing, until at length it began to give way; then huge beams swung loose in the air, iron rails struck fire as they fell upon the stone piers, and several spans came crashing down into the turbulent river.

We are now completely isolated from home, and must remain so for many weeks. Sherman is on the rampage. He will go down to posterity as "The Great Raider." We all feel that we are on the grandest raid of the war. This isolation in the heart of rebeldom produces a feeling of loneliness beyond anything we have yet experienced.

TUESDAY, Nov. 15th.

We do not move early this morning, and may improve the time in noting down a few items.

Lieut. B. is chief of our mess. A Georgia contraband, not very intelligent but apparently a faithful boy, cooks for us. He states that his master was killed in one of the battles of Atlanta. Asked him if his master had been very wealthy. "No, not very; only had three black 'uns," was his reply. The negro is here the standard of wealth, and the chivalry would make him the corner stone of their confederacy.

As we write, a dark, dense cloud of smoke rolls up from Atlanta. Much public property is being destroyed. Is not A. H. Stephens' picture of desolation about to be realized?

Night.—It is almost midnight. We left camp about 10 o'clock this morning. Have moved at a snail's pace, owing to the slow movement of an immense wagon train, which we must guard. Have had no supper. We are now in Decatur, a very pretty little village, seven miles east of Atlanta. As darkness came on this evening, the western sky was lighted up with a more brilliant glow than that imparted by the sun's declining rays; it was the light of burning buildings.

WEDNESDAY, Nov. 16th.

Well, the upshot of it was, we marched all night. At daylight halted for breakfast; have just finished the meal, and are again about to move. We are now only thirteen miles from Atlanta.

Evening.—Reached camp at 7½ P. M., having marched with but one or two hour's intermission since yesterday morning. Too tired and sleepy to write much to-night. We are passing through a very good country. Forage is becoming abundant. Our camp to-night is at Yellow Creek.

THURSDAY, Nov. 17th.

The sun is sinking low in the west as we write—during a temporary halt of the column. Judging from appearances, we could subsist on the country for months without recourse to government rations. We are living on the fat of the land.

* * * * * *

Marched until 8 o'clock this evening. We have had fresh pork, chickens, mutton, molasses, honey and yams brought into camp to-day in great abundance. One company of our regiment drove in about thirty head of cattle. We are living like kings, but are marching in wretched order.

We will close this day's record with a specimen of orthography transcribed from tombstones at a place on the line of march. One of the slabs mentioned the name of the deceased, and added the words, " who was *bond* the 1 of Sept 1853 " The next bore the name " Sarah *An* who was *bornd* the 3d of March 18— and *dide* the 6th of Sept 18—." There also seemed to be some doubt as to the proper mode of spelling the word *who*, for on one of the slabs it was chiseled " hoo."

In justice to the enlightened portion of the South, we will state that these inscriptions were found in a rural district, and some charitable persons with us suggested that it might have been the work of negroes, which may be true.

Marched eighteen miles to-day, and camped near Flat Creek.

FRIDAY, Nov. 18th.

We were up at four o'clock this morning, and marched until 8 P. M. Distance fifteen miles. Passed through the town of Social Circle, a beautiful little village. Later in the day, passed through the town of Rutledge. These places are located on the Atlanta & Augusta Railroad. The country becomes more beautiful and more productive as we advance. We are now feeling about the heart-strings of the Confederacy.

The face of the country and the style of the buildings strongly remind us of Illinois. Instead of the rugged hills of northern Georgia, we here have gently undulating plains.

The rebels, as yet, do not impede our progress.

SATURDAY, Nov. 19th.

We had a glorious sleep last night. Our camp was in a field where the coating of fine grass made an excellent bed. We were up this morning at half-past four.

A REBEL SENSATION ITEM.

Late rebel papers have been received. They confirm the reported election of Lincoln. One of the papers also says, the rumor is prevalent that Sherman has evacuated Atlanta, destroyed all the railroad between that place and Chattanooga, and is about to march to Charleston. The editor discredits the statement. As it is an Augusta paper, he may soon have convincing proof that there is some foundation for the startling rumor.

We wish it were in our power to describe a "raid" such as we are at present making. To be appreciated it must be participated in. We see much that is revolting, much that is exciting, and much that is amusing. Usually the line of march is indicated by the smoke of burning buildings; nevertheless, but few private residences are destroyed, and the people are dealt with as mildly as could be expected under the circumstances. The troops, it is true, help themselves, indiscriminately, to everything eatable on the line of march, but if the Southern people are as generous as they claim to be, no one need suffer. Beyond the range of our foragers there is evidently food in abundance. Of course, we would not countenance indiscriminate foraging, yet where such immense bodies of troops are passing through a country, everything good to eat must rapidly disappear. Doubtless many innocent little children go hungering; and while this is to be regreted, it is difficult to see how it may be avoided.

As we write, the column has halted in Madison, the county seat of Morgan county. This is the most beautiful town we have seen in Georgia. The old flag is unfurled.

* * * * * * * *

We halt again in the court house square. The band of our brigade is playing patriotic airs. The men have obtained files of old papers, and are scattering them by hundreds through the different regiments.

The buildings in Madison are almost all of the first class. Some of them are very elegant. We see here numerous evidences of taste and refinement.

* * * * * * * *

The day's march is over. It has been short, but very interesting. The march through Madison was a triumphal procession. Fair ladies and old men looked upon the flag they had discarded, and thinking of this, the color-bearers bore their colors more proudly. The citizens manifest a kind of moody indifference The colored people are overjoyed. Many fall in with the column of Yankees, and we think a majority would go with us, but some are restrained by considerations aside from any feeling of loyalty to their masters.

We obtained a paper that was published in Madison on the 9th of November, 1859, about the time of the John Brown raid. It contained an editorial which opens in this style, "The Abolitionists of the North are advancing upon us," and the South is advised to "put on her armor." That editorial would hardly be an inappropriate one for Nov. 19th, 1864.

The men came into camp this evening loaded as usual with fresh pork, molasses and yams. As we were marching along this afternoon the foragers kept up an almost uninterrupted fire upon turkies, chickens and porkers. All along the column could be seen the fruits of their work. One man carried a chicken, another a turkey or two, and another a headless sheep. Still others had transfixed on the points of their bayonets, pieces of fresh pork—the choice parts—with the hide and hair all on :

Georgia takes the palm for sweet potatoes, or as they are termed here, yams. They are becoming a drug in camp. Geographically speaking, this State is remarkable for the wonderful crops of negroes and yams which it produces, and the great amount of molasses which its citizens manufacture. The cultivation of cotton is almost abandoned; still, there have been vast quantities stored away. We saw a large lot of it burning to-day. It is the basis of Southern credit, and we derive a peculiar satisfaction from seeing it burn. Some one asked an ancient negro—who lived at the plantation where it was burning—why he set it on fire. "You Yankees did it," said he, "and I'm glad of it—*it would never have done me no good.*"

Everything indicates that we will concentrate at Milledgville.

We are camped four miles south of Madison.

SUNDAY, Nov. 20th.

Marched at 5 A. M. Considerable rain fell last night, and the roads have been very bad; nevertheless our expedition grows more interesting. Our regiment was in the advance to-day, and of course had the choice of chickens and other game·at the roadside. No description can convey an idea of the scene as the regiment came into camp this evening. Almost every one was loaded with something to eat. Still, an unlucky flock of sheep being discovered in the corner of the field, in which we had just halted to go into camp, an exciting chase commenced. A dozen or more men broke ranks and charged upon the flock. A line of battle confronted the doomed animals on one side, and a fence confronted them on the two other sides of a somewhat irregular triangle. Hither and thither they dodged; hither and thither the boys dodged after them. When one was successful, he almost invariably tumbled down with his captive, and then the laughing and cheering in the regiment was unrestrained. In vain the officers commanded attention; in a few moments the sheep were all captured, and most of them fell into the hands of the 102d.

To-day, for the first time within six months, we have tasted butter. What think you of this, epicurean Northern friends?

While passing an elegant mansion to-day, we observed the first manifestations of Union sentiment on the part of citizens since the march commenced. A number of ladies at the mansion waved their handkerchiefs as we passed, and the men cheered heartily.

Have marched fifteen miles, and camped two miles north of Eatonton. It is raining as we write, at nine o'clock P. M., and we may expect rough marching to-morrow.

MONDAY, Nov. 21st.

The prediction made last night has been more than fulfilled. We marched at daylight, in a steady, pitiless, driving rain, which continued during the greater part of the day—literally waded through mud. Our camp is twelve miles from Milledgeville. Distance marched, fifteen miles.

TUESDAY, Nov. 22d.

Moved at a late hour this morning, and reached Milledgeville, the capital of Georgia, at a late hour this afternoon. Met with no opposition. The town is pretty; but aside from the capitol building and a few other structures, is rather insignificant. We have seen no state capital yet that is as. small as the capital of Georgia. It is located on the Oconee River, and the only railroad that reaches it is a branch of the Georgia Central road.

The weather is very cold. We are to remain in camp here to morrow.

WEDNESDAY, Nov. 23d.

Another cold day—cold at least for this climate. The men have been very busy washing and preparing everything for another forward movement.

Our fingers are numb with cold, so we will cut short this day's record of events.

THURSDAY, Nov. 24th.

We marched from Milledgeville this morning. Before proceeding with notices of subsequent events, we must give some additional items concerning the city and its inhabitants.

Yesterday we visited the State House, which is a neat structure. Looked into the Senate and Hall of Representatives, where treason had so long held supreme sway, and thought the "beggarly array of empty seats" were eloquent, though silent speakers. There is a fine library in one of the rooms. Many of the books had been thrown out at the window. Choice literary and scientific works lay piled upon the ground, and a crowd of soldiers in selecting from the lot, walked over and trampled upon them, and we observed a horseman ride through the crowd purposely to let his horse trample the books. It was a very bad exhibition of a very lawless nature. Also visited the Arsenal, which contained a large assortment of military goods. Among other weapons of warfare were a few thousand pikes, and as many cutlasses—formidable looking weapons, indeed, but of little value when pitted against Spencer rifles. In the State House were twenty or thirty cases of muskets. The Arsenal was burned yesterday evening.

The manufacture of cotton goods has been carried on quite extensively in this city. By the destruction of the machinery the business is effectually suspended. By this suspension many poor people are thrown out of employment. In addition to, this misfortune, they have had much of their personal property taken from them. Thus the hardships of war fall most heavily on those least able to bear them, and who are least responsible for the existence of war.

Nearly all of the citizens have left the place. When we marched in, keeping step to inspiring martial music, the sidewalks and doorways were thronged with delighted negroes. Some of their ecstatic demonstrations were ludicrous in the extreme. The white friends of the Union, if such there are in that section, were not visible. We are, indeed, in a land of enemies.

FRIDAY, Nov. 25th.

Our march of yesterday, which commenced early in the morning terminated this morning at 3 o'clock. Distance, ten miles. Our Division guarded the wagon trains, and the frequent miring of the teams in mud holes was the cause of our slow progress. The night was very cold, and great fires were built along the line of march, simply by kindling the pine rail fences, which burned very rapidly. Among the rough experiences of the soldier, there is hardly anything to be named that is more disagreeable than a night march, especially if the night is cold, and he must keep pace with a slow moving wagon train.

We are moving in the direction of Sandersville.

* * * . * * * * * *

The enemy having burned the bridge over a small creek, the column halts to-night five miles from the camp we left this morning.

We are passing through a very swampy country. The soil is sandy. The water in the swamps is clear, and the sandy bottom, where washed by the waters, is beautifully white. The forests of pine become more grand as we advance. We noticed patches of cane brake near the edge of the swamps; have also seen the palmetto tree. We still have an abundant supply of rations,—drawn from the country. The rebels can have no excuse for starving our prisoners. There is no scarcity of provisions in this country.

SATURDAY, Nov. 26th.

"Becalmed" in the heart of the Confederacy! Such, at least, seems to be our present condition. We are in a region of swamps. These are dull, hazy, dreamy days, and the column moves tediously along, sometimes halting for hours. We moved this morning quite early, and it is now afternoon; yet we are not more than one mile from the camping ground of last night. As if to relieve the tedious hours of waiting, the band is playing. It has just played Annie Laurie.

Contrabands are constantly coming to us. They are greatly excited throughout this section of the country. This Yankee raid is a huge event in their eyes, and the ruling thought in their minds is thus expressed whenever neighboring darkies meet: "*Is you g'wine?*"

We have passed the Buffalo Creek swamps, and are now on higher ground, and may expect better roads. Wheeler's cavalry is hovering about us. They attacked the advance of our column yesterday, and there has been some skirmishing in the front to-day.

Went into camp this evening at Sandersville, before sunset. Camping at such an early hour is something of a novelty with us, and it may be attributed to the proximity of rebel cavalry. Distance marched, eleven miles. In the skirmish yesterday, the 9th Ill. Mounted Infantry lost one man. He was buried in a field by the roadside.

We hear but little of the right wing of our army. The 14th Corps is now on our left.

SUNDAY, Nov. 27th.

This has been a warm, Indian-Summer day. Our march has been quite interesting. The negroes are literally flocking in to join the Yankees—old and young, and of all shades of color. Their grand exodus from this part of Georgia will seriously damage the cause of rebellion. It must be excruciatingly painful for the slaveholders to see their property walk off thus, thousands of dollars at a time! Some of these wretched children of Ham present a repulsive appearance, as they trudge along in their miserable rags, seeking their freedom.

There was another skirmish to-day in the advance. The column was not delayed by it. Towards night we passed a burning mansion, which had been an elegant structure. We were told that it had been fired because the rebels attacked our advance at that place.

This is a rich section of country. The foragers bring in fresh pork, chickens, turkies, yams, molasses, and no one knows how great a variety of preserves. Talk of starving the Southern Confederacy! The idea is hugely ridiculous. The people have as much to eat as our own people have, and they raise a greater variety of edibles.

The business of foraging is most effectually done. For instance, in our own regiment four or five men are detailed every day from each company, and these men roam almost unrestrained through the country. The column of troops takes everything at the roadside. The foragers go far away, and at night come in loaded with provisions. They bring in a great many horses and mules. The citizens endeavor to secrete many things, and thus save them from the "rapacious Yankees," but they have not always been successful. Some men of Co. C found a barrel of sugar secreted in an orchard to-day. It is very white and nice. Indeed, but little can escape these experienced foragers. On an average our forces are "cleaning out" a scope of country forty miles wide, through the heart of the Confederacy.

Marched fifteen miles to-day. Crossed the Georgia Central Railroad at Tenille. Part of the Corps has been at work destroying the track. We are encamped near Davisboro. As I write—about 8 o'clock P. M.—the camp is hilariously jubilant. The soldiers yell, cheer and laugh like wild men. At times a spontaneous cheer breaks out in one regiment, and is echoed and repeated, apparently, by the whole corps. Just now a band is playing. O, who that participates in this raid can ever forget these scenes? An army, apparently, on a "bender!" Doubtless the Great Raider is in his element, and as happy as his men. There is only one thought to sadden the thoughtful: amid this waste and destruction, many who are innocent must suffer.

Immense quantities of cotton are burned every day, as we advance. As the dense columns of smoke roll up towards the sky, we mentally exclaim, "Cotton is *not* King!"

The band at this moment plays that noble air, "Hail Columbia." If there are any rebels within hearing distance they must think all Yankeedom is here, having a grand jubilee.

Distance marched to-day thirteen miles.

MONDAY, Nov. 28th.

The above day and date have just passed, it being now after midnight—that is the morning of the 29th. We have been busy in our line of duty up to this hour. Must now secure a few hours of sleep.

TUESDAY, Nov. 29th.

It is now almost noon, and we still remain in camp. The weather is very warm. We marched yesterday eleven miles and camped before night. The bridge across the Ogeechee River, just ahead of us, having been destroyed by the enemy, we were compelled to halt. The plantation of Herschel V. Johnson is about three miles from our camp. Men of our regiment who visited it state that it is well stocked with negroes. The household property had been buried on the premises. The soldiers discovered the place where it was buried, exhumed the boxes and helped themselves.

Our rations are still of the best quality. Our mess had for breakfast this morning "corn pones," fresh pork, sweet potatoes, sausages and butter.

It is becoming apparent that unprincipled men are taking advantage of the license given them to forage, and are pillaging. No one can tell what outrages may not be committed by these villains. Many have abandoned all principles of justice and morality, and only seek to gratify their own desires. Alas! when will the days of rapine and bloodshed be past?

Marched four miles and crossed the Ogeechee River and Rocky Comfort Creek. The bridge across the Ogeechee which the rebels destroyed was an important structure. We crossed on pontoons.

Passed through the small town of Louisville, the shiretown of Jefferson county. It has an ancient appearance.

WEDNESDAY, Nov. 30th.

Have remained in camp to-day. Nothing of importance to chronicle.

THURSDAY, Dec. 1st.

The day's march is now over, and we camp six miles from our camp of last night. We learn this evening that the mounted men of our brigade had an exciting little fight some miles away from the road. The squad was out taking horses and mules. A detachment of rebel cavalry attacked them, and when our men found they could not drive the enemy, a retreat commenced, and a running fight ensued. Three of our men fell into their hands. Some of the captured property was abandoned to the enemy.

We witnessed a scene to-day that would attract no little attention at home. It might be termed a negro family in search of freedom. A small, tough, and somewhat venerable negress led the way, bearing a bundle which was poised upon her head. A young negro child was clinging to her back, and was sustained in its position by her hands. Following her was a girl perhaps twelve years old. She also carried a young one in her arms. All were most wretchedly clothed. Their dresses, which had been patched and re-patched until the original cloth had lost its identity, were faded and greasy, and it would seem that they had worn no others for years. The old negress had a disconsolate but determined look, and pressed on perseveringly with her burden.

We realize more fully the grandeur of this great raid. All the principal railroads of the Confederacy will be rendered useless during the remainder of the war. *We are fighting railroads!* When these are thoroughly destroyed, the rebel army will be in a sorry condition to oppose us.

FRIDAY, Dec. 2d.

How ridiculous to write December above these lines! The sun's rays are intensely warm, and the sky has not the appearance of our Northern winter sky.

* * * * * *

Our brigade is in the rear of the column, and we are therefore in close proximity to the contrabands who follow us. When we halt they continue on, in order to be more surely protected by our arms. A squad of six women, ten or twelve children and one man has just passed. They have the squalid and forlorn appearance common to the fugitives from this part of the South.

* * * * * *

11 *o'clock* P. M.—At length we are ready to go to bed. Marched fourteen miles, and camped long after dark.

SATURDAY, Dec. 3d.

We have halted for dinner five miles west of Millen. Moved quite early, but have marched slowly. The country is very sandy and very swampy.

To-day, for the first time, we have seen cypress swamps. These are so full of cypress trees that they seem almost impenetrable. In the vicinity of these swamps, Spanish moss is very abundant. Those who have never seen it may realize what its appearance is from such an illustration as this: Imagine a tree that has all of its limbs draped with long, wavy tufts of flax, ready for the spinning-wheel. These tufts hang very straight when not stirred by the breeze, and beautifully fringe the limbs from which they depend. This moss is much used in the upholstery business.

The pine groves through which we are passing are more beautiful than any we have heretofore seen. Laurel and live oak are very common.

We passed a mill pond to-day which formed a pretty picture. The pond was surrounded with cypress trees, which were all heavily draped with moss, and the edges of the pond were full of water lilies. The old mill with its waterfall made the picture complete.

We passed near the ground where the Union prisoners have been confined, a few miles from Millen. Those who visited the spot state that it was a wretched prison.

The only houses the prisoners had were made of sod, and were not more than two or three feet high. The remains of Union prisoners were found there unburied. The prisoners were hastily removed from the place very recently.

We crossed the remains of the Savannah and Augusta Railroad. Several brigades have been at work destroying it, and many miles of it have been rendered useless.

Marched fifteen miles, leaving Millen to the right, and camping five miles east of the railroad.

The 15th and 17th corps have been marching on parallel roads a few miles south of us. We have as yet met with no serious opposition. Kilpatrick had a fight the other day, the particulars of which we have not yet learned. Aside from this there has only been occasional skirmishing.

SUNDAY, Dec. 4th.

Marched ten miles through a swampy region. Nothing of material interest to chronicle.

MONDAY, Dec. 5th.

Still among the swamps! Camp this evening seven miles from our camp of last night. The Savannah River at the nearest point is about twelve miles distant. The enemy skirmished with our advance this morning, but made no stubborn resistance.

The country through which we pass is terribly scourged. We can hardly convey an idea of the visible effects of this stupendous raid. At times the whole circle of the horizon is dark with the smoke that arises from fires which are far away from our own column. During several days past the grass has been burning in the woods, and everything combustible is in a blaze. Seen far in advance at night, these fires often lead the weary soldiers to believe that they are approaching camp, and they press on with renewed vigor, only to be deceived, and to discover other fires still farther ahead. The dead pine trees often catch fire, and the creeping, writhing flames ascend from their base to the topmost branches. They may be seen miles away. These scenes are indelibly impressed upon the mind. Boys who are with us will one day take their grand-children upon their knees, and tell them of these strange, wild scenes; and as they tell them they will vainly endeavor to repress the tears which such memories, with all their glowing associations, cannot fail to bring.

The face of the country since we left Stone Mountain, near Atlanta, has been uniformly level. We see no hills—simply elevations. A kind of tough, wire grass, such as is common on bottom lands in Illinois, grows quite heavily here, and forms so thick a coating that we have soft beds, ready-made when we camp.

TUESDAY, Dec. 6th.

We are not more than thirty-five miles from Savannah. Have been marching parallel with the river, and camp ten miles northwest of Springfield. The rebels endeavored to impede our progress by felling trees across the road. The obstructions were easily removed or evaded.

WEDNESDAY, Dec. 7th.

The 102d has been in advance of the Corps to-day, and with the other regiments of the brigade, has just entered the town of Springfield. A company has been detailed as provost guard, and is guarding the houses of citizens. But alas, for these over prudent citizens! They buried their household goods in grounds adjoining their houses, and the soldiers have discovered them. An almost endless variety of articles have been exhumed. Some are bringing away clothing, others blankets, others fine dishes, silver spoons, etc. One man has just passed us dressed as a lady, only his toilet was rather rudely made.

* * * * * *

We camp to-night in Springfield, which is the county seat of Effingham county. It is in a swamp country, and is so old and moss-grown that it appears to be a product of the swamps. There are several churches in the place, all of a rude style.

This afternoon we found the road obstructed with fallen trees at a point where it crossed a swamp. The rebels had worked very hard, and had thrown a great many trees across the road. They undoubtedly supposed we would find the difficulty almost insurmountable. Well, what did we do? Why, simply marched *around* the obstructions! It is true, we found the new road a very rough one; but the general delay caused by the prodigious efforts of the enemy will not fulfill their expectations. The tide of Yankees rolls oceanward, and will hardly be stayed by anything that stands in the way.

TUESDAY, Dec. 8th.

We write this at 7 o'clock P. M., by the light of burning buildings. We are about to resume the march.

* * * * * *

Midnight.—Still on the road! Swamps impede our progress. Heavy canonading is heard in the direction of the river.

A Springfield negro who accompanies us has given us a full account of a case of hanging which took place in Springfield on the 11th day of July, 1861. On that day, a prominent citizen, named Brad. Jones, was taken by a mob composed of his fellow citizens, and was hanged by the neck until dead. His crime was loyalty to the Union! We were informed that our regiment camped near the spot where he was executed. His aged mother still resides in Springfield. He was her only son, and, it is said, was a good man. We learned these facts after leaving Springfield. The torch did not do its perfect work there.

FRIDAY, Dec. 9th.

It is now almost midnight again, and we have been constantly on the road since yesterday evening, and have had no sleep since that time. Have marched sixteen miles since leaving Springfield.

SATURDAY, Dec. 10th.

Were in motion again by daylight this morning. Have marched nine miles, and halted four and a half miles from Savannah. The rebels are in line of battle immediately in front. Skirmishing is going on quite lively, farther to the right, and there is considerable artillery firing—the old familiar sounds again!

We have omitted to mention that the advance of our corps captured two small earthworks yesterday. They are located about three miles north of the railroad, and were defended by about 400 men, with two or three pieces of artillery. They fired a few shots, skirmished a little, and then skedaddled.

We camp to-night in line of battle. (*End of the Diary.*)

Our "siege of Savannah" lasted ten days. The permanent line of battle was established on the 11th of the month. No approaches were made after that time, until the rebel line was abandoned. The cannonading on the part of the enemy was much of the time heavy but did little damage. The skirmishers were close together and kept up a lively contest.

On the 15th of the month we received official notice of the capture of Fort McAllister, and consequent opening of communication with the Federal fleet.

The celebrated swamp bridge was commenced on the 13th. This bridge was designed to span a wide, deep swamp which for some distance separated the opposing armies. The work was prosecuted at night, and often under a heavy fire of artillery, the enemy throwing grapeshot and shells. The water was from two to four feet deep, and the bottom in many places was composed of loose black mud, which seemed to extend downwards *ad infinitum.* Working under fire, and floundering around in the mud, the fatigue parties had an unenviable task to perform.

It seemed absurd to suppose that a column moving by the flank across a narrow bridge, could make a successful assault on the enemy's works. Daily the question was discussed in camp, and nocturnally the work progressed. Fortunately the bridge was never used.

There, as at other places, the opposing pickets sometimes became communicative. Captain Merritt, in his diary, reports the following colloquy between a Union and a rebel picket, about the time the work on the bridge was progressing.

The rebel commenced thus: "O! Yanks, where do your rations come from?

Federal. From Fort McAllister. Who runs the rice mills on the river?

Rebel. (Dodges the question.) Who was elected President?

Federal. Lincoln.

Rebel. Hurrah! for Jeff. Davis.

Federal. We have a rope to hang him.

Rebel. Come over.

Federal. Can't get over.

Rebel. Come over on the new bridge you are building across the swamp!

The firing of a big rebel gun at that instant interrupted the conversation and it was not immediately resumed.

Our rations during those ten days consisted mainly of rice. Immense quantities of this cereal were in store near the river and on the islands. In a brief space of time the rice mills were all at work, and the negroes, men, women and children, were hulling rice with mortar and pestle. If all other resources had failed, the army could have been subsisted on rice for an indefinite length of time. As it was we had rice for breakfast, rice for dinner, rice for supper, prepared in all conceivable styles. It was cheap living, and rather a light diet.

The scene at the rice mills on the river banks was one of the greatest activity. Heavy details of soldiers were busy running the mills, day and night. Teams loaded with rice, or rice straw, were constantly coming and going. But the most grotesque feature of the scene was that in which the African figured. Every shade, every caste, every size; all varieties of form and physiognomy were there represented—the handsome octoroon, the *natural* negro, and the uncouth, animal looking blacks who seemed scarcely one remove from the ourang-outang—all or nearly all clothed in the most wretched manner. Many of them used the French language and could not understand a word of English.

We observed one old negress, whose features appeared to have been toughened by a hundred years of work and exposure. Her hide must have been almost bullet proof.

She could "talk English" but did not know her own age. Crouched on the floor of her cabin, her repulsive features just visible above her knees, as she worked with mortar and pestle, she seemed to be a type of the very lowest form of humanity. Poor creatures, they scarcely realized their own wretchedness.

The soldiers made frequent expeditions to the islands in the river and occasionally crossed to the South Carolina shore. Company "I" was for a time on detached service seven miles up the river, on an island, running a rice mill.

Running rice mills was a novel experience in the life of the raiders, but they were ready for anything that would aid the cause and gratify their epicurean appetites.

The change from the mountain regions of Northern Georgia to the flat country around Savannah, was very striking. The weather was much of the time delightful, but was rendered less so by the heavy fogs which prevailed each morning. We had never seen such fogs before. The vapor was so dense that the water would drop from the trees like rain for hours every morning.

Among other novelties in that vicinity, the huge live oaks attracted universal attention. These grow to a fabulous size, spreading their broad arms over an immense area of ground. They are usually draped with Spanish moss. In those pleasant December mornings, standing beneath the beautifully draped evergreen branches of the huge oaks, while the fog wreaths could scarcely be distinguished from the wavy tresses of moss, one could hardly resist the impression that he had been transported into "fairy land."

Amid so much that was novel and interesting time did not drag heavily as we waited there for mail and hardtack. The first mail came on the 17th, bringing letters and newspapers. Then the soldiers were happy. Hard bread was received and issued on the 20th; none had been issued to the men for twenty days.

Early on the morning of Dec. 21st, we were informed that the rebels had abandoned their works, and that the 2d Division of our Corps was in motion towards the city.

Our Brigade, (except the 79th Ohio Regiment, which had moved to the right,) was soon on the road. At 9 o'clock A. M., we marched into an open field a quarter of a mile west of the city and went into camp. The Stars and Stripes were then waving from the City Hall. Savannah, with all its rich stores, was in the hands of the Federal army.

CHAPTER X.

A Look Northward. The short rest at Savannah. Crossing the Savannah River. Cheves' Farm. Hardee Farm. Hardeeville. Robertsville. THE MARCH THROUGH THE CAROLINAS.

As the Federal picket paced to and fro on the South bank of the Savannah River, his eye often wandered northward, across the wide stream to the dark woods of South Carolina.

"When we move again let us go into South Carolina." This sentiment pervaded all hearts, and the wish expressed on every hand was soon to be realized.

Our stay at Savannah was even more brief than we had anticipated. While there Colonel Smith obtained a leave of absence with permission to visit his home. The Colonel had won golden opinions as a brigade commander. Colonel H. Case, of the 129th Illinois Regiment, succeeded him in command of the Brigade. At Savannah Captain H. H. Clay was mustered in as Major.

Regular camps were then laid out, and the men worked busily from the 21st to the 31st of the month constructing board quarters. A grand review of the army by General Sherman took place while there. The 20th Corps was reviewed on the 30th of the month. Next day the 3d Division was put in motion to cross the river. We left our little village of newly finished huts at daylight—1st Brigade in advance—102d in advance of the Brigade. Crossed on a pontoon bridge to Hutchinson's Island. This island is several miles in length, and from a mile to a mile and a half in breadth. It is barely above water when the tide is out. Embankments thrown up for the purpose prevent the overflow of the island. It is well cultivated and produces immense quantities of rice. By a system of canals with locks, it is overflowed at certain periods for the benefit of the growing crop. The canals traverse the island from one channel of the river to the other, and when the tide was in, the water in them was much higher than the surface of the island.

On the embankment of one of these canals we marched to the second channel. There the rebel pickets on the South Carolina shore opened fire upon us. Artillery was brought up, and by several well directed shots the enemy was driven away. One man in the Regiment was slightly wounded. Efforts were being made to lay a pontoon bridge. Companies A and F were sent across in small boats to an island in the channel, to keep back the enemy's skirmishers while the work on the bridge progressed. It was "a cold, misty, rainy day." In the afternoon the wind arose and the channel became so rough that it was impossible to continue the work of laying down pontoons. It was difficult and dangerous to communicate with the companies on the little island. This was done, however, by Captain T. H. Andrews and George Dew, ("the sharpshooter.") The wind was blowing at the time, most fiercely and the white caps were rolling magnificently. Their frail boat was in imminent danger of being swamped, but they managed it skilfully and crossed safely.

Late in the afternoon the 102d, except the two companies on the little island, was marched back to the Savannah landing. There we boarded the steamer Black Diamond, and went down the river with the intention of flanking the island and effecting a landing on the Carolina shore. As we turned the lower point of the island and began to move up towards the channel north of it, the rebel cavalry pickets could be seen on shore skedaddling in fine style. But we were again thwarted in our purpose. The tide being out, the pilot said he was afraid to attempt the passage of a bar near the point of the island. It was finally arranged that the vessel should steam back to the wharf and make another attempt at high tide next morning—*or rather next year!*

The evening of the 31st of December, 1864, was very cold at Savannah—cold at least for that region. Ice formed during the night a half inch in thickness.

On that miserable little boat, nearly destitute of rations, shivering with cold, we passed the closing hours of the year 1864, and witnessed the dawn of the new year. The men were stowed away in every nook and corner of the vessel; as many as possible crowded about the boiler works.

Next morning, the 70th Indiana joined us on the boat, and by noon a landing on the opposite shore was effected without opposition.

We marched the same evening, five miles out, to Cheves' Farm, crossing the bottom land north of the river. This lowland is also below tide water, and like Hutchinson's Island, is cultivated by the aid of embankments, canals, &c. It extends nearly five miles back from the river.

The rebels were near by, and had been busy near Cheves' Farm felling trees to obstruct our progress. Their labors subsequently occasioned some heavy fatigue work, but the road was cleared as soon as the army was ready to proceed beyond that point.

We camped that evening (Jan. 1st) where the timber was principally pine—which, in its green state, makes very poor fire-wood. The night was cold; the men had suffered during the previous night, and were therefore more determined to make themselves comfortable. It did not take them long to decide *how* this should be accomplished—*they were in South Carolina!*

There were several unoccupied houses and barns near by, and we had been in camp but a few moments when the work of demolition commenced. The entire brigade was represented in the work of destruction. The crashing of falling timbers, the ripping loose of the siding, and the general clatter of hammers made such an uproar that some of the men who had lain down to sleep actually thought the enemy was making an attack.

Our camp was on the premises of Hon. Langdon Cheves—once a prominent South Carolina secessionist. While we were in the vicinity, his home was used for Division headquarters. Among his papers were numerous printed copies of a speech made by him at Nashville, in the year 1850.

Speaking then of the course the Yankees would pursue, in case the South seceded, he said:

"Will they invade us—where is their army?"

It is enough to say that we were then encamped upon his premises; but ah! thought we, where is Mr. Cheves? We were informed that he fell in battle at Charleston, the victim of his own false teachings.

There was much beautiful shrubbery in the grounds adjoining his residence. But while we were there everything about his once peaceful home was rapidly going to destruction.

We moved on the 4th to a new camp on the Hardee Farm, a mile north of Cheves' Farm. The camp was established in rear of some grass-grown fortifications—"said to have been constructed by the rebels in 1862, at a time when Butler was making a demonstration on the coast."

At that place another dash was made on vacant buildings. The men had scarcely broken ranks, when the click of a solitary hammer was heard; it was quickly followed by others, and soon dozens were at work, creating a perfect bedlam,—*hack, bang, rip, rattle, squeak, crash,*—and the boards flew and the beams fell faster than they were ever made to fly or fall by any Hook & Ladder company. Men were all over and all through the houses, perfectly reckless of flying boards and falling timbers. At length they commenced cutting the corner posts of one of the buildings. Soon it began to totter. The men were on tip-toe. A few more strokes of the axe were sufficient, and down came the structure, raising a cloud of dust. There was a *yell, a blind rush* and a *scramble.* A few moments sufficed to remove the last stick of timber, leaving the ground ready for the plow.

At the Hardee Farm we remained until the 17th of January. As usual much labor was expended in constructing little board huts. Fatigue duty was then quite heavy. A great deal of "corduroy" road was built across the bottom land between the camp and the river.

The enemy hovered near, constantly watching our movements. In one or two reconnoisances made at that time, sharp skirmishes took place, but none of our men were hurt. While encamped there, large quantities of fresh oysters were obtained from an oyster island at the mouth of the Savannah River. Those who participated in the oyster expeditions had rare sport; a good ride and a general good time.

We abandoned the camp at Hardee Farm on the 17th of Jan., and marched ten miles to Hardeeville, a little town on the Charleston and Savannah railroad. Camped at two o'clock P. M.

Again the work of destroying buildings commenced, Among others, a large beautiful church was attacked Men of various regiments were engaged in the work. First the pulpit and seats were torn out, then the siding and the blinds were ripped off. Many axes were at work. The corner posts were cut, the building tottered, the beautiful spire, up among the green trees, leaned for a time several degrees out of the perpendicular, vibrating to and fro. A tree that stood in the way was cut. By the use of long poles the men increased the vibratory motion of the building, and soon, with a screeching groan the spire sunk down amidst the timbers which gave way beneath, and as the structure became a pile of rubbish, some of the most wicked of the raiders yelled out: " There goes your d——d old gospel shop."

Next day scarcely a vestige of the church was visible.

It was barbarous, yet it verified the words of the Bible: —*" For they have sown the wind and they shall reap the whirlwind."*

While at Hardeeville, the weather was wretchedly bad. Once more the men constructed small houses, only to leave them when fairly finished.

The 79th Ohio Regiment returned to the brigade on the 18th of February.

Forage in that region was very scarce. The men scouted far away from the camp, and obtained a few yams and small quantities of meat. Rice—our staff of life—was found in abundance.

As soon as we were fairly in South Carolina, the citizens commenced burying their property. One old man had buried his treasure beneath the roots of an old tree near our camp. Becoming fearful that the prying Yankees would discover it, he obtained permission of the military authorities to dig it up. It was buried in an earthen jar, and amounted to over two thousand dollars in gold and silver.

The troops were at length ordered to be in readiness to move at seven o'clock on the morning of the 29th. Early in the morning the board quarters were fired, and as the air was very cold, the men gathered about the fires in groups, awaiting the command to fall in. When the order came they marched cheerfully away from their burning village—the third little village of the kind, built and abandoned subsequent to the occupation of Savannah. Marched eighteen miles in the direction of Robertville. Camped in a plowed field. Resumed the march next morning and by noon reached the vicinity of Robertville, four miles east of Sister's Ferry, on the Savannah river.

Remained in camp at Robertville during the 31st of Jan., and the 1st of February.

Up to that time the army had been "getting into position" to commence the raid. Irregular communication had been kept up with the outer world. Our supply of rations was there slightly increased, letters were sent out, and there on the 2d of February we abandoned communication and "swung loose." Sherman's grand army being again "lost in Dixie."

We soon found rebels. Our brigade was in the advance. The 105th Ill. Regiment in the advance of the brigade. We were marching in the direction of Lawtonville. About a mile from the town, the skirmishers from the "105th" became engaged with the enemy, driving the rebels slowly to a strong position in thick woods at the edge of a swamp. Sharp firing then commenced, the rebels blazing away from behind trees and logs, while many of the "105th" boys stood up in the road without any protection, firing rapidly, round after round, at the concealed foe. But the rebels were not disposed to give back. The 70th Indiana and 102d Ill.

8

were deployed in line of battle in rear of the 105th. The 79th Ohio, and the 129th Ill., were ordered to make a detour to the left. Other troops came up and deployed in line of battle on our left. Artillery was brought up, and a number of shells were thrown with good effect. The enemy kept up a galling fire, killing one man instantly in our regiment and wounding two others—one of them mortally. We were then in line of battle, partially under cover of a hill. At length their fire ceased in front, and an advance was made, but the enemy had abandoned the position. The flank movement made by the "79th" and "129th"—and most brilliantly executed—had compelled them to "get up and travel."

It was one of Sherman's battles *in miniature*. The distinctive features of his strategy were well illustrated in the movements of the "1st Brigade."

Part of the brigade entered Lawtonville that evening, but being in an isolated position the force was withdrawn. We camped near the enemy's vacated line.

Resumed the march next morning, moving on the Barnwell road. It was a lovely morning. We passed through some beautiful country. A half mile from Lawtonville we passed a charming palatial residence. The grounds were ornamented in the finest style, with a rich variety of shrubbery. The house was magnificently furnished. The richest of carpets covered the floors; splendidly bound books ornamented the library; a sweet-toned piano was in the parlor. The property belonged to a rebel officer, and had but recently been used by Gen. Wheeler for headquarters. In accordance with orders received *from a proper source*, the building was burned.

A number of similar dwellings were burned during the day, in each case "according to orders." Forage was becoming more abundant. We marched at half past seven A. M., February 4th, following a by-road. At Smyrna Church passed into a public road which led to Allendale, and thence to Barnwell C. H. In the afternoon we passed a beautiful lake, bearing the outlandish name—"Swallow Savannah." The lake is seven miles in circumference and is bordered with cypress trees. We camped that evening two miles from Allendale.

Next morning, advanced on the Barnwell road about five miles, then turned to the right and moved in the direction of Beaufort Bridge. Camped that evening near Salkehatchie swamp through which a tributary of the Conbahee river runs. Beaufort bridge, previous to our arrival, spanned the stream, but the rebels had partially destroyed it, and the troops were delayed several hours. The position had been strongly fortified. It would have been impossible to drive the enemy from their earthworks by approaching along the narrow causeway across the swamp, and over the bridge. But the position was turned, or outflanked by troops operating on other roads, and the rebels were compelled to retire without realizing any benefit from their naturally impregnable position.

Marched at five o'clock, the morning of the 6th. Crossed the bridge, turned to the left, and moved in the direction of the Charleston and Augusta railroad.

Foraging operations grew more extensive with each succeeding day. The four weeks experience in Georgia had prepared the men for more desperate work in South Carolina. Now they struck boldly out, from ten to twenty miles from the column. The whole country was alive with men who made foraging their sole business. Officers were sent out with detachments, but hundreds were constantly out independent of all control. Those who went out with officers usually became separated from them in a short time. Many roamed through the country solely to plunder, and in their nefarious work threw off all restraint—fearing neither God nor man— nor his mythical majesty, the Devil.

On the right, on the left, and in front, dark columns of smoke rolled up, as the great army, with its flankers, the foragers, pressed forward.

We camped, the evening of the 6th near Little Salkehatchie, which is also a tributary of the Combahee river.

Late in the evening, Feb. 7th, the brigade reached the Charleston and Augusta railroad, at Graham Station. A cold chilling rain had been falling since morning, rendering the march very disagreeable. The troops moved slowly, crossed several swamps, built a number of bridges and made considerable corduroy road.

On the 8th, commenced the work of destroying the railroad track. After tearing it up effectually three fourths of a mile, we went into camp at Graham. In the afternoon, left knapsacks, etc., in camp and moved out to work on the railroad. Marched four miles; found nothing to do—other troops were ahead. We were obliged to retrace our steps to camp. The men could not see the wisdom of the movement, and some of them swore savagely. Reaching the camp we ate a hastily prepared supper, then packed up and resumed the forward movement, under orders to halt where the 1st Division ceased destroying the road.

"Misfortunes never come singly," says the old adage, and it was verified during the day's maneuvers. About night we took the wrong road and marched at least a mile out of the way. Reached camp at half-past eight that evening, very tired and almost suffocated with the smoke of the burning railroad, and other burning property. Our camp was four miles, direct, from Graham. The night was very cold, and we slept uncomfortably.

The work of destroying the railroad was accomplished most effectually. For at least three days the bulk of Sherman's army was thus engaged. The smoke of the burning ties, rising mile after mile, and mingling with the smoke of burning buildings, burning fences and burning cotton, enveloped the whole country.

The road was torn up by sections as the columns advanced.

The brigades halted alternately to work at destroying the road. The following plan of operations was observed. Having stacked arms and unslung knapsacks each regiment formed in line of battle opposite the track. Sections of the road were assigned to the different companies, and at the command of the officers, the men advanced to the attack. Acting in concert they lifted the structure and tumbled it over at the side of the grade. The ties were then loosened and piled upon the grade, very much in the manner that boys construc-

b-houses. The iron rails were placed upon the piles—
e ends projecting. Fires were then kindled beneath
em, and when the rails became heated to a white heat
ey were easily twisted into various shapes.

The morning of the 9th was cold and a heavy frost
overed the ground. We continued the march in the
rection of Augusta. The column moved slowly, and
henever it halted we made ourselves comfortable by
tting fire to the light, combustible pine rails at the
adside. Reached the dilapidated village of Blackville
before noon. Halted in the "suburbs." Built large
es, but were made miserable by the all-pervading
noke. Momentarily expecting to move, we awaited
ders until late in the afternoon, and then went into
mp for the night. At Blackville we received a light
ail. It was brought up by a brigade that abandoned
mmunication a day or two after the campaign com-
enced.

Next morning we continued on towards Augusta.
orked on the railroad again, "finishing it" as far as
e little town of Williston. It had been a pretty town,
ut did not look well amidst the smoke and dust that
as raised by our destroying army. Camped near Wil-
ston.

Abandoning the railroad on the 11th, we moved
orthward—the next objective point being Columbia.
rossed the South Edisto that afternoon. Passed
rough a rough, hilly region. Observed several varie-
es of hard-wood timber. It was a pleasant change
om the level country and pine barrens through which
e had been so long marching.

We went into camp the evening of the 11th on the
outh side of a small stream that empties into the North
disto. Forage somewhat scarce.

A heavy frost covered the ground on the morning of
e 12th. The air was very cold. The enemy having
urned the bridge across the little stream above men-
oned, the troops were compelled to wade it. Many of
e small streams along the sea coast in the South are
carcely distinguishable at first view from swamps.
hey are literally swamp streams.

In this case there was a great sheet of water sprea[d] out over swamp land, which was thickly grown wit[h] cypress trees and a maze of underbrush. The swam[p] stream was about a quarter of a mile in width and fro[m] one to three feet in depth, a sluggish current movin[g] the waters in the centre. Some of the men strippe[d] their feet and rolled up their pants to wade it; othe[rs] went in without any preparation. All the horses th[at] were tractable "carried double."

The water was so cold that many of the soldiers b[e]came almost paralyzed. It was bitter cold work wadin[g] swamps in mid winter. After crossing, the troops we[re] halted—large fires were built of rails, and an hour w[as] passed in drying off.

Crossed Goodland Swamp Creek during the day, an[d] went into camp a half mile south of the North Edist[o]. The 2d Division of our Corps met with strong oppos[i]tion at the river, but effected a crossing after losin[g] several men.

The 3d Division was in the advance next day—Febr[u]ary 13th. The 1st Brigade being in advance of the D[i]vision, and the 70th Indiana in advance of the Brigad[e]. We crossed the river on a temporary bridge. T[he] enemy hovered near in front and did not drive we[ll]. Skirmishers from the 70th Indiana were deployed a[nd] they exchanged shots with the enemy at intervals un[til] the column halted eight miles from the river.

A squad of foragers from the "70th" was surprise[d] and completely routed about the time we went in[to] camp. They had ventured too far to the front and we[re] attacked by a force of rebel cavalry. In the affair t[he] detachment lost seven men, wounded and missing. [A] number of horses and mules fell into the hands of t[he] enemy. Some of the foragers who escaped came badly demoralized—minus hats, guns, accoutrements a[nd] horses. The "70th" then marched out to retaliate, b[ut] could not find the enemy.

We remained in camp until 10 o'clock A. M. of the 14t[h] Moved then on the Columbia road, until we reached road leading to Lexington C. H. Five miles out on th[e] road at a point where the Columbia and Augusta wag[on] road crosses it, the troops went into camp.

The art of foraging had by this time become thoroughly understood. Forage was yet abundant. Had it been otherwise the skill of the foragers would, in a measure, have made up all deficiencies. Let me diverge here and sketch a day with the foragers.

As usual the camp is aroused long before daylight. In the gray dawn the foragers, all mounted, form in line and move off—we will suppose towards the right. Following strange roads, guided sometimes by the compass, sometimes by the sun, and sometimes "going it blind," they dash away from the main column—over high hills, across deep hollows, fording deep and rapid streams, riding on through the wilderness of pines, until at length a farm house is descried. Then they "go for it." Who will be first? The rowels sink deep into the flanks of the horses—and mules. Away they go—neck and neck. "Go it, old barebones;" "go it, donkeys;" and like wild Arabs the party approaches the dwelling—but hold! there are blue coats all over the premises—"what is the use of riding so hard." The speed is slackened. The party rides by, determined to be first at the next plantation. On through the woods, mile after mile, they go—passing insignificant houses with the remark, "O, they're poor folks—they've got nothing there." Finally a large rich looking plantation is discovered. Again they are on the gallop—they dash up to the gate—throw it open. Old men and terror-stricken women come to the door. The entire party rides in at the gate. In an instant they have dismounted. Some of them go for the meat house, others for the pantry, and others rush into the parlor. A squad attacks the bee-hives. "Knock off the top,"—"get water and drown them,"—"smoke them," any way to get the honey,"—thus they talk and thus they act. Soon a swarm of bees fills the atmosphere. The men are no more afraid of them than they are of bullets, but run to and fro among them with choice honey trickling from their fingers. A small squad is at work at the yam hills. The meat is brought out—choice hams; they will have no other. The flour barrels are soon emptied; the meal is gobbled up, and the molasses running into the canteens. One or two of the sharpest take a darkey to one side, quiz him, threaten him, show him a revolver; he tells them something—no matter what—they are off. In a neighboring swamp, amid the thick jungle, on a piece of dry ground that is surrounded on all sides by water, a number of fine horses and mules are found—saddles and bridles too. They are quickly "rigged." The captors gallop back to the farm house. Those who remained there have loaded their animals with a miscellaneous assortment of forage. There is more than they can conveniently carry. What shall be done? The "old gentleman" has a nice carriage in his carriage-house, and the captured horses, two of them, can draw it—certainly—not another word parleying—they do not speak, but act. The carriage is brought out—if harness are lacking they are supplied by Yankee ingenuity. Old straps, old ropes, old tugs are brought together in the semblance of harness. The vehicle is then loaded down until the springs click together. Meanwhile the house has been thoroughly pillaged. There is a class of pillagers as well as a class of foragers at work. Cellars, parlor, chamber, garret, all have been ransacked. Things are in the most perfect, chaotic confusion. Other foragers have arrived—other pillagers also. Drawers are thrown upon the floor—contents turned out. Trunks are broken open. Clothing and other valuables taken. Men of various brigades, divisions and corps are engaged in the despicable work. Who can control them? It is a whirlwind let loose, and must sweep on with all its horrors. "Does the old gentleman protest?" Most assurredly he does, and the old lady, and the pretty young girls, with tears in their eyes, implore protection. As well address their words to the idle winds. The foragers must have something to eat; the army must live by foraging. They feel for the poor and sometimes spare them, but from the wealthy they take without stint. And the pillagers show no compunctions of conscience. With a look of stolid indifference, peculiar to the hardened criminal, they prosecute their abominable work amid the tears and vain entreaties of the helpless citizens.

At length our foragers set out for camp—perhaps passing another house, where they load an old cart or buggy with more provisions. Reaching camp just after dark, the forage is soon distributed, and the soldiers are happy over many good things to eat.

And this is but one day out of many long weeks of such work; scarcely a house escaping the visitation, as the great army swept onward over a tract of country at least fifty miles in breadth.

And we have only looked at the surface; at what was done when numbers of the foragers and pillagers were congregated. We may well imagine that a darker chapter could be written of the work of marauders, who, banding together for the purpose of pillaging and committing other crimes, visited the lonely homes of defenseless women and children, far away from the marching columns. God pity any people that are subjected to the tender mercies of a raiding army.

The foragers became every day more daring, and their services were of great value in a strategic point of view. By their eccentric maneuvres the movements of the main armies were rendered inexplicable to the enemy.

Among the regular foragers were many of the most daring and devoted men in the army. In the saddle they were at home. A little incident which occurred about the time of which I write will illustrate the spirit of these mad-caps. Far away from the main column a party of five foragers descried thirteen rebels, well mounted and armed. Four of the foragers were unarmed, but they made a sudden dash upon the rebels, took them by surprise and completely routed them; capturing six horses.

The 15th of February we marched twelve miles through a rough country—forage not abundant. Chilly, damp weather. The leading division skirmished heavily with the enemy. Went into camp two miles south of Lexington, and about nine miles from Columbia. Another day would determine whether the enemy intended to fight for Columbia.

Every preparation was made on the morning of the 16th for a fight. Non-combatants were sent to the rear. The trains were halted, artillery and ambulances were o dered forward, nd the gentry with stretchers, who were more obnoxious to our finer sensibilities than the village sexton could ever be, were at hand. They were a worthy and useful class to be sure, but their discolored stretchers were very suggestive of disagreeable reflections. Leaving Lexington to the lef, we crossed the newly constructed grade of the projected Columbia and Augusta railroad, and advanced slowly towards Columbia.

No skirmishing ahead. Surely they will not yield the city witho t a struggle. At length we approach th summit of a hill not more than two and a half miles from the city. At the summit there is a farm house and a fence. From that point something ext aordinary is visible. The men far in the rear are sure of this, for those in front are climbing the fence in regular succession to "take a loo] ." In our tu n we do the same, and beyond the Congaree river behold the famed city of Columbia—the cradle of secession.

Then we recollected the occasi n when, four years pre ious, the words flashed over the wires to our Northern homes, "*South Carolina has seceded*,"—and people miled incredulously. But the issue was real, and at the opening of the y ar 1865, Sherman's grand army carried the Stars an Stripes to the gates of Columbia, with a protest which in words simply meant, "*South Carolina cannot secede*." It was a delicate reproof that reached the ears of the Columbians that evening, when the field bands, with grand enthusiasm, played "Hail *Columbia, happy lanc !*"

The enemy had crossed to the north bank of the stream and still occupied the city, but not in force. Skirmishers from the ri ht wing of the army were exchan ing shots wit.. th rebel pickets, and there was light artill ry firing. We camp ed i.. line of battle abc ut two m les from the city.

In that po ition we remained until near noon, February 17th; t en marched to the rear and right, under orders to cross Saluda and Broad rivers, and continue northward towards Winnsboro.

The day's march was most disagreeable. A high wind was blowing; the woods were everywhere on fire. Pine knots and the scarred surface of the turpentine trees burned brightly and sent up their blackening soot, and the pine rail fences were all in a blaze. It was then the universal prayer—"O! for one breath of pure air!" Near the Saluda river the Brigade was sent out on the Lexington road and ordered to be on the alert for Cheatham's forces, which were reported to be harrassing the rear of Kilpatrick's cavalry, which was then coming in. As patiently as we could, gasping in the thick smoke for the breath of life, we awaited further developments. No enemy came. About night, moved a short distance towards the river and went into camp.

Immense wagon trains were corralled near by. Our turn to cross the river would come when they had all passed over. All night they kept moving. By noon next day, (Feb. 18th,) we were enabled to cross.

The Saluda is a pretty little stream, one hundred and twenty-five yards wide, and has a swift current. A short distance above Columbia it unites with Broad river, forming the Congaree. The Brigade camped after dark at the right of the road a few miles south of Broad river.

Moved at half past six on the morning of the 19th; proceeded five miles, then halted and relieved a Division of the 14th Corps, which was guarding approaches to the pontoon bridge across Broad river. "There we went into camp expecting to remain all night, but an hour later were ordered to 'pack up and march immediately.' No one was in a condition to move. Some of the men were cooking, others washing their clothes, and many were out foraging. Everything was in confusion and everybody swore, *or felt like it*—but we were soon all ready and in motion."

We followed a by-road to the right, and camped on the hills immediately south of Broad river.

While encamped there an order was received directing the troops to make preparations for continuing the campaign forty days. Already the men had made severe marches. Many were footsore and ragged. All were blackened with dirt and smoke. Soap had played out.

Those "forty days" loomed forth like a little eternity, but it was in accordance with the plans of our trusted leader, and therefore al. right. Wall tents were to be no longer tolerated in the army. Previous to that time each regiment had been allowed three of these. They were then ordered to burn them, reserving only the "tent flies." Baggage was again cut down. Many articles that had been taken from the country, and were being carried along in view of reaching a "water base" in a short time, were abandoned. Numbers of splendidly bound books of the highest intrinsic value were committed to the flames.

In resuming the march on the 20th, it was our fortune to be again in the rear. All day the troops and trains were crossing the river. The Brigade was deployed in line of battle facing to the rear, to be in readiness for an attack by Cheatham's forces.

The country in the vicinity of Broad river is rolling and picturesque. Between the two rivers there are some fine plantations. Forage was abundant.

At dusk we moved closer to the river. Formed line as before. Again we have a tedious time of waiting. "Why don't the army move?" some one asks, in imitation of Northern croakers. Be patient—it will.

The shadows deepen. The scene in the gloaming of the evening is beautiful: Bright lights twinkle on the hills beyond the river. Are they camp fires? Be patient; we shall see.

At length the order came to fall in. We marched down the steep hill, across the broad and rapid river, and halted a mile north of it, but not to go into camp. Again it was our business to wait—wait until the trains and troops had all passed on ahead. In the thick woods we built fires, rolled ourselves in our blankets and slept. An hour and a half later the Brigade refrain, "Hail Columbia, happy land," aroused us, and we continued on after the slow-moving column.

A night march! how it tries men's souls! The patient man of old was never subjected to that terrible affliction. Let us look at the regiment on a night march. The teams of course are stuck somewhere ahead, and the column has for the moment halted. The pine rails are all ablaze. Stumps and pine knots are set on fire. Groups of sleepy soldiers are gathered about them. Some have dropped down and are sound asleep.

Forward again. Slowly the column re-forms and moves on; but only for a few hundred yards. There is another dead lock. The men stand still, only stamping their feet to produce circulation of the blood. Another move, and this time it continues for perhaps a mile, when there is a brief halt; then a move more brief, and another halt—and another move—the column crowding on by "fits and starts." What is wrong ahead? Doubtless the men are walking a log across some stream—passing in Indian file. Foot by foot we gain ground, and at length the little stream and the file of soldiers are developed. Thanking God that our turn has come at last, we cross over in the same manner, then "lengthen our steps and march rapidly." No one in the way now! what has become of them? Double quick—forward! The horses go off in a trot, and the long-drawn-out column closes up. Again we march regularly. We look up at the star-gemmed heavens—and wonder if there is war and night marches in those far-off worlds. Our eyes wander northward to the great dipper and the polar star. "N. N. W."—yes, just a little to the left of the great dipper—that is the direction of *home.* All are asleep there. If they could know that we are marching at this hour—tired, footsore, cold and sleepy, would they rest as easily! Ah! it is well—

"Where ignorance is bliss 'twere folly to be wise."

It is long after midnight. Some one rides towards the rear, and the oft-repeated question is reiterated, "How far is it to camp?" "Three miles." "Three miles, *indeed;* I'll bet it's *six,*" retorts the soldier, who did not intend to believe the man when he asked the question.

But it is only three miles. We may get to sleep some yet. Away vain hope—teams are mired somewhere ahead, or there is another log to cross in Indian file. Slowly the column drags along. The "first faint streaks of dawn" light up the eastern sky. The sound of a distant bugle is heard. It is far ahead—and now we can hear the roll of drums. It is reveille in camp—no sleep to-night. Day advances; the sun shoots great red beams up towards the zenith. We reach the camp where the advance Division had halted long before midnight. There is some disappointment—some little irritation. The 1st Brigade is boisterous—the men laugh, cheer and yell—they will not be deprived of *that* privilege. The head of column is turned into an open field; the regiments halt, stack arms, unsling knapsacks, and are allowed one hour for breakfast.

Thus we marched, and thus perchance many soliloquized during the night of February 20, 1865.

After our hasty breakfast, February 21st, we moved in the direction of Winnsboro. Passed through a good section of country—found plenty of forage. Reached Winnsboro by noon. It is a beautiful town, pleasantly located. After dinner we marched through the town in review, before Generals Sherman and Slocum. Camped before night two miles east of Winnsboro, in a nice pine grove, at the right of the Rocky Mount road.

Next day, February 22d, we continued on towards Rocky Mount; passing in the morning through a region which was so rough that the foragers could scarcely get away from the column, or once away could hardly return. The road wound along a high ridge from which we had a good view of the country miles away on either hand. The scenery was beautiful, and afforded a pleasant relief from the monotony of the pine woods through which we had been marching. Far away, right and left, clouds of smoke indicated where other corps were moving.

We pressed forward close upon the heels of the rebel cavalry, and during the day the advance guards had a slight skirmish with the enemy. About noon Butler's Division of rebel cavalry crossed the road not more than a mile ahead of us. Our foragers under Captain Woolley had a sharp skirmish with a detachment of rebels and drove them. Forage was found in the greatest abundance. The men brought in a great variety of edibles, including the best of hams and large quantities of flour. All of the teams were loaded, and a large amount of forage was thrown away for want of transportation. We camped before night on the west bank of the Catawba, at Rocky Mount—a place of no consequence aside from the interest which attaches to it on account of a fight which took place there during the war of the Revolution. It is about eight miles above the celebrated Camden battle ground.

A few moments after our camp had been selected, General Sherman called at Division headquarters. While conversing with General Ward, an orderly rode up with a message announcing the fall of Charleston. After reading it, Sherman looked up and said: "Well, General, you can inscribe Charleston on your banners. It is a part of the programme. A skilfull surgeon may kill a man with the smallest needle, while another would cut him up with a butcher knife and then fail to kill him." The General then added that he "proposed to march his army through Washington in less than three months."

Tents were put up, supper was disposed of, and many had gone to bed, when an order came directing us to move across the river—the pontoon bridge having been finished. Packed up and—waited. Troops were crossing ahead, and the column moved slowly. At midnight we marched down the precipitous bluff, crossed the rapid stream, and ascended to a level piece of ground a mile beyond. There we slept until daylight—then, without breakfast, marched three miles. Halted and went into camp, at the left of the road, in thick woods. Rain commenced falling during the afternoon. It rained heavily during the night.

Next day, February 24th, we marched three miles over a corduroy road—"and still it rained." The trains moved with the greatest difficulty. The soil was as treacherous as the people of that State. The rain had thoroughly saturated the ground. Horsemen riding off the road, on ground which appeared firm, suddenly found themselves floundering amid quicksands.

The morning of the 25th it was still raining. We were under orders to move at half past six. Tents were struck—the rain still pouring down. Happily for us, the order was countermanded. The 20th Corps was compelled to wait for the 14th Corps, which found great difficulty in crossing the Catawba, then much swollen by the heavy rains. Rain continued to fall during the night of the 25th.

The 26th was a fair day. We moved early in the morning, and the right wing of the Regiment built "corduroy road."

It may interest those who were not there, to know how such roads are constructed. Usually the troops took rails from adjoining farms and made a *perpetual bridge of rails*. The rails were placed so near together that the mules could walk over the road without stepping between them into the mire. These roads were constructed very rapidly. It required but a brief space of time for a Brigade to "turn out" a forty acre lot—leaving the fence for the farmer to extract from the mud after the army had passed by. At times no rails could be obtained and young pines were cut and used instead.

We went into camp before noon, at Hanging Rock—a place of revolutionary notoriety. A sharp little fight occurred there between the colonists and the British. The rock—an immense boulder—is poised on a large ledge of rocks at the brow of a steep hill. It is apparently so nicely balanced that it seemed dangerous to walk out on the overhanging edge—lest it be precipitated into the valley below. Capt. Merritt in his diary writes: "The rock is notorious as the scaffold from which the British hanged six American soldiers after the battle near it, Aug. 13, 1780."

An equally singular rock is near it; a huge boulder with the lower part of the face " scooped out," forming a concave wall and roof of smooth stone. It has the appearance of a work of art. Its singular formation is attributed to the action of fires, which it is argued have been kindled beneath its overhanging brow, by successive visitors, during ages that have passed. A whole company could find shelter beneath the rock-roof from the storms. It is said the revolutionary patriots made it a place of frequent resort. Near it a squad of men from the 102d stood picket. The locality was visited by hundreds of officers and soldiers, many of whom carried away relics.

Feb. 27th—Remained in camp. Owing to the slow movements of the troops, forage was becoming scarce. The foragers were compelled to go far to the front and fight for what they got. Capt Woolley was out with the detachment from the 102d. He encountered Wheeler's force of cavalry; had a sharp skirmish, and was compelled to retire. Lost two men captured. It rained heavily during the night of the 27th; next day we marched and "corduroyed." Moved eight miles in the direction of Cheraw corduroying two-thirds of the entire d stance. Camped after dark, in the woods. Capt. Woolley came in with his detachment of foragers and gave an account of the capture of the Bank of Camden by his men. It occurred in this way: When the detachment was far away from the main column, Jesse McQuade, of Co. I, and Charles Hartsell of Co. E, espied a fresh wagon track, which led off into the woods. Leaving the main party they traced it into an obscure place where they discovered three covered wagons. Putting spurs to their horses they dashed up towards them, and when very near, were fired upon by citizen guards. McQuade received no less then twenty small shot in his shoulder, left arm and side.. Hartzell received about a dozen in his right arm. This repulsed them, as both were disabled. McQuade's wounds were serious, and he retired a short distance, then becoming faint, slipped from his horse to the ground, where he remained until Hartzell brought up the main party. Some of the citizen guards had by this time fled to the woods, and those who remained surrendered without further opposition. The bank property consisted of four safes, containing about $700 in specie, $2,500, in bullion, and $35,000 in Confederate bonds. Also a quantity of silver plate, jewelry, &c. In addition to all this, three wagons, one buggy, one horse and twelve mules were captured. The property was turned in by Capt. Woolley at Corps headquarters.

In disposing of the property Capt. Woolley adhered to the letter of the law as a responsible officer, but it is to be regretted that the brave men who were wounded in the affair, did not receive a portion of the money at least, as a reward for their daring.

We crossed Lynch's Creek, on the 1st of March, and went into camp two miles north of the stream, at a point where the road forks—one leading to Charlotte, N. C., the other to Chesterfield. Lynch's Creek is about twenty yards wide. It was spanned by an excellent bridge, which the rebels for some reason, left unburned. A large flouring mill stood near the bridge. The foragers had been running it for two days. They carried their grists to the mill on the backs of their donkeys.

March 2d—Advanced on the Chesterfield road. The foragers, during the previous day, had been in North Carolina, where they obtained forage in abundance. They struck out again in that direction. The column marched only ten miles, being delayed by the breaking down of a bridge over a small stream.

The troops moved at 6.30 A. M., March 3d. The weather was disagreeable and the roads in an execrable condition. Several miles of corduroy were made. Reached Chesterfield at 1.30 P.M., and marched through the town with colors flying and bands playing. The column passed Gen. Sherman's headquarters. The General was standing in front of his tent, looking as pleasant as a May morning, apparently not at all burdened with the responsibility of conducting the greatest raid on record. We camped a mile east of the town.

Lieut. A. H. Trego, in his diary furnishes the following reminiscence of Chesterfield:

"While passing through the town I saw one of the saddest and most affecting spectacles that I have witnessed since coming into the army. In the road we met two women who evidently belonged to the poor white class. Their dresses were of home-made cloth—soiled and worn. They were barefoot, and apparently destitute of all clothing save their dresses and bonnets. Their features plainly indicated the marks of poverty and distress. On the face of one there was an expression of the deepest grief. Upon inquiry I found that *she carried a dead babe in her arms*. It was her own child, which had been dead but a short time. She had lived almost alone. Only her aged mother was with her. The rebels had conscripted her husband. She was destitute of means, and was therefore compelled to carry her dead child to her friends to have it buried. She had already carried it three miles, and was obliged to carry it eight miles farther. If ever I felt pity and sorrow for any human being it was for this poor heart-broken woman. How little is known of the suffering among the poor people of the South by the loyal people of the North."

We were informed at Chesterfield, that twenty-five thousand rebels awaited us beyond the Great Pedee River, and would dispute the crossing. The rebel cavalry had been acting for weeks as an advance guard for the Federal army—trotting ahead as some one observed, "to announce its coming." Some apprehensions were entertained that a fight would occur near the borders of North Carolina. But the enemy could not interpose a force sufficient to oppose the resistless tide of blue. Cheraw, on the South bank of the Pedee, was captured on the 4th, with immense stores and many pieces of artillery.

On the 4th our division made a flank movement on the Wadesboro road, and camped that afternoon in North Carolina, a mile and a half from the line, and near the Yadkin river—called the Great Pedee after it passes into South Carolina, probably out of regard for the sensitive feelings of that State, on the question of State rights.

Sunday, March 5. Remained in camp. A beautiful day.

Marched at noon the next day, down the river in the direction of Cheraw. A dense, dark smoke, black as if sent up from the heart of the bottomless pit, loomed up like a gathering storm-cloud away over in North Carolina. At length it hung like a pall between the earth and the sun, and the sun was the color of blood. At first we could not comprehend the cause of the immense smoke-cloud, but learned afterwards that it arose from burning stores of rosin. We halted near Cheraw and awaited our turn to cross the river—waited till after dark, built fires and slept—waiting finally till near morning. Awhile before daylight, marched through the remnant of the town. An "accidental" fire had destroyed

the place. In the dim light of the morn-
the Great Pedee—a river that had ever
with glorious memories of the war of
by the daring deeds of Gen. Francis
miles north of the river, at a house off
d a white-haired old gentleman whether
s buried in Cheraw. I had previously
hat such was the fact. "If he was, I
I've never heard nothing about it,"
1 man, indicating profound ignorance
 my inquiries. Truly, "A prophet is not
ave in his own house."
edee is a rapid stream, and had been
wollen. As we marched across the bot-
of the river, the trees at the roadside
d with rubbish that had lodged there
m was up. This rubbish was lodged
ier than the heads of men on horseback.
Great Pedee we entered the turpentine
vast wilderness of pine trees—just such
 represented by a wood-cut in the school
e woods so dense that they resemble a
gnified into a forest. The trees are many
 limbs for a hundred feet from the base,
an arrow. The only inhabitants are the
nd rosin manufacturers. They live con-
 secluded homes, isolated from all the
 about as distinct ideas of the real active
d, as we have of the mythical inhabit-
1.
ies of rosin were stored up in the wilder-
t places.
rom the column one day with a friend,
d of smoke was observed at no great
ling towards the heavens. We ap-
e, and our attention was attracted to a
ng, seething sound, which mingled with
 flames. "What was burning?" We
The flames seemed to rise up from the
round. We drew nearer. The fire was
 a small hollow. Before the brilliant
were spreading and shooting up great

tongues of fire, a boiling liquid substance, like melted lava, ran down the ravine on the surface of a small stream. "Have the Yankees set the world on fire!" thought we. Dismounting we procured some of the boiling liquid and found it was rosin. A great quantity was burning. Awe-stricken, we stood spell-bound for a time watching the magnificent column of black smoke, —black as blackness can be—rising and rolling into a thousand beautiful shapes, which seemed crystalizing into substantial forms in the region of the clouds. Far upwards in the centre of the column the flames ascended, and their red light was occasionally brought to view by the evolutions of the smoke.

Stores of rosin consisting of hundreds of barrels were often burned.

We camped the night of March 7th, at Laurel Hill, eighteen miles northeast of Cheraw. During the day, a number of the foragers who had remained out all night came in. The detachment under Lieut. T. G. Brown had been engaged the previous day in a sharp fight with Wheeler's cavalry. I give Lieut. Brown's report of the affair in his own words:

"On the morning of March 6th, I started up the Pedee river with twenty-men for the purpose of procuring forage. I proceeded up the river about sixteen miles. Near Wadesboro, found a steam mill; ordered the proprietor to fire-up and go to work grinding meal for us. In the mean time the boys succeeded in finding as many nice hams as the horses could carry. We got our meal ground about an hour before sundown and mounted our horses to start for camp, when, on looking down the road I saw a party of mounted men, I judged about one hundred. Thinking they were too strong for us I thought it policy to retreat, but as soon as we started the "Johnnies" gave a "corn-meal yell" and came for us. We issued our hams and meal, quicker than any commissary could have done it. The rebels being better mounted were soon upon us. A running fight was kept up for nearly quarter of a mile, and I saw they were gaining on us all the time. About a dozen of them being right among us, while several of the boys had abandoned their horses and taken to the timber. In order to avoid capture, on coming into a lane I ordered a halt. The boys all sprang from their horses and began pumping their Spencers, which soon made the rebs turn their backs upon us. We followed them back some distance. Saw four of the poor devils that we had shot, one of them was not quite dead. He said there were one hundred and fifty of them. After we drove them back they made a flank movement and attempted to charge us across an open field, but we soon made them seek the timber for safety. We then started for camp. Taking a small path through the timber, we traveled at a 2-40 rate for about ten miles. When within about five miles of where we left our brigade in the morning, we learned from one of our boys—who had become separated from us in the beginning of the fight, and was in advance of us—that Butler's Rebel Division was camped on the road a short distance in front of us. Here was another dilemma. After due deliberation we left the road, which ran parallel with the river, and took through the country, keeping between the road and river. We had to cross creeks and ravines of every size and description. We reached the 14th A. C., about one o'clock in the morning, tired and hungry, did not overtake our own command until after 11 o'clock the next night. In the fight St. George of Co. "B" had his coat sleeve torn off by a big reb who ordered him to surrender. He said he "couldn't see it." Several of the boys were struck with pistols and carbines. Quite a number of hats were lost, but the boys soon "cramped" others of the South Carolina chivalry. I had four men captured, but only one man wounded—Walker of Co. "A,"—very slightly."

During the march from the Great Pedee to Fayetteville, forage was exceedingly scarce. Foragers sometimes rode all day and saw only a few wretched huts. To take from the poverty-stricken inhabitants was to rob the poor. It was the only alternative, and the majority of the few citizens that lived in that region were left utterly destitute.

The soldiers were often deeply affected by the scenes of destitution and want. The foragers sometimes visited houses where everything had been taken and the children were crying for bread. Having compassion upon them, they would leave with them some of the forage collected at other places, but would scarcely be gone before another party, less humane, would visit the house and take all that had been left by their predecessors.

I will relate an incident that occurrred at a small house which the column passed when we were almost through the pine wilderness. An intelligent lady with two children occupied the house; one was a pretty curly-haired girl of about seven years, and the other a blue-eyed boy about four years old. Everything fit to eat, and almost every thing else had been taken. Many soldiers were in and about the house; one was lying on the floor very sick. The little boy, with tears standing in his eyes, was crying—"Ma,—ma—I'm hungry; I want something to eat."

"I have nothing," said she, "but an ear of corn; I made my dinner on that—ask the soldiers for something."

The soldiers were almost entirely destitute, but they could not resist such appeals—although the little boy did not ask them, as the mother suggested. They gave the family pieces of corn bread, small bits of pork, and one or two yams.

The column marched all day the 8th of March through the "pine barrens," and saw only one house—a mere hut. It rained all day. Camped five miles south of Lumber river.

We moved at 6 o'clock in the morning, March 9th; followed a by-road four miles and then halted to await the completion of a bridge across Lumber river. After waiting over three hours we moved forward, and during the next two hours marched one mile. Night overtook us in the midst of a heavy rain storm—still south of Lumber river. General Ward had determined to cross that evening. General Geary had "outflanked" him during the day, and camped his division before night. Ward was therefore swearing mad, and declared he "would not let Geary get ahead next day if it cost half the men in the Division." But the old General was compelled to succumb to inevitable fate that evening, and he abandoned the idea of crossing before morning. We camped as best we could, hungry, wet and cold. Hard bread was issued that night—the first for over a month.

We moved at six in the morning, March 10th. Crossed Lumber river and three swamps in passing over the first mile. The heavy rains had raised the water until the bridges were surrounded. The road was very narrow, and through the mud and water the wagon train, the foragers and the infantry, huddled all together, pressed forward. The men were compelled to wade one of the swamps. The water was eighteen inches deep and very cold.

Although on the road from six o'clock in the morning until ten o'clock at night, we marched only seven miles. Camped near Rock Fish Creek—twenty miles from Fayetteville.

During the morning of the 11th the troops corduroyed three miles of road. In the afternoon struck a plank road, and at ten o'clock P. M. reached Fayetteville—having marched the last ten miles in two and a half hours.

At Fayetteville, Gen. Sherman communicated with the Federal forces in Wilmington, and we had an opportunity to send letters home, a privilege we had not enjoyed since leaving Robertville, South Carolina, over five weeks previous.

We rested at Fayetteville on the 12th, and marching in review before Gen. Sherman through the city, crossed Cape Fear river on the 13th.

The brigade—excepting the 102d—camped a short distance north of the river. Our regiment was sent forward on a reconnoisance. Musketry firing was heard not far ahead. The foragers were driving the enemy. This they had been doing for many days, but they were destined soon to "run against an obstacle," which could not be overcome by their loose system of warfare.

The regiment did not come up with the enemy, but went into camp about five miles north of the river. From that position another reconnoisance was made the following day. We were accompanied by the 20th Conn. and 33d Massachusetts regiments. The foragers drove the enemy from several barricades, but at Silver Run, nine miles from our camp, on the Raleigh road, the rebels were found in a strong position, from which they refused to be driven. A skirmish line was deployed. Co's A, I, C and E, went out from the 102d. A sharp skirmish took place, lasting over an hour. But the rebels were entrenched, and to all appearances had a superior force. At dusk the reconnoitering party withdrew, and we made a tedious march back to camp.

The troops advanced next morning on the same road. At Silver Creek only a light skirmish line of the enemy was found. The foragers could drive them without difficulty. We camped that evening a short distance north of Silver Creek. It rained furiously. Our camp was in a pine wood that had recently been burning. Everything was black, including ourselves. There was plenty of water but no soap. The enemy had become stubborn during the evening, and skirmished heavily with Kilpatrick's men.

March 16th. The troops moved early and soon found the enemy. When about four miles south of Averysboro heavy firing commenced in front. The 1st Brigade, except the 70th Indiana, which was "train-guard," was formed on the right of the road in line of battle, and preparations were made for an advance. Finally we moved by the left flank, crossed the road, and made a detour of about three-fourths of a mile to the left. Then moved to the front, the skirmishers becoming quickly engaged. As we advanced cautiously through the young pines to the edge of an open field, it was perceived that the Brigade had completely flanked the rebel position. Not more than a hundred and twenty-five yards in advance they were visible in great numbers, running forward to their front line of works to reinforce the rebels there engaged. At that instant a number of our men yelled out, "Don't fire—they are our own men." For a moment our line was undecided. It was thought barely possible that we had become bewildered and were about to charge our own troops. Many months of active campaigning had rendered the uniform of the opposing armies almost undistinguishable. Many of the rebels wore blue, and many of the Federals, having worn out their blue, were dressed in citizen's gray. The enemy in the meantime had kept up a galling skirmish fire, and heavy artillery and infantry firing was going on in the front, where the 3d Brigade confronted their breastworks. Soon all doubts as to the identity of the rebels in our front were dispelled. The Brigade raised a yell, and, as if by an intuitive perception of the duty required, rushed forward—the 102d on the right, the 79th on our left; the 129th and 105th in the second line. The rebels, completely surprised and outflanked, instantly broke. Yelling like wild men, the Brigade swept magnificently forward, directly in rear of and parallel with the rebel line of works. Three pieces of artillery fell into our hands and many prisoners—recumbent in a trench behind their works—held up their hands and handkerchiefs begging for mercy. But the main body of the charging column rushed by them and continued on after the flying enemy, who abandoned blankets, haversacks, canteens, guns, cartridge-boxes—everything that could impede their progress. Reaching heavy timber, the pursuing column halted, re-formed the line of battle, and rested for a time, keeping up a sharp skirmish fire with the enemy. Capt. Wm. M. Armstrong, of Co. B, who had gallantly led his company in the charge, was at that time severely wounded and was carried from the field. At length, other troops having moved forward to our support, a general advance was made. The second line of rebel works was found abandoned, but as we approached the third, which was very strong, we were met by a rapid fire of musketry and artillery, the enemy throwing grape shot and shells. The advance was made over level ground, in a pine wood that was quite free of underbrush. The enemy had an almost unobstructed view of our lines.

It seems reasonable that troops should not be advanced into such a position unless a charge is intended. But no charge was ordered. Our bugle at intervals sounded the Brigade refrain "Hail Columbia," &c., then the "forward." The enemy knew what the bugle meant as well as we, and the moment the column moved, poured in a heavy volley of musket balls and grape shot, which checked the advance—the men lying down; some protected by trees and logs, others in open ground. The affair in the morning had been managed magnificently but the afternoon's work was done in a bungling manner. Finally the Brigade threw up breastworks a hundred and twenty-five yards from the enemy's line.

Night came on with rain. It had been a day of excitement and fatigue. Cold and wet, we passed a miserable night. But the rebels must have been more miserable, for, as we discovered next morning, they retired during the night, and were obliged to pass along a most wretched road, rendered almost impassable by the rain.

Thus terminated the battle of Averysboro. In the 102d two men were killed and nineteen wounded. The killed were Cornelius Lott, Co. I, and Samuel D. Hutchinson, Co. K. Among the wounded were Capt. J. Y. Merritt, Co. K, Capt. O. B. Matteson, Co. D, and Lieut. A. H. Trego, Co. C, then A. A. G. on staff of Brigade Commander.

1st Sergeant J. C. Simpson was shot through the left arm, which was afterwards amputated. H. J. Fisher was accidentally shot by a comrade, the ball passing through his left leg, which was subsequently amputated.

The advance regiment of the Division pursued the enemy through Averysboro. The Division remained near the town until next morning to keep up the show of a movement on Raleigh.

General Sherman, in his report of the "Campaign of the Carolinas," makes the following, among other remarks in regard to the battle at Averysboro. After giving an account of the position of affairs on the evening of the 15th, he says:

"Next morning the column advanced in the same order and developed the enemy, with artillery, infantry, and cavalry, in an entrenched position in front of the point where the road branches off toward Goldsboro, through Bentonville. On an inspection of the map, it was manifest that Hardee, in retreating from Fayetteville, had halted in the narrow swampy neck between Cape Fear and South rivers, in hopes to hold me to save time for the concentration of Johnston's armies at some point to his rear, namely, Raleigh, Smithfield, or Goldsboro. Hardee's force was estimated at 20,000 men. It was necessary to dislodge him, that we might have the use of the Goldsboro Road, as also to keep up the feint on Raleigh as long as possible. General Slocum was therefore ordered to press and carry the position, only difficult by reason of the nature of the ground, which was so soft that horses would sink everywhere, and even men could hardly make their way over the common pine barren.

"The 20th Corps, General Williams, had the lead, and Ward's Division the advance. This was deployed, and the skirmish line developed the position of a brigade of Charleston heavy artillery, armed as infantry, (Rhett's) posted across the road behind a light parapet, with a battery of guns enfilading the approach across a cleared field. General Williams sent a brigade (Case's) by a circuit to his left that turned this line, and by a quick charge broke the brigade, which rapidly retreated back to a second line better built and more strongly held. The whole line advanced late in the afternoon, drove the enemy well within his entrenched line, and pressed him so hard that next morning he was gone, having retreated in a miserable stormy night over the worst of roads. Ward's division of infantry followed to and through Averysboro, developing the fact that Hardee had retreated, not on Raleigh, but on Smithfield."

He also states that the Division captured "three guns and 217 prisoners, of which 68 were wounded." * * * That "one hundred rebel dead were buried by us," and that the loss of the left wing of his army in that affair was 67 killed and 477 wounded.

Everything indicated that the rebels had been badly cut up in the fight. Their dead and wounded were found in almost every house in the vicinity of Averysboro—one house contained sixteen of their dead. In the town itself we found thirty of their wounded. An abandoned ambulance, which we passed, contained a dying rebel officer. The poor fellow moaned piteously.

We followed the main army on the Goldsboro road, the morning of the 18th. Crossed a number of swamps; roads very bad—in some places almost impassable for teams. All night we were on the move or waiting to move, and between sunset and sunrise passed over but three miles of the road.

The march was continued on the 19th. In the afternoon of that day the battle of Bentonville took place. Gen. Joe Johnston then hurled all of his available force on the left flank of Sherman's army. The cannonading early in the afternoon became very heavy directly in our front. We were then guarding a wagon train, but the Division was ordered forward to assist those engaged, and the teams were left to come up at leisure. Then there was a rush towards the front—cavalry, artillery and infantry all crowding along one narrow road. As we approached the scene of action the roar of the conflict became perfectly terrific. The advance brigade of Carlin's Division, 14th Corps, had been repulsed, and affairs looked somewhat critical. Our batteries were being served with wonderful energy. The crashing roar of musketry reminded us of Resaca. Our Division was quickly hurried to a position on the left of the 1st Division, and breastworks were thrown up by the 1st Brigade in almost no time. The men thought they would be needed, but they were not. The extreme left did not become engaged.

During the day a squad of eight foragers from our Regiment had a severe fight with a party of rebels. In regard to the affair, Corporal E. S. Ricker, one of the eight, writes:

"I wish to do honor to the memory of a gallant lad who fell mortally wounded on that occasion—Wm. H. Hampton, of Co. K. Eight of us were attacked by over thirty rebels. Hampton was wounded in the leg just above the knee but continued to fight on until he had discharged his piece *ten times*, and then fell on his face fainting. You cannot do him and others of like character full justice by any eulogium. He displayed the finest qualities I ever saw exhibited in action."

The others of the party were not hurt. Hampton was taken to a field hospital, and a week later he died.

On the 20th, orders were issued for a general assault upon the enemy's works—to take place next morning. This order was not communicated officially to the troops, but it was soon noised around, and that evening there was much sober thought about the work to be accomplished on the morrow. In such a case the soldiers dislike to be in suspense. One who distinguished himself on every field where the regiment fought, describes his feelings on that occasion in the following words: "After hearing this news, we were a sober, silent party. For it is desperate work to charge the enemy's lines over open fields, where, if we should fail, there would be but slight hope of escape from death or imprisonment. We all went to bed early—silent and thoughtful. Were up at 5.30 next morning and ready to move on the enemy's works. I cannot describe the feelings then experienced, nor the thoughts that passed through my mind, as I sat by the fire, waiting for the time when the work should commence. I almost longed for the time to come that the work might be finished and off my mind. This thinking of a battle so long before it is to take place, and knowing it must be fought, almost makes a coward of the thinker."

But the contemplated assault was abandoned.

We remained in the vicinity of the Bentonville battle ground until the morning of the 22d; in the intermediate time built a new line of works—marched to them—returned to the old line—then back again to the new. There was picket firing and cannonading on the right much of the time. The morning of the 22d, the enemy having retired to Smithfield, we resumed the march to Goldsboro. A high wind was blowing; otherwise the day was beautiful. A star (Venus) was visible at noonday in the clear sky. It attracted general attention, and the soldiers called it "Sherman's Star," and was sure it was the star of peace. At dusk we reached Falling Creek. The bridge across the creek was in a miserable condition—indeed it was the worst bridge we crossed during the campaign. Our brigade occupied two hours in getting over.

On the 23d we crossed Neuse River. Previous to crossing we waited for a time in a plowed field. The wind was blowing a hurricane, and we were almost suffocated with dust that was swept up in great clouds from the field. During the day we passed some of Major Gen. Terry's troops—two divisions, one composed of white troops the other of blacks. Some of the men from the white division complained very bitterly of their hardships. They "had been cut off from communication and had been without letters *seven days.*" Our men answered them very consolingly, saying, "It is too bad—a real shame—but then we have had no letters since January 12th—our latest news from home is only seventy days old." We camped near Beaver's Creek that evening nine miles southwest of Goldsboro. The rebel cavalry skirmished there with the pickets. The 102d being detailed to guard the pack mules into town, we were up at 1 o'clock A. M., March 24th. Moved without breakfast an hour nd a half later—reached Goldsboro at daylight. Finally the Brigade went into camp and constructed breast works two miles north of the town.

During the raid the 102d lost 44 men—killed, wounded and captured.

Excepting one or two intervals of rest, we had been raiding fifty-two days, and, according to Gen. Sherman's own statement, had marched nearly five hundred miles. The troops were ragged beyond all description. Swarthy, smoked and worn out—many without shoes—no wonder the negro soldiers of Terry's command said, as the raiders marched by, "Sherman's men are a hard lookin' set, *suah.*" If the army could have marched through a northern city, appearing as it did, the people would have held up their hands in amazement and inquired, "What wretched ragamuffins are these?"—and some independent soldier would have replied, "Only Sherman's Greasers."

CHAPTER XI.

Rest and recuperation. New clothes. The fighting at Richmond and Petersburg. The glorious result. Advance on Raleigh. News of the surrender of Lee's Army. GOING HOME. THE HOMEWARD MARCH.

The army needed a long rest at Goldsboro, but did not get it. We remained there from the 24th of March until the 10th of April. During the intermediate time new clothes were drawn, and the great ragged army came out in an entirely new suit of blue.

While at Goldsboro, Capt. Isaac McManus rejoined the regiment. He had been commissioned Lieutenant-Colonel, but, as we had two field officers, could not be mustered into that grade. Col. McManus had earned the position by his valuable services and his sufferings, and he is therefore generally accorded the title which was withheld from him by a mere technicality. At the date of this writing he is still suffering from the wound received at Pine Mountain—his left arm being hopelessly crippled.

The news of severe fighting at Petersburg and Richmond reached us about the 4th of April. On the 6th there was a grand review of the division by Major-Gen. Mower, who had succeeded Gen. Williams in the command of the 20th Corps. As we were coming in from the review, we heard heavy cheering far away in the direction of Goldsboro. Gradually the wave of enthusiasm approached our part of the line—one regiment following another in such outbursts of deafening cheers as can only be heard from soldiers in the hour of victory.

What could it mean? We approached our camp and the glad news was then on every tongue—"RICHMOND IS OURS." Then the old "First Brigade" swelled the deep chorus of voices that went up from all the hills and valleys around Goldsboro. Everybody became happy.

That afternoon, business was almost suspended in high military circles. The army was wild with joy. Additional news in regard to the great victories, occasioned new outbursts of feeling. With enthusiasm that knew no bounds, the troops received the order of Gen. Grant announcing the result, and saying substantially to Gen. Sherman: "Move immediately against Johnston, and let us finish up the job at once."

The morning of the 10th, we were in motion. Our brigade moved through Goldsboro, made slow time, and camped about six miles southwest of town near Mockasin River. The next day we made a rapid march to Smithfield. The day was very warm and great numbers of the soldiers fell out by the way, completely exhausted. Several men died of excessive heat. Others were in spasms, and many were doubtless injured for life.

It appeard afterwards that there was no necessity whatever for the rapid march. No enemy was found at Smithfield.

Camped the night of the 11th a quarter of a mile east of the town. Moved at sunrise next morning—on the road leading westward through Smithfield. As the head of the column approached the ancient little town, cheer after cheer reached us from other columns and from the camps of other troops. "More good news" the soldiers said and pressed forward to hear it announced. An Aid soon rode along the column, and the electric words thrilled every heart, "LEE HAS SURRENDERED WITH HIS WHOLE ARMY!"

Then the cheering surpassed all previous manifestations. Hats flew into the air as thick as the flying leaves of autumn. Oh! the unspeakable joy of that moment to the war-worn soldiers. The glorious words needed no comment. All felt that the war was virtually over—the Union saved. A few moments later we passed Gen. Sherman, who was walking rapidly to and fro on the sidewalk, his hands crossed behind him. He was evidently absorbed in deep thought, but his thoughts could only have been of a happy nature, for he had just issued an order in which the following noble sentiments were uttered, substantially in these words:

"*All glory be to God! And all honor to our brave comrades towards whom we have been marching! A little more toil; a few more days of labor, and the great race is won; and our government stands before the world redeemed and disinthralled.*"

The march on that day was also severe. We crossed Neuse river and camped twelve miles from Raleigh, on the west side of a small creek.

Moved at daylight the 13th, and reached Raleigh without opposition at 2 o'clock P. M. Went into camp southeast of the city. The rear of Johnston's army had retired during the previous night.

Saturday, the 15th, according to previous orders we were ready to move at six o'clock in the morning. But the order was countermanded. Joe Johnston, as we subsequently learned, had offered to talk with Gen. Sherman about surrendering.

While negotiations were pending, the news of the assassination of the President reached us. The army during many days, had been intoxicated with joy, but when this terrible news was confirmed, the general joy was turned into mourning. Had all the bright omens of peace been suddenly swept away the reaction could not have been as violent as it was under the effect of this one harrowing thought—*Lincoln slain in the hour of victory.* O! how the great heart of the army throbbed and swelled; first with the wild thirst for vengeance, and then with a profound sorrow, that would heed no words of consolation.

Two days after the receipt of this news, Gen. Sherman announced that he had effected an arrangement with Johnston, which if approved at Washington would secure peace, and he would soon be enabled to "conduct us to our homes." Peace and home—sweet words. But this great news was scarcely sufficient to arouse the army from the deep lethargy into which it had fallen. Patiently we awaited the return of the messenger that had been sent to Washington with the "memoranda" of Gen. Sherman's arrangement with Johnston. With the announcement of his return we expected to receive orders to commence the homeward march.

The citizens of Raleigh and vicinity, were anxious for a restoration of peace and a return to the old order of things. Some of them had never been disloyal, while the disloyalty of others had been most effectually subjugated. An old citizen, whom our foragers visited in the country, entertained very peculiar ideas in reference to the state of the country. "I always told them so," said he, alluding to his fire-eating neighbors. "I always told them 'Uncle Sam' would be our next President, and now its going to be just as I told 'em. 'Uncle Sam's' bound to be our next President."

Raleigh is a beautiful city. The site is elevated, and the ground undulating. The State house is large and commodious, but not remarkable for its beauty. In front of it there is a magnificent bronze statue of Washington, representing him clad in the panoply of war. The Insane Asylum is an imposing structure, six hundred feet in length and of a proportionate height. There is also in the city an asylum for the deaf and dumb.

Those of our regiment who were in Raleigh the morning of the 24th, witnessed a grand pageant—the review of the 17th Corps by Gens. Grant and Sherman. Grant had arrived that morning. Very few were aware of his presence in the city. As the hour for the commencement of the review approached, an immense concourse of spectators, soldiers and citizens, collected about the reviewing stand. Guards kept the streets clear. At length the familiar form of Sherman, on horseback, caught the eye of the crowd. But who was that with him, riding on the right—short, heavy-set, iron-featured; looking travel-worn, yet having the bearing of the quiet great man. It was Grant, fresh from the scenes of his victories in Virginia. The glorious old 17th Corps marched proudly that day. It was a pleasure to them to dip their tattered flags to the chief whom they had known at Vicksburg.

The Generals remained seated upon their horses at the reviewing post. Grant was quiet and calm as usual. Sherman who was stationed then on his right—a very little retired—exhibited a slight degree of restlessness—looking occasionally to the right and to the left, and then fixing his eyes for an instant on the ground as if in deep thought. He had that morning received the information that his arrangement with Johnston was disapproved.

Other distinguished Generals were there—Howard, Schofield, Logan, Jeff. C. Davis, Slocum, Blair, and a host of other Major Generals, with a small regiment of Brigadiers.

At the close of the review, as Sherman and Grant rode through the crowd, there was a spontaneous outburst of cheering, and their way was almost blocked by the surging mass of humanity—weak humanity it is true, and yet it is no mean quality to honor the truly great.

That evening, without one word of explanation, we were ordered to be in readiness to march the following morning. Rumors were rife that President Johnston had disapproved of Sherman's proceedings, and that we were to "go for them" again. The troops were nervously excited, and not a little angry with the new President. "Grape-vine" said that Sherman had tendered his resignation, but the men could not tolerate the thought. They wanted no other leader.

The morning of the 25th the new campaign opened. It was destined to be short. A few moments after the march commenced Col. Smith and Adjutant Snyder rejoined the regiment, both having been "absent with leave, and "on detached service." Our new chaplain, Rev. C. M. Wright, had joined the regiment a few days before—also Capt. D. W. Sedwick and Lieut. Wm. H. Bridgford.

Our regiment, with the corps, marched out about fourteen miles on the Holly Springs road. Camped six miles from the springs, and remained there during the 26th and 27th. In the meantime Johnston surrendered. We returned to Raleigh the morning of the 28th, and immediately commenced preparations for the homeward march.

Being sick at the time and unable to march with the troops, I have obtained of Corporal E. S. Ricker, of Co. I, a brief sketch of the march from Raleigh to Alexandria. Friend Ricker is an accomplished writer, but has had no time to furnish more than the mere outline of the march. He says:

"At seven A. M., on the 30th of April, we left Raleigh *en route* for Washington, via Richmond. Marched thirteen miles and c mped on the west side of the Neuse river, near Faust's Paper Factory. Ward's Division in the rear. May 1st.—Early in the morning crossed the river—marched twenty miles—Ward's Division in the rear. May 2d.—Marched thirteen miles, and went into camp on the north bank of Tar river. May 3d.—Marched *twenty-five* miles and passed from North Carolina into Virginia. Crossed Roanoke river after night, and camped near that stream. Our division (Ward's) which had been previous to that time considerably in the rear, came up with the corps at the Roanoke, and passed over the river in advance. May 4th.—Moved at half-past four A. M., Gen. Ward in advance. Crossed Meherrin river, at Saffold's Bridge. Marched twenty miles that day. May 5th.—Moved again at half-past four in the morning. Ward in advance. 102d in the rear of the division— acting as train guard. Reached camp at three o'clock P. M., on the north side of the Nottoway river, having marched eighteen miles—weather very warm. May 6th —Moved out soon after daylight, marched about fifteen miles—passed through Black's and White's and Wellville stations, on the Petersburg and Lynchburg railroad. At the former place found some of the Sixth Corps— Army of the Potomac—on duty. Went into camp at noon; weather excessively warm. A ration of whisky was issued to the men. Moved May 7th, at 4.30 A. M. Harrison's Brigade in advance of the corps. Crossed the Appommatox River before noon and reached camp at Clover Hill, twenty-one miles from Richmond, at 12.30 P. M., having marched about eighteen miles. May 8th.—Moved at 4.30 A. M., and went into camp at noon, seven miles from Richmond; weather very warm. May 9th.—Moved two and a half miles in the direction of Manchester. Orders were received from Gen. Halleck, directing the army to resume the march towards Washington on the following morning. The order announced that the troops would pass in review before Gen. Halleck's headquarters. That evening Gen. Sherman arrived from Savannah. May 10th—Orders received on the previous day were countermanded. May 11th, at 11 A. M., the march was resumed, but the troops did not march in review through Richmond. Passed Castle Thunder and Libby Prison. We were treated with marked attention by the people. They supplied the thirsty soldiers with water and in some cases with wine. We camped four miles from Capitol Square, on the road leading to Washington, and at the point where Kilpatrick trained his artillery on Richmond in one of his dashing exploits when connected with the Potomac army. May 12th.—Marched nine miles. Roads in bad condition. Waited in the morning for the 17th Corps to pass. The 14th Corps was in advance of the 20th—crossed the Chickahominy and camped one mile south of Ashland. May 13th.—Crossed the South Anna in the forenoon, marched fifteen miles and camped at night on the south side of Little River. May 14th.—Crossed Little River and the North Anna. Ward's Division in the rear. Marched about 17 miles and camped within seven miles of Spottsylvania, C. H. May 15th.—Marched fifteen miles; passed through Spottsylvania; saw many evidences of the hard fighting that took place there; camped that evening on the old Chancellorsville battle ground. May 16th.—A march of four miles brought us to the Rappahannock, which we crossed at United States Ford. Camped at sunset near White Ridge—a hamlet of half a dozen houses. Distance marched about twenty-one miles.

Early that morning, Adjutant J. H. Snyder, with a mounted orderly, W. O. Jones, of Co. I, rode off from the column to view the battle-ground. *They never returned, and no clue to their fate has since been obtained.*

May 17th.—Marched fifteen miles and camped at Occoquon Creek. May 18th.—In the forenoon crossed Bull Run, a wide, shallow stream, with gravelly bottom, and clear water. Marched eighteen miles, and camped two miles northeast of Fairfax C. H. Weather excessively warm. May 19th.—Moved at an early hour and reached camp two and a half miles from Alexandria, a little after noon."

ADJUTANT J. H. SNYDER.

In the preceding notes of the homeward march, reference is made to the mysterious disappearance of Adjutant Snyder and Private W. O. Jones. As far as known, the circumstances attending this sad affair were as follows:

The regiment being camped on the old Chancellorsville battle ground, there was an opportunity to visit the interesting localities in that historic region. When the regiment was in line ready to move, May 16th, Adjutant Snyder and W. O. Jones, rode away from the column to view the battle-ground. A short time afterwards they were seen by a member of Co. C, about two miles from the column on the left. They were then inquiring the distance and direction to the moving column. A squad of about twenty citizens was passing at the time. They said they were "going to Fredericksburg to take the oath." When we reflect what villains a majority of the oath-loving citizens were, we may well suspect that those men were none too good to waylay and murder a Union soldier.

It was for a time supposed that they had tarried on the field until the pontoon bridge was taken up and had been compelled to seek a crossing at Fredericksburg. But as day after day passed and nothing was heard of them, it became apparent that they had met with foul play. From Washington, Lieut. Trego went back to Fredericksburg, and with a small squad of men, searched in the vicinity of the Chancellorsville battle ground, but could get no clue to the fate of the missing men.

Adjutant Snyder was in many respects a remarkable young man. Noble, generous and brave, his character was in every respect above reproach. The best faculties of the mind ruled his life. Temperate, honest and intelligent; with a refined love of the beautiful, the true and the pure in nature and in human character, and possessing withal a genial disposition, he was the soul of every social circle in which he moved, and was ever in the sunshine of life. An enthusiastic lover of music, he excelled in that noble accomplishment. Since returning home the men of the regiment often hear the strains he used to sing, and memory instantly recalls the old camp ground and the Adjutant with his guitar.

It is to be regretted that a more careful search was not made for the lost men before the Regiment left Washington. Even at this late day some clue might be obtained that would account for their mysterious disappearance. As members of the 102d, we owe it to the memory of our lost comrades to have another and a thorough search made. Until this is done we cannot feel that we have properly discharged our duty in the premises.

W. O. JONES.

Private Jones, who was lost with the Adjutant, was then acting in the capacity of mounted orderly, and was a good boy. Faithful in the discharge of duty, he was mild and patient under all circumstances. Often he talked of the approaching day of peace, and of returning to the home he was destined to see no more. He was esteemed throughout the Regiment as a faithful soldier.

While encamped near Alexandria, preparations were made for the g and review in Washington, and on the 24th, at an early hour in the morning, the army was in motion. It was a beautiful morning, and as the columns, following a serpentine course, passed over Arlington Heights, the scene was magnificent. There the soldiers caught the first view of the grand dome of the Capitol building. About 9 o'clock A. M. we crossed the Potomac over Long Bridge, and felt that we were out of the land of Secessia. The head of the column was halted at Capitol Hill, and from that point the review commenced.

Marching around the Capitol building, we passed into Pennsylvania Avenue, thenceforward for two miles—to the President's house—dense masses of humanity occupied the pavement on each side of the street, and at some places crowded upon the marching column. Every available place of observation was taken up. The noble army of the Potomac had marched by, the previous day. And these were "Sherman's raiders." How would they acquit themselves? In column by company, with eyes fixed to the front, the regiments moved as one man—sixty thousand bayonets gleaming in the sunlight, and each regiment bearing aloft the old flag. "*Sherman has been abused*," they said, and marched more proudly. There was music, but no music was needed to secure a uniform motion. The steady *tramp—tramp—tramp—* of each company on the paving stones, was heard distinctly above the hum of voices and the strains of music. The pride and strength of the Great West swept down Pennsylvania Avenue. Kind words of welcome in appropriate mottoes, greeted the eyes of the soldiers, and bevies of beautiful ladies smiled a welcome still more prized. Onward the column moved. Cheers rang out on all sides. In its turn, with soldiery tread, the 102d—preceded by the 70th Indiana, and followed by the 79th Ohio, 129th and 105th Illinois—"dipped" the old flag to the President, Grant, Sherman and a brilliant galaxy of other distinguished men of our own and other lands.

After the review we marched to a camp near the northeast corner of the District of Columbia—one company of the regiment being camped around the cornerstone.

Thus we have traced the career of the Regiment to its virtual close. In reviewing what has been written, I am conscious that no delineations in the foregoing pages have adequately portrayed the worth of the brave men who shouldered their muskets on the banks of the Ohio, and from that point carried our good old flag through Kentucky and Tennessee into Georgia—where its bright folds gleamed on many sanguinary fields—and thence bore it onward in "the march to the sea," the "campaign of the Carolinas," and finally exhibited it, tattered and torn, in the capital of the nation which they went forth to save. How they toiled onward when weary limbs almost refused them support, still looking forward to the hour of final victory, let the words of a Christian warrior tell. They are the noble words of Major General O. O. Howard, and were spoke at Gettysburg, July 4th, 1865:

"I would point you to the soldier pursuing his enemy into the strongholds of Dalton, behind the stern impassable features of Rocky Face, Resaca, Adairsville, Cassville, Dallas, New Hope Church, Pickett's Mill, Pinetop, Lost Mountain, Kenesaw, Culp's Farm, Smyrna,

Camp Ground, Peach Tree Creek, Atlanta, from so many points of view, and Jonesboro, are names of battle fields upon each of which a soldier's memory dwells. For upwards of a hundred days he scarcely rested from the conflict. He skirmished over rocks, hills and mountains; through mud, streams and forests. For hundreds of miles he gave his aid to dig that endless chain of intrenchments which compassed every one of the enemy's fortified positions. He companied with those who combatted the obstinate foe on the front and on the flanks of those mountain fastnesses which the enemy had deemed impregnable, and he had a right at last to echo the sentiment of his indefatigable leader, 'Atlanta is ours, and fairly won.'

" Could you now have patience to turn back with him and fight these battles over again, behold his communications cut, his railroad destroyed for miles and miles; enter the bloody fight of Alatoona, follow him through the forced marches, *via* Rome, Georgia, away back to Resaca, and through the obstructed gaps of the mountains of Alabama, you would thank God for giving him a stout heart and an unflinching faith in a just and noble cause. Weary and worn, he reposed at Atlanta, on his return, but one single night, when he commenced the memorable march toward Savannah. The soldier has become a veteran; he can march all day with his musket, his knapsack, his cartridge box, his haversack and canteen upon his person; his muscles have become large and rigid, so that what was once extremely difficult he now accomplishes with graceful ease. This fact must be borne in mind when studying the soldiers' march through Georgia and the Carolinas. The enemy burned every bridge across stream after stream; the rivers, bordered with swamps—for example, the Ocmulgee, the Oconee and the Ogeechee—were defended at every crossing. That they were passed at all by our forces, is due to the cheerful, fearless, indomitable private soldier.

" Oh, that you had seen him as I have done, wading creeks a half mile in width and water waist deep, under fire, pressing on through wide swamps, without one faltering step, charging in line upon the most formidable works, which were well defended! You could then appreciate him and what he accomplished as I do. You could then feel the poignant sorrow that I always did feel when I saw him fall bleeding to the earth. I must now leave the soldier to tell his own tale among the people; of his bold, bloody work at McAllister against the torpedoes, abattis, artillery and musketry; of his privations at Savannah; of his struggles through the swamps, quicksands, and over the broad rivers of the Carolinas; of the fights, fires, explosions, doubts and triumphs suggested by Griswoldville, Rivers' and Binnaker's bridges, Orangeburg, Congaree Creek, Columbia, Cheraw, Fayetteville, Averysboro, and Bentonville. I will leave him to tell how his hopes brightened at the re-union at Goldsboro. How his heart throbbed with gratitude and joy as the wires confirmed the rumored news of Lee's defeat, so soon to be followed by the capture of the enemy's Capital and of his entire army. I will leave him to tell to yourselves and your children how he felt and acted; how proud was his bearing; how elastic his step as he marched in review before the President of the United States at Washington! I would do the soldier injustice not to say that there was one thing wanting to make his satisfaction complete, and that was the sight of the tall form of Abraham Lincoln, and the absence of that bitter recollection which he could not altogether exclude from his heart—that *he* had died by the hand of a traitor assassin."

While we were in camp near Washington, General Sherman issued the following farewell order:

HEADQUARTERS MIL. DIV. OF THE MISS.,
In the Field, Washington, D. C., May 30, 1865.

Special Field Orders No. 76.

The General Commanding announces to the Army of the Tennessee and Georgia, that the time has come for us to part. Our work is done, and armed enemies no longer defy us. Some of you will be retained in service till further orders.

And now that we are about to separate to mingle with the civil world, it becomes a pleasing duty to recall to mind the situation of national affairs, when but little more than a year ago, we were gathered about the towering cliffs of Lookout Mountain, and all the future was wrapped in doubt and uncertainty. Three armies had come together from distant fields with separate histories, yet bound by one common cause, the Union of our country and the perpetuation of the Government of our inheritance.

There is no need to recall to your memories, Tunnel Hill, with Rocky Face Mountain and Buzzard Roost Gap, with the ugly forts of Dalton behind. We were in earnest and paused not for danger and difficulty, but dashed through Snake Creek Gap and fell on Resaca, then on to Etowah, to Dallas, Kenesaw, and the heats of summer found us on the banks of the Chattahoochie, far from home, and dependent upon a single road for supplies. Again we were not to be held back by any obstacle and crossed over and fought four hard battles for the possession of the citadel of Atlanta. That was the crisis of our history. A doubt still clouded our future, but we solved the problem and destroyed Atlanta, struck boldly across the State of Georgia, severed all the main arteries of life to our enemies, and Christmas found us at Savannah. Waiting there only long enough to fill our wagons, we again began our march, which for peril, labor and results, will compare with any ever made by an organized army. The floods of the Savannah, the swamps of the Combahee and Edisto, the high hills and rocks of the Santee, the flat quagmires of Pedee and Cape Fear rivers, were all passed in mid winter with its floods, and rains, in the face of an accumulating enemy, and after the battles of Averysboro and Bentonsville, we once more came out of the wilderness to meet our friends at Goldsboro. Even then we paused only long enough to get new clothing, to re-load our wagons, and again pushed on to Raleigh, and beyond, until we met our enemy suing for peace instead of war, and offering to submit to the injured laws of his and our country. As long as that enemy was defiant, no mountains, nor rains, nor swamps, nor hunger, nor cold had checked us, but when he who had fought us hard and persistently, offered submission, your negotiations followed, which resulted as you all know, in his surrender. How far the operations of this army have contributed to the final overthrow of the Confederacy, and the peace which now dawns on us must be judged by others, not by us; but that you have done all that men could do has been admitted by those in authority, and we have a right to join in the universal joy that fills our land, because the war is over, and our Government stands vindicated before the world, by the joint action of the volunteer armies of the United States. To such as remain in the military service, your General need only remind you that success in the past was due to hard work and discipline, and that the same work and discipline are equally important in the future, to such as go home he will only say that our favored country is so grand, so extensive, so diversified in climate, soil and productions, that every man may find a home and occupation suited to his taste, and none should yield to the natural impatience sure to re ult from our past life of excitement and adventure. You will be invited to seek new adventures abroad, but do not yield to the temptation, for it will lead only to death and disappointment. Your General now bids you all farewell, with the full belief, that as in war, you have been good soldiers, so in peace you will make good citizens, and if, unfortunately, a new war should arise in our country, "Sherman's army" will be the first to buckle on its old armor, and come forth to defend and maintain the Government of our inheritance and choice,

By order of   Maj. Gen. W. T. SHERMAN,
[Signed.]   L. M. DAYTON, Asst. Adjt. Gen.

Before the regiment left the camp at Washington, Col. Smith was promoted to the rank of Brevet Brigadier General.

Until the 6th of June the officers were busily at work making out rolls, &c., preliminary to the discharge of the regiment. On that day, in accordance with General Order No. 77, War Department, and Instructions from the Adjutant General's office, we ceased in reality to be soldiers of the Union army—and became as the men expressed it, *brevet* citizens.

Reveille sounded that morning at two o'clock, and our camp at once became the scene of busy preparations for the journey home. At four all was ready. The splendid band of the 79th O. V. I., had assembled at regimental headquarters. A number of pieces were played in the best style, and the band preceded the regiment as it moved away. Joyfully, yet almost sadly we marched away from the brigade encampment. Long years of hardships and dangers had united the regiments as one family. Amid the parting adieus and good wishes of all we marched away from the 70th Ind., and by the camps of the "79th," "129th" and "105th." Halting a moment at Brigade Headquarters, we gave three cheers for "Little Ben," (Brevet Brig. Gen. Ben Harrison) then looked for the last time at the lone-star-triangle, the battle flag which had fluttered before us from Chattanooga to Atlanta, from Atlanta to Savannah, and from Savannah to the last encampment. Then we passed on to Gen. Ward's headquarters—gave three cheers for the old General, and moved forward. After reaching the main road to Washington, the band filed off at the roadside and continued playing. Fainter the music grew as we marched away, and among the last pieces we heard was the "Star-spangled Banner." Long live the memory of the "79th." The 102d fully appreciated this last generous compliment.

At nine o'clock A. M., we boarded a train of box cars at Washington. It was an immense train—over a quarter of a mile in length, and blue with soldiers. Slowly we moved away through the green fields of Maryland—*homeward bound at last.*

Lovely Maryland! pity that thy lauraled hills, thy green fields, thy noble forests should ever have been associated with the dark history of treason.

Late in the afternoon we reached Baltimore and at dusk moved away westward, on the Penn. Central road. By daylight next morning we reached York, and during the morning followed up the Susquehanna—a broad shallow stream with a rugged, rocky bottom, and here and there pretty little islands. At Bridgeport, looking across the river we had a good view of Harrisburg

Some distance above Harrisburg we left the Susquehanna and followed up the Juniata, and some of the soldiers were reminded of the occasion when far away in Georgia, the " Blue Juniata " was played so delightfully by the " 33d Mass. " Band, and Gen. Sherman desired them to repeat the enchanting strain.

Upward—upward—crossing and recrossing the little stream, we approached the summit of the Alleghany Mountains. At the little town of Johnstown we were greeted with patriotic demonstrations of the most enthusiastic character. All over the town at almost every door and window white handkerchiefs fluttered in the breeze. There was a universal rush for the depot. The children were evident y all out, and they exhausted every method of exhibiting their enthusiasm. The love of liberty has a generous growth in those wild and free mountain regions. Passing through a tunnel beneath the comb of the Alleghany range, we were soon whirling down the western slope, and a short time after midnight reached Pittsburg. That noble city extended us a most hospitable welcome. Even at that hour of the night, the good citizens were ready to work for the soldiers. We were conducted to the City Hall, and there partook of an excellent breakfast. A band discoursed sweet music while the soldiers were enjoying the meal. When the repast was finished the regiment gave three hearty cheers for the citizens of Pittsburg. One of the gentlemen who assisted in caring for the soldiers, said in response to the cheers: " I wish there were enough of us to give *you* such cheers, for you are the men who deserve the compliment." Noble and generous Pittsburg. In many Western homes the memory of thy disinterested hospitality will be cherished by those who, being tired and hungry, were fed and sent on their way rejoicing.

But I have not space to dwell upon the incidents attending our homeward ride. During the 8th, we moved through the fertile fields of Ohio; at night, passed into Indiana, and reached Chicago in our own Illinois, on the morning of the 9th.

Chicago was in the midst of a great Sanitary Fair, and the citizens were so occupied with this philanthropic enterprise, that they did not know of our coming. No one was ready to receive us. We left the cars in a cold rain. Finally marched into an amphitheatre at the Sanitary Fair grounds, and after waiting two hours and a half, cold and hungry, partook of an indifferent meal at the Soldier's Rest. "And this is in Illinois," mused the soldier—"this—Chicago—*not Pittsburg!*" But Chicago was in the midst of a GREAT NATIONAL SANITARY FAIR! What wonder that while engaged in such a magnificent field of philanthropy she was forgetful of the wants of one little Sucker regiment.

We were assigned quarters at Camp Fry. There we received our pay and final discharge on the 14th of June, and the men took the first trains for their respective homes. Each company on reaching the town or neighborhood, where organized, met with a magnificent welcome, which went far towards removing the impression produced by the cold comfort extended us by the chief city of our State.

With the disbanding of the regiment the thread of our story ends—yet I am loth to quit the interesting theme. There is a charm connected with active military service which no other pursuit can give. Emotions are awakened, which, as citizens, we can never feel again. We almost long to experience the sensations produced during the most eventful moments of the great campaigns; to hear again the grand roll of artillery, to observe the bursting shells, and to shout once more the shout of victory.

Since the dark cloud of war has passed by, it seems even more black than when the storm was at its height. But the sunshine of peace is upon us once more.

In the midst of the sunshine there are shadows. Our minds revert to the Southern battle-fields, and to the many thousand graves which mark the route followed by the great army. "Sleeping for the flag," among the pines of northern Georgia, along the line of the march to the sea, and in the far-off Carolinas, our hero-comrades rest—but not unremembered. The "Old Flag," consecrated afresh by their blood, floats unopposed in every State where its defenders are buried.

SUPPLEMENTARY.

Col. Smith's Report of the Atlanta Campaign.

    HEAD QUARTERS 102D REG'T ILL. VOLS.
      ATLANTA GEORGIA, SEPT. 20TH, 1864.
COLONEL D. DUSTIN,
  COMMANDING 3D DIV., 20TH A. C.,

  Sir: I have the honor to report that on the morning of the 2d day of May last, in obedience to orders received May 1st, I broke camp at Wauhatchie, and moved with the brigade, South from Chattanooga, passed through Rossville, and camped for the night near Gordoh's Mills, Georgia.

  On the morning of the 4th of May my regiment (or six companies of it,) was detached to guard the Division Supply and Ordnance Train, under my own command.

  At 6.30 A. M., we moved in the direction of Ringgold. Three companies of my detachment were deployed as flankers on the South side of, and at a distance of a hundred yards from the road.

  That evening I camped at Pleasant Grove Church, one and a half miles from Ringgold.

  On the moroing of May 6th, at 6 oclock A. M., I moved, with the brigade, and encamped for the night at Leed's Farm.

  At 2 o'clock on the morning of the 7th, I received marching orders and moved with the brigade, crossing Taylor's Ridge, at Gordon's Gap, at 11 oclock A. M.,—our advance surprising the outposts of the enemy, on the Ridge, and again near Gordon's Springs, —encamping that night near Villanow.

  We remained at this point until the morning of the 11th of May, when at six o'clock we moved south and into Snake Creek Gap. At 12 o'clock we went into camp, and were soon actively engaged with the brigade in clearing, repairing and widening the road through the "Gap".

  Remained at this work until 12 o'clock, on the 12th, when we moved south to the opening of the Gap, where we encamped for the night.

On the 13th, moved with the brigade towards Resaca, about three miles, where my command was formed in line of battle on the left of the 70th Ind.,—which regiment was on the immediate left of the 15th Army Corps—and skirmishers were thrown out, who advanced with the skirmishers of the 15th Corps, under a scattering fire of shells and musketry. No casualties occurred on this day. After dark, on the 13th, my command took position near the centre of the line, in front of the enemy's works—relieving a part of the 14th Corps. The position of my line was on the crest of a ridge, skirting a flat, cleared field of bottom land, some eight hundred yards in width, through which ran a small muddy creek, parallel with my line, and about two hundred yards from it. The bluff opposite was occupied by the enemy, whose rifle-pits and entrenchments were plainly in view.

Brisk skirmishing commenced at daybreak on the 14th, (my skirmishers holding a fence at the foot of the ridge,) which continued until about 10 oclock, A. M., when an order was received to cease firing.

At about 11 oclock A. M., an order was received to advance the skirmish line as far as possible, with the view of creating a diversion. I therefore reinforced the skirmish line, with a view of holding the former line, and advanced the front line to or near the creek above mentioned; which line was held during the day.

At about three o'clock P. M., my line of battle was advanced about forty yards, over the crest of the ridge, in accordance with orders, —which position was mantained until dark, when the command was withdrawn to its original position.

My skirmish line was also relieved after dark, by detachments of the 105th and 129th Ill's regiments..

During the night, rifle-pits were constructed on the crest of the hill fronting my command.

The casualties of this day were three men killed and nineteen wounded, of which number, one was killed and three were wounded in advancing the line of battle. The other casualties occurred on the skirmish line, mostly during the advance across the open field, at which time a murderous fire was opened by rebel sharpshooters, on the front and flanks.

I have evidence that the enemy suffered severely from the fire of my skirmishers—especially from the fire of the Spencer Rifles.

On the morning of the 15th my command was relieved by a portion of the 14th Corps, and marched to the left of the line of operations, where it was drawn up for an assault upon a formidable rebel position—consisting of a battery of four guns, supported by a line of breastworks, in the rear. My line was formed in rear of the 70th Ind., which led the assault. The position of the brigade was on the northern slope of a hill opposite the enemy's fortifications.

The charge was ordered at 11 o'clock A. M., and my command advanced down the southern slope of the hill upon which it had formed, thence across the Dalton and Rome road, through an open field under a most terrible fire, until it reached the enemy's battery and planted its colors upon the rebel works. Part of my command —members of Companies I and E—captured five prisoners, including the captain of the battery. A portion of my command also advanced to the second line of works, but owing to some misunderstanding, failed to carry it.

The battery was held during the remainder of the day, although several attempts were made to recapture it. The casualties of this day were eighteen men killed, seventy-six wounded and one missing. Six of the wounded have since died. My color bearer was twice shot down, and my regimental banner received fifty shots in the folds and two in the staff. This was the first flag planted upon the fort.

The line officers of my regiment behaved with conspicuous gallantry, with scarcely an exception,—all advancing to the front with promptness, and sharing in the capture of the battery; the majority remaining at the fort until dark, when they were relieved by a regiment of Gen. Geary's command.

The greater part of the 16th was spent in burying the dead.

On the morning of the 19th my command was advanced in line of battle on the Adairsville road to near Cassville, my skirmishers being thrown out in a semicircle around the front and left of the left flank of the Brigade.

The regiment was at this time exposed to a fire of shells from the Battery of the enemy, and lost one man killed.

The balance of the day was spent in maneuvering, in which no casualties occurred.

The total loss of my command during the seven days, was twenty-two killed, ninety-six wounded, and one missing.

On May 20th, encamped with the Brigade, near Cassville, Georgia, and remained there until the morning of the 23d of May, when with the army I moved forward and crossed the Etowah River, encamping at night about one mile from the crossing.

Slight skirmishing between our cavalry and the enemy in front, continued from four o'clock P. M., until nearly dark.

On the morning of the 24th, at sunrise, the march was resumed in the direction of Dallas, and continued without obstruction until the afternoon of May 25th, when the 2d Division of the 20th A. C., encountered the enemy near Burnt Hickory.

At 4 o'clock P. M., the Brigade moved in the direction of the enemy in line of battallion in mass, until it came under the enemy's fire, when, by order of Brig. Gen'l Ward, we were deployed in line of battle.

Soon thereafter, my regiment, with the 70th Ind., was ordered to halt and hold itself in readiness to act as a reserve for the Brigade.

In obedience to said orders I moved my regiment a short distance by the right flank, occupying a good position under the crest of the hill fronting the enemy. Here I remained, awaiting orders, until dark, when I was ordered by Maj. Gen'l Butterfield, Commanding the 3d Division, to move forward with my regiment and make a vigorous attack upon the enemy's right wing.

I immediately commenced a forward movement, but was soon directed by a member of the General's staff to halt until the 70 Ind., Vols., under Col. Harrison, approached, as he was also ordered forward.

As Col. Harrison's command came up I again moved in the direction of the enemy, passing over four lines of our troops lying upon the ground, until I arrived at a line of skirmishers sent forward from the 2d Brigade, (Col. Coburn's) where I halted, preparatory to making the attack.

At this point I found that I was separated from the 70th Ind., and here I was informed by Col. Coburn that the enemy was very strong (six lines deep) in my immediate front, and not more than two hundred yards distant.

At this juncture a member of Gen'l Butterfields staff appeared, who, upon being informed of the situation of affairs, directed me to remain in that position, and, if possible, (through the darkness of night) find Col. Harrison.

I immediately sent my Adjutant to the rear for that purpose, and he found him about two hundred yards in that direction.

He, having been put temporarily in command of the Brigade, sent me an order to return and join the Brigade, which I did, getting into position about 10 o'clock P. M. At two o'clock on the following morning I was ordered to move my regiment to the right half a mile and relieve the 5th Conn. I arrived at that point at three o'clock, and found the ground occupied by them on the right of the 2d Division, (Gen'l Geary) and extending to the left of the 2d Brigade, Col. Coburn. The 5th Conn. had not constructed works of any kind, I therefore immediately commenced to build breastworks, advancing my lines a little and occupying a semicircular ridge, convexing toward the enemy.

At daybreak the enemy's sharpshooters opened a most galling fire upon my working parties, compelling me to stop work upon the fortifications. I deployed one company of Spencer Rifles, under the command of Captain Sedwick, Co., E., and ordered him to drive the sharpshooters from my front, which he performed handsomely, and at 8 A. M. he had driven them behind their works. At two o'clock it was reported to me that the enemy was bringing forward two pieces of artillery directly in my front.

I immediately reinforced my skirmish line with eight picked sharpshooters, who hastened forward to such positions as to cover the guns sought to be put into position, soon compelling them to abandon their guns and retire beyond musket range.

At 5 o'clock P. M., I was directed, by Gen'l Hooker, to take such measures as would prevent the enemy from putting the guns in position, or from removing them.

In obedience thereto I sent forward, at dark, twenty sharpshooters, with Spencer Rifles, to a rise of ground about seventy-five yards in front of the guns, and fifty yards in front of the enemy's breastworks, with instructions to keep a vigilant lookout during the night, and at all hazards to prevent their removal.

At 11 o'clock at night, some fifty of the enemy collected about the guns for the purpose of quietly removing them beyond range of our guns, when my sharpshooters opened on them with a rapidity of fire only to be obtained by the Spencer Rifles, scattering them like chaff before the wind, and leaving the guns in a position where neither party could obtain them, in which position we held them until 3 o'clock P. M., of the 27th, when we were relieved by a regiment of the 2d Division, and we rejoined the brigade on the right of the Corps, and were allowed to rest until dark, when we were ordered into the front lines and remained there until the 28th at 9 o'clock A. M., when the brigade was relieved and retired to the rear for rest.

Our loss during the four days operations amounted to four killed and fourteen wounded.

On the night of the 29th my regiment was ordered to move to the right half a mile for the purpose of closing a gap between the 20th and 15th Corps, where it remained until the 31st of May, when we were relieved by the 129th Ills., (Col. Case.)

On the 1st day of June I moved, with the Brigade, to the left, and nothing of particular interest occurred until the 15th, when, at 12 o'clock M., we received orders to strike tents, and moved at 12½ o'clock P. M., with the Corps still farther to the left in the direction of Big Shanty. At 2 P. M. the Brigade was halted and I was ordered to deploy my regiment as skirmishers, which order I immediately executed, holding four Co's in reserve, and advanced across an open field for twelve hundred yards, joining Gen'l Knipe's Brigade of the 1st Division, on the left, and the 2d Brigade of the 3d Division on the right.

After advancing about one thousand yards, and when within two hundred yards of a piece of woods, I received the fire of the enemy's sharpshooters, who appeared to be armed with a variety of arms, principally squirrel rifles.

Still advancing, I drove the enemy's skirmishers and gained a position one hundred yards in the woods, where I ordered a halt and awaited orders.

Here I was informed by Capt. Oliver, A. D. C. to Gen'l Butterfield, that the 105th Ills., had been sent forward to my support and was then in close proximity in my rear.

I was ordered by Gen'l Butterfield to advance and feel of the enemy, ascertain his position and the strength of his works.

Slowly, but steadily, my men advanced under a brisk fire of the enemy's skirmishers until I found myself within one hundred yards of their rifle pits, which, from their construction, were supposed to be a continuous line of breastworks.

Yet undaunted, my men continued to advance through the thick underbrush until we were within fifty yards of the enemy's works, which were then discovered to be rifle pits for skirmishers.

This information ascertained, and learning, also, that the 105th Ills. was ordered to the right, leaving me no support, I ceased to advance and ordered my men to cease firing and keep under cover, and thus remained until 5 o'clock P. M.

At this time the firing was resumed, and heavy skirmishing in my front caused me to fear lest my weak skirmish line would be overwhelmed.

I immediately communicated my fears to Gen'l Butterfield, not knowing where to find Gen'l Ward, Brigade Commander, as I had received no orders from him after commencing the advance.

Gen'l Butterfield ordered the 105th Ills. to move by the left flank and take position on the left of my reserve. This movement was discovered by the enemy, who undoubtedly supposed it to be a preparation for an advance, as they retired from their rifle pits which were immediately taken possession of by our men, and held by them until the brigade arrived, (midnight) when we commenced the construction of works, and at daylight, had a strong line of defense in our front.

About 1 o'clock on the 16th of June I received a slight wound in the fleshy part of the thigh, while reconnoitering the enemy's position, at Gen'l Butterfield's request, which unfitted me for active duty in the field until the 10th of August, when I again reported for duty.

My loss during the two days operations was thirteen wounded, including Capt. I. McManus (of Co. G.) and myself.

I beg leave to state that of the operations of my regiment during my absence, I can only speak from the report of my Lieut. Col., who was in command during that period.

On the 20th of June, Co. B. of my regiment, was deployed as skirmishers in front of the 136th New York Vols., of the 3d Brigade, losing on that day one killed and one wounded. On the 22d of June the Brigade was ordered forward in support of the 3d Brigade. Casualties of the day, three wounded.

On the morning of July 3d my regiment, having the advance, was deployed in line of battle with two companies deployed as skirmishers under Capt. D. W. Sedwick, and moved forward in the direction of Marietta, encountering in our advance the rear guard of the enemy, or a portion of it, consisting of a thousand cavalry, with which a brisk skirmish was kept up by my skirmishers, driving the cavalry through the town of Marietta, when we were halted during an engagement between Captain Geary's battery and a battery of the rebels, after which we were moved forward—passing to the right of town.

Nothing of further importance occurred until the afternoon of the 20th of July, when we were deployed in line of battle; my regiment holding the right of the Brigade and also of the Division, under the cover of a hill south of Peach Tree Creek. At 3.45 P. M., we were ordered forward by Col. Harrison, commanding 1st Brigade, to take a position on the crest of a hill in our front.

The enemy was discovered advancing in heavy column, in a direct line toward the left of the Brigade, and moved directly in front of the 79th O. V. I., and 129th Ills., and 70th Ind., the latter occupying, on this occasion, the left of the brigade, the 105th Ills. moving forward in the rear, as a support, or reserve line—the shock falling heaviest on the 79th O. V. I., and the 129th Ills.

There being no enemy in our immediate front, we changed our position by wheeling slightly to the left, and opened upon the advancing rebel column an enfilading fire, pouring volley after volley in quick succession—such as the Spencer Rifle only can give—until we had the proud satisfaction of seeing the enemy vanquished, and seeking safety in flight.

From the favorable position of my regiment, during this sanguinary engagement we dealt upon our enemies severe punishment, with trifling loss to ourselves, losing two killed, and eleven wounded. Nothing of importance occurred from that time up to the 13th of August, when the lines were advanced a few rods, without any molestation.

Until the 25th of August the regiment lay in the advanced works, the brigade lying on the right of the Atlantic & Western R. R., the regiment in its usual place, second from the right.

About the 17th, a truce between the pickets was agreed to, and during the remainder of our stay there, all was quiet. But one casualty occurred, and that was the result of imprudence.

A member of Co. K ventured out too far from the rifle pits, and received a severe flesh wound in the face; this was speedily avenged, and all was again quiet.

On the 25th of August, at 8 o'clock, in common with the remainder of the Corps, the regiment evacuated its works, and during that night moved back to the Chattahoochie River bridge, a distance of six miles, where the brigade was held in reserve while the 1st Division posted itself securely on the eminences surrounding the bridge.

On the 27th the regiment moved across the river and was posted in the rear of the extensive depots and corrals there, on the left of the 70th Ind., the companies distributed in the following order, Co's B, E, H, G in stockades (built by the rebels on their old line of works) about two hundred yards apart, Co's A, F, D, I and C occupying a line of breastworks on the summit of a commanding hill to the right of the R. R., and Co. K in a stockade two hundred yards to the left of Co. C, and on the extreme left close along the R. R.

The regiment remained in this position, doing very heavy picket and fatigue duty, until Sept. 16th, when it moved to Atlanta; there, with the brigade (except the 105th Ills,) it went into camp one mile southeast of the Court House, where it at present is, preparing a comfortable camp.

I cannot close this report of operations of my command during the campaign, unparalleled for its duration and severity of labor, without expressing my profound satisfaction with the gallant conduct of the officers and men, who, actuated by the highest motives of patriotism, have borne its fatigues and exposures, performing long and rapid marches and laboring upon fortifications under the blistering rays of the sun, as well as during the pelting storm, night as well as day, often upon short rations, without a murmur; always facing the enemy, never yielding an inch of ground, and at all times unshrinkingly facing the hazards and dangers of war.

Respectfully,
F. C. SMITH,
Col. 102 Ill. Vols.

A LEAF FROM OUR REGIMENTAL RECORD.
Vindication of Lieut. Aaron G. Henry.
BY LIEUT. COL. ISAAC McMANUS.
(EXTRACT.)

The nature of our duties at Lavergne, Tenn., rendered it necessary to mount the command and arm them with more efficient weapons.

This involved a new kind of duty, viz: the PRESSING of horses and mules, and the training of the men to some extent in cavalry drill. To procure the necessary amount of stock was a work of great labor. Raids for this purpose were made in all directions, far and near, with greater or less success.

It was during one of these raids that an incident occurred, long to be remembered by those connected with it. I refer to the burning of the house of one Thomas Greenfield, and the seizure of the property of one James Greenfield; both claiming to be loyal citizens of the United States, and having protection papers from Maj. Gen. Rousseau—then commanding the Military District of Nashville.

The troops engaged in this expedition were: Co. G—commanded by myself and Lieut. A. G. Henry—and Co. C, commanded by Capt. Shaw and Lieut. Jordan; the entire detachment being subject to my orders, as I was the ranking officer. The instructions given me by Col. Smith were, in substance as follows: "Take stock from disloyal persons only, (except where loyal persons wish to dispose of such property to the government,) and for this purpose the following classes of persons shall be deemed disloyal: 1st. All persons residing within our lines who have not taken the oath of allegiance, in accordance with existing orders. 2. All such persons as, having taken the oath, continue to harbor guerrillas, and furnish material aid and assistance to the rebellion." It was astonishing what a number of persons came within the limits of this order; especially along the valley of Duck River, in Murray county; where the treasonable propensities of the people had been encouraged by a Copperhead Colonel—then in command at Columbia. Such an inviting field of operations was not to be overlooked, and with as little delay as possible, I moved in that direction—determined to "clean out" the scoundrels, and deprive them at least of the MEANS of rendering material aid to the rebellion.

Hearing of a family of Greenfields, who were engaged in the patriotic (?) business of harboring guerrillas, it was thought advisable to give them a call. The result proved the information correct,—three guerrillas were captured at the house of James Greenfield. Finding himself caught, and fearing the consequences, honest (?) Jim fell back on his loyalty—an old trick among rebels—and rushing up to Lieut. Henry thrust a protection paper in his face, demanding protection for himself and property. This was too much for that patriotic young man, whose soul burned with indignation at such duplicity. Looking the rebel full in the face, he said: "D——n you and your protection papers—you ought to be hung with them." This sentiment was heartily concurred in by every officer and man who understood the circumstances which called it forth. And although the expression made by Lieut. Henry was afterwards tortured into an insult to his highness, Gen. Rousseau, and was used to his damage by a court martial, composed of men who were EXCEEDINGLY anxious to do their duty, every loyal, patriotic heart will exonerate him from all blame, and approve the sentiment that would hang a traitor and make a shroud of protection papers that had been wrung by dissimulation and treachery from a weak-headed General. A few moments later I rode up, and Mr. Greenfield, not to be diverted from his purpose, renewed his demand for protection, at the same time exhibiting his protection papers. Without replying in words to his request, I ordered Serg't Reynolds to take Mr. Greenfield and place him under guard with the rest of the prisoners, and then proceeded to seize his property for the use of the government; thus treating his protection papers with contempt, in actions if not in words, as the circumstances of the case evidently justified. It will appear from this that I fully endorsed all that Lieut. Henry had done, and went infinitely further in disregarding the farcical protection of rebels and rebel property—laying a heavy hand on both.

Passing thence to the plantation of Thomas Greenfield, who had been harboring a gang of seven or eight guerrillas, for several months, as we were told, we found, concealed about his house, carbines, revolvers, fixed ammunition, government saddles and blankets, and such stores as thieving guerrillas had either captured or stolen from our men. This so aroused the indignation of the men, that when the column marched away, a few of them who remained behind applied a torch to the building, and the vile den was soon in ashes. This act, though unauthorized, was not to be wondered at when we consider the provocation. And now, after all is past, and the truth of history must be vindicated, it will seem strange that Lieut. Henry is almost the only sufferer. But although he has been shamefully abused, his record is that of a gentleman and a soldier, and as such, he will ever be esteemed by the officers and soldiers whom he served.

CONCLUDING NOTES.

Owing to the limited space remaining unoccupied, several important items connected with the history of the regiment are unavoidably omitted. Statements of prisoners—including sketches by Abner T. Morford of Co. E, and Corporal George S. Trego of Co. C—giving an account of their experience in rebel prisons—are crowded out.

It will interest the members of the regiment to know that the rank of BREVET MAJOR has recently been conferred upon two of our most worthy officers, viz: Capt. Dan W. Sedwick and Capt. Ed. H. Conger. The following is a copy of the order promoting Capt. Sedwick:

WAR DEPARTMENT,
WASHINGTON, D. C., June 19th, 1865.

SIR:

You are hereby informed that the President of the United States has appointed you, for gallant and meritorious conduct during the war, a MAJOR of VOLUNTEERS by BREVET, in the service of the United States, to rank as such from the 13th day of March 1865. Should the Senate at their next session advise and consent thereto, you will be commissioned accordingly.

EDWIN M. STANTON,
BREVET MAJOR DAN W. SEDWICK, U. S. VOL.   Sec'y of War.

A similar order was received by BREVET MAJOR E. H. Conger. By faithful services both of these officers had earned the honor conferred upon them. The fact that others, equally worthy, failed to secure a like recognition of their merits, should cause no feeling of dissatisfaction. Titles are not objectionable, but better than all titles is the consciousness of duty well performed.

In preceding pages the proper meed of praise has been in one or two instances inadvertantly withheld from officers who deserved special mention. An instance is recalled at this moment. Lieut. R. S. Peebles of Co. F, who was one of the first in the enemy's fort at Resaca, and who stood upon the earthworks in the midst of a shower of bullets, urging the men to hold their ground, is not mentioned in the account of the battle. The "inevitable Bob" was of course in the thickest of the fight.

Another name comes up in my mind, as I recall the bloody scenes of Resaca. That of 1st Serg't John Morrison, of Co. A, who was mortally wounded there. Serg't Morrison was entitled to a Commission as Lieutenant, long previous to that time. But his merits were not recognized, and another got the place which he had earned by his fidelity and courage.

In the sketches of the great raids, special credit should have been awarded Lieut. A. H. Trego of Co., C, for the able manner in which he discharged the responsible duties of Assistant Adjutant General; which position he filled from the time the Brigade left Atlanta until it was disbanded at Washington.

Other equally important omissions have occurred. Many of the enlisted men—the private soldiers who did the real hard work of the war—won laurels which entitle them to enduring fame, but where so many were heroes it is impossible to make special mention of all.

APPENDIX.

FIELD AND STAFF AND COMPANY ROSTERS.

ROLL OF THE FIELD AND STAFF.

LIST OF MEMBERS MUSTERED OUT WITH THE REGIMENT.

Brevet Brig. Gen'l, Franklin C. Smith, Oneida, Ill.*—wounded at Pine Mountain.
Major, Hiland H. Clay, Galesburg, Ill.
Surgeon, William Hamilton, ——
Chaplain, Cornelius M. Wright, Keithsburg, Ill.
Quartermaster, Hobart Hamilton, ——

RESIGNED.

Colonel William McMurtry, February, 1863.
Lieut. Colonel James M. Mannon, Sept. 1864.
Major L. D. Shinn, at Stewart's Creek, Tenn., 1863.
" C. H. Jackson, July 9th, 1864.
Surgeon D. B. Rice, at Stewart's Creek, 1863.
Assistant Surgeon T. S. Stanway, August, 1864.
1st Lieut. and Adjutant J. Pitman, Jan. 1863.
" and R. Q. M. Francis H. Rugar, at Lavergne, 1863.
Chaplain M. K. Tullis, at Gallatin, 1863.
" Jesse E. Huston, Sept., 1864.

TRANSFERRED.

Assistant Surgeon, David P. Bigger, May, 1865, to 9th Ill's Infantry.

MISSING.

1st Lieut. and Adjutant Jacob H. Snyder, since May 16th, 1865.

NON COMMISSIONED STAFF.

MUSTERED OUT WITH THE REGIMENT.

Serg't Major, Stephen F. Fleharty, Galesburg, Ill.
Q. M. Serg't, Clarence V. Shove, Kewanee, Ill.
Com. Serg't, Edward C. Courtney, Oneida, Ill.
Hospital Steward, James B. Knapp, Knoxville "—wounded near Atlanta.
Allen V. B. Taylor, Principal Musician, Galesburg, Ill.
John W. Ames, " " " "

DISCHARGED.

Hospital Steward, John B. Shaw, at Gallatin, Tenn., 1863.
Com. Serg't, G. Frank Clarke, at Lavergne, 1863.

*Present Post Office Address.

APPENDIX.

ROLL OF COMPANY "A."

LIST OF ORIGINAL MEMBERS DISCHARGED WITH THE REGIMENT.

Captain, Theodore H. Andrews, Galesburg, Ill.
1st Lieut., William H. Brown, Galesburg, Ill—wounded at Resaca.
1st Serg't, Adam N. Tate, Ionia, Ill.
Serg't James L. Moredock, "   "
  "   Hugh French, Henderson, Ill.
  "   Daniel B. Randall, Viola, Ill.
  "   George W. Miller, Ionia, Ill.
Corporal, William C. Cashman, Ionia, Ill.
  "   Enoch W. Gentry,   "   "
  "   John T. Lawson, Galesburg, Ill.
  "   Andrew J. Bowlinger, Ionia, Ill.
  "   George R. Hill, Oxford, Ill.
  "   Amos Crow, Abingdon, Ill.
James Rittenburg, Musician, Oxford, Ill.
William C. Wightman, Wagoner, Ionia, Ill.

PRIVATES.

James B. Abbott, Ionia, Ill.
John C. Brown, Keithsburg, Ill.
Thomas Brittingham, Henderson, Ill—wounded at Resaca.
Crawford A. Bruner,   "   "
Simon Burger, Abingdon, Ill—wounded at Resaca.
Lyman S. C. Bailey, Cameron, Ill.
Benjamin W. Briles, Ionia, Ill.
Riley Brazzell, Eaglesville, Mo.
George W. Crosby, Ionia, Ill—wounded at Resaca.
Richard Dowell,   "   "
Samuel Eicher, Woodhull, Ill.
Richard Foster, Ionia, Ill.
Henry M. Glass,   "   " .
Patrick H. Gilgan, Henderson, Ill.
George Hopple, Cameron, Ill.
Henry Mingles, Ionia, Ill.
James McCartney, Ionia, Ill—captured in S. C.—exchanged.
Joseph Mann, Pope Creek, Ill.
Charles W. Mosier, Ionia, Ill.
Perry McLaughlin, Pope Creek, Ill.
Swan H. Olson, Galesburg, Ill.
Andrew Pearson, Oquawka, Ill.
Daniel Richardson, Knoxville, Ill.
Alvin Richardson, Galesburg, Ill—accidentally wounded, June 6th, 1864.
Riley Short, Ionia, Ill.
Fielding E. Scott, Ionia, Ill.
William R. Terrill, Eddyville, Iowa.
Albert G. Talbott, Ionia, Ill.
Otis B. Vanfleet, Galesburg, Ill.

APPENDIX. III

ENLISTED SUBSEQUENT TO ORGANIZATION OF THE REGIMENT.

John Walker, Ionia, Ill.
Ransom A. Walker, Ionia, Ill.

RESIGNED.

Capt. R. R. Harding, Jan., 1863. Capt. Robert W. Callaghan, July 12th, 1863. 1st Lieut. Levi F. Gentry, Jan. 27th, 1863. 1st Lieut. M. L. Courtney, July 15th, 1864. 2d Lieut. Charles M. Barnett, Jan. 19th, 1863.

DIED.

1st Serg't. John Morrison, July 3d, 1864, of wounds received in action at Resaca. Corporal Eli Judd, of disease, at Chattanooga, July 27th, 1864. Corporal Hugh Butterfield, killed at Resaca. Wm. H. Augustine, of disease, at Gallatin, Tenn., Feb. 10th, 1863. Alfred Boyd, of disease, at Gallatin, Jan. 15th, 1863. Robert T. Carl, of disease, at Gallatin, Jan. 7th, 1863. Albert P. Cooper, killed at Resaca. Ebenezer Daggett, of disease, at Gallatin, Jan., 22d, 1863. John Edwards, of disease, at Nashville, Dec. 18th, 1862. John K. Holmes, of disease, at Mill Creek, Tenn., Nov. 3d, 1863. Orlando Kinney, of disease, at Scottsville, Ky., Nov. 20th, 1863. William Miller, of disease, at Gallatin, Jan. 28th, 1863. Lawrence Nash, killed at Resaca. Franklin Offut, of disease, at New Albany, Ind. Nov. 10th, 1862. Charles H. Rodgers, of disease, at Frankfort, Ky., Oct. 21st, 1862. George A. Rodgers, at Louisville, Jan. 10th, 1864, of disease. Arthur F. Sabin, killed at Resaca. Oliver N. Tyler, of disease, at Gallatin, Jan. 17th, 1863. Elias N. Vestal, of disease, at Bowling Green, Ky.,—no date given. Jacob A. Walton, of disease, at Gallatin, Tenn., Jan. 17th, 1863.

DISCHARGED.

Corporal Calvin Martin, Jan. 21st, 1863. Wm. T. Anderson, March 16th, 1863. Wm. H. Black, Feb. 17th, 1863. Solomon Brittingham, March 12th, 1863. Ambrose D. Blake, Jan. 16th, 1863. Wm. H. Crandall, March 12th, 1863. Neally Daggett, Sept. 30th, 1864, on account of wounds received at Resaca. Thomas G. French, Jan. 18th, 1863. Christopher C. Fulton, Oct., 1864, to accept commission in Colored Regiment. Thomas A. Greenwood, Nov. 22d, 1862. John A. Miller, Jan. 18th, 1863. William Morris, Jan. 20th, 1863. James C. Routh, Oct. 28th, 1864. Asa Richardson, Jan. 29th, 1863. Cyrus Weaver, Dec. 9th, 1862. John Wells, March 4th, 1863.

TRANSFERRED.

Allen V. B. Taylor, to Non. Com. Staff. Rigdon B. Walker, to Veteran Reserve Corps.

ROLL OF COMPANY "B."

LIST OF ORIGINAL MEMBERS DISCHARGED WITH THE REGIMENT

Capt., William M. Armstrong, Utah, Ill—wounded at Averysboro
1st Lieut., Ambrose Stegall, Utah, Ill.
1st Serg't., John W. Terpening, Utah, Ill.
Serg't, John J. Armstrong, Utah, Ill—wounded at Resaca.
" Alonzo Beswick, Utah, Ill—wounded at Peach Tree Creek.
" Michael Dougherty, Utah, Ill.
" Michael Rees, Utah, Ill.
Corporal Dwight Corning, Galesburg, Ill.
" Orrin E. Beswick, Utah, Ill.
" James Walton, Princeton, Pa.
" William B. Armstrong, Utah, Ill.
" Ezra D. Bugbee, Utah, Ill.
" Charles B. Parsons, Utah, Ill.
" Elisha E. Russell, Utah, Ill.
" James M. Black, Galesburg, Ill.
John Hodges, Musician, Galesburg, Ill.
Samuel R. Curtis, Wagoner, Utah, Ill.

PRIVATES.

David Artlip, Centre, Iowa.
John H. Brown, Galesburg, Ill.
Daniel R. Boyd, Utah, Ill—wounded at Peach Tree Creek.
Jeremiah Badger, Rio, Ill.
Thomas P. Bruington, Galesburg, Ill.
Samuel Church, North Henderson, Ill.
Walter S. Chapin, Oquawka, Ill—captured before Atlanta—exch'd.
John E. DeWitt, Duck Creek, Ill.
Lemmon DeWitt, "   "   "—wounded near Franklin. Ky.
Thomas Davis, Galesburg, Ill.
Morton M. Durand, "   "—on detached service during last year.
Geo. W. Dunn, Utah, Ill—wounded near Franklin, Ky.
William D. Graham, Utah, Ill.
John Gregg, Galesburg, Ill—captured near Averysboro,—exch'd.
Simeon G. Heflin, Utah, Ill.
Andrew Kiser, Utah, Ill.
Robert Maxwell, Galesburg, Ill.
Newton Nelson, "   "
William H. Rees, Monmouth, Ill—wounded at Resaca.
Gideon D. Russell, Utah, Ill—wounded at Kenesaw Mountain.
Thomas M. Snyder, Aledo, Ill—wounded at Averysboro, N. C.
James W. Snyder, Aledo, Ill.
George Sherman, Monmouth, Ill.
James Sohoman, Galesburg, Ill.
Manuel Trout Henderson, Ill—wounded at Peach Tree Creek.
Samuel Terpening, Utah, Ill.
Richard B. Woolley, Henderson, Ill.

APPENDIX.

William R. Wimmer, Ionia, Ill.
Benjamin Webber, Henderson, Ill.
Lewis A. Woods, Utah, Ill.

ENLISTED SUBSEQUENT TO ORGANIZATION OF REGIMENT

Lorenzo D. Chapin, Oquawka, Ill.
John Walton, Princeton, Penn.,—wounded at Resaca.
Thomas St. George, Utah, Ill.
John Armstrong, Utah, Ill.
Richard Brown, Utah, Ill.
Albert Smith,   "   "
Nathan A. Terpening, Utah, Ill.

RESIGNED.

Captain Elisha C. Atchison, April 9th, 1863. 1st Lieut. James C. Beswick, Jan. 14th, 1864.

DIED.

David Hocker, of disease, at New Albany, Ind., Nov. 4th, 1862. Josiah M. Kellogg, killed at Resaca. John Rich, of disease, at Gallatin. Henson Blake, of wounds received in action near Franklin, Ky—died April 28th, 1863. Stephen Cussins, killed at Resaca. Charles W. Fort, died of disease, while at home on furlough. Leonard Harsh, drowned in Stewart's Creek, Tenn., July 2d, 1863. John Hewson, of disease, while at home on furlough, Feb. 15th, 1865. Charles Hollenbeck, of disease, March 23d, 1864, at Lookout Valley. Thomas J. Maxey, killed in action near Kenesaw Mountain, June 21st, 1863. Harvey Rodgers, of disease, at Gallatin, Tenn., Jan. 1st, 1863. Henry Reynolds, of disease, at Gallatin, Tenn., Dec., 1862. Lyman B. Straw, killed at Peach Tree Creek. Jacob Snavely, of wounds received in action near Franklin, Ky., April 28th, 1863.

DISCHARGED.

1st Serg't John B. Gregg, Serg't Henry C. Miles, Corporal Lewis Trout, David Ingersoll, (Musician.) Henry B. Burton, Thomas M. Hite, James B. Dunn, Elias K. Ferris, Fielding F. Miles, John M. Miles, Thatcher Porter, Robert St. George, Daniel B. Stivers, at Gallatin, Tenn. John W. Brown, at Frankfort, Ky. Alfred Brown, at New Albany, Ind. James Donnelly, on account of wounds, at Springfield, Ill., Oct. 7th, 1864. Francis M. Duffy, Andrew Peterson, at Smyrna, Tenn. Washington G. Sallee, at Jeffersonville, Ind. Daniel S. Weiser, Bowling Green, Ky.

TRANSFERRED.

Geo. Coziah, to Vet. Vol. Engineers.

DESERTED.

Samuel C. Davis, March, 1863.

ROLL OF COMPANY "C."

LIST OF ORIGINAL MEMBERS DISCHARGED WITH THE REGIMENT.

Captain, Almond Shaw, Centre Ridge, Ill.
1st Lieut., Alfred H. Trego, Galesburg, Ill—wounded at Pine Mountain, and at Averysboro.
2d Lieut., Byron Jordan, Rural, Ill.
1st Serg't, George W. Gregg, Centre Ridge, Ill.
Serg't, Sampson M. Tenney, Pre-emption, Ill.
" Henry Bridgford, Richland Grove—wounded at Resaca.
" Reading L. Carver, Pre-emption, Ill—wounded at Resaca.
" Brainard Vance, Pre-emption, Ill.
Corporal Phœnix R. Briggs, Richland Grove, Ill.
" John H. Lippincott,—wounded at Resaca.
" George S. Trego, Centre Ridge, Ill—captured near Cheraw, S. C.—exchanged.
Corporal James M. Shull, Centre Ridge, Ill.
" Charles I. McIntyre, Hamlet, Ill.
" William J. Long, Rural, Ill.
" Wilford Pitman, Pre-emption, Ill.
" Lester H. Cooper, Hamlet, Ill.
Thomas Merryman, Musician, Centre Ridge, Ill.

PRIVATES.

Thomas Allely, Rural, Ill.
Theodore Asquith, Hazlitt, Ill.
Richard B. Barnes, Geneseo, Ill.
James F. Barnett, Centre Ridge, Ill.
Christian F. Bharinger, Richland Grove, Ill.
James M. Beardsley, Rock Island, Ill—captured at Bentonville,—exchanged.
David Beck, Richland Grove, Ill.
Christian Bloom, "   "   "
Louis Bloom, Richland Grove, Ill—captured Nov. 15th, 1864—escaped next day.
William Blackfan, Orion, Ill.
Manuel M. Briggs, Richland Grove, Ill—wounded at New Hope Ch.
Samuel G. Chaney, Centre Ridge, Ill.
James Cottenburg, Richland Grove, Ill.
Jacob Clause, Richland Grove, Ill.
Wm. H. Cooper, Hamlet, Ill.
William E. Davis, Centre Ridge, Ill.
George Eckley, Centre Ridge, Ill.
Ed. L. Emerson, Keithsburg, Ill—captured Jan., 1863—exchanged.
Samuel B. Ewing, Orion, Ill.
James Gorman, Perryton, Ill.
Horace J. Gridley, Hamlet, Ill.
Louis Hetzel, Richland Grove, Ill.
Nathaniel Hamor, Rural, Ill.

Charles Joseph, Rock Island, Ill—wounded at Averysboro' and captured near Goldsboro'—exchanged.
Jacob Krause, Richland Grove, Ill.
Charles J. Lawson, Centre Ridge, Ill—wounded at Averysboro'.
Joseph Littlefield, Centre Ridge, Ill—wounded at Resaca.
Harvey McElhinny, " " "
Matthew H. C. McElhinny, Centre Ridge, Ill.
Freeman Merryman, Centre Ridge, Ill—wounded at Resaca.
John H. Martin, Centre Ridge, Ill.
Gottlob Maier, Richland Grove, Ill.
Adam Maucker, Centre Ridge, Ill.
Albion Nichols, Hamlet, Ill—wounded at Resaca.
Charles W. Norman, Centre Ridge, Ill—captured near Louisville, Georgia—exchanged.
John P. Olson, Paxton, Ill—wounded at Resaca.
David Pfitzenmaier, Richland Grove, Ill.
Joseph M. Piersol, Rural, Ill.
Joseph N. Roberts, Centre Ridge, Ill.
Isaiah N. Rhodenbaugh, Centre Ridge, Ill.
Frederick Schurr, Richland Grove, Ill.
Peter Smith, Richland Grove, Ill.
John Smith, " " "
Henry W. Suter, Centre Ridge, Ill—wounded at Resaca, and captured near Louisville, Ky.,—exchanged.
Warner Twining, Pre-emption, Ill.
Gideon M. Tomlinson, Richland Grove, Ill.
Thomas Wilson, Pre-emption, Ill.
Joseph White, Richland Grove, Ill.
William E. Wallace, Rural, Ill—wounded at Resaca.
Franklin M. Weaver, Keithsburg, Ill.
Wilford J. Ungles, " "—captured Nov., 1864—exch'd.

ENLISTED SUBSEQUENT TO ORGANIZATION OF REGIMENT.

Stephen A. Bartlett, Richland Grove, Ill.
Charles T. Blackfan, Orion, Ill.
John J. Brice, Centre Ridge, Ill.
Edwin T. Jordan, Rural, Ill.
Gilbert A. Jordan, " "
James G. Love, Centre Ridge, Ill.
Alexander McKay, Rock Island, Ill.
William McGill, Rural, Ill.
James Marshall, Richland Grove, Ill.
Lewis N. Peyton, Centre Ridge, Ill.
William Parks, ———
Valentine Smith, Rock Island, Ill.
Harrison Trego, Centre Ridge, Ill.
Alfred R. Tomlinson, Richland Grove, Ill.
William W. Vansant, Centre Ridge, Ill.
Thomas H. White, Rock Island, Ill.

APPENDIX.

RESIGNED.

Captain F. Shedd, April 6th, 1863. Lient. Watson C. Trego, Nov. 18th, 1862.

DIED.

Serg't Geo. W. Allen, of disease, at Gallatin, Tenn., May 7th, 1863. Serg't I. N. Roberts, of disease, at Gallatin, March, 4th, 1863. Charles Anderson, of disease, at Gallatin, Tenn., Dec. 15th, 1862. Francis M. Freeman, killed at Resaca.

Henry Herr, of disease, while at home on furlough, June, 1863. George H. Huffman, of disease, at Gallatin, Tenn., Jan. 6th, 1863. Edmund Kinsey, killed at Resaca. Thomas B. South, of disease, at Gallatin, Jan. 4th, 1863. George Bharinger, of disease, at New York City, 1865.

DISCHARGED.

Serg't Rodney C. Manning, Sept. 12th, 1864, on account of wounds received at the battle of Resaca. George Bressmer, Dec. 16th, 1863. Henry G. Cooper, Oct. 7th, 1864, on account of wounds received at Resaca. Myron N. Jordan, Jan. 15th, 1863. Major McMullen, Jan. 15th, 1863. James Spivey, May 9th, 1863. Leonard Stark, June 20th, 1864. Jacob R. Trego, Jan. 15th, 1863. Jacob Robb, Feb., 1863. William Thorpe, at Bowling Green, Kentucky, 1863.

TRANSFERRED.

Corporal S. F. Fleharty, to Non. Com. Staff. James H. Jackson, to Pioneer Corps. Clinton Olin, to Vet. Reserve Corps. Jason E. Young, to Pioneer Corps. Chas. Pierce, to Vet. Reserve Corps.

DESERTED.

Jonas Swab, April 20th, 1863, at Gallatin, Tenn.

APPENDIX. IX

ROLL OF COMPANY "D"

LIST OF ORIGINAL MEMBERS DISCHARGED WITH THE REGIMENT.

Captain, Orville B. Matteson, Galesburg; Ill—wounded at Averysboro'.
1st Lieut. Irving L. Clay, Galesburg, Ill.
1st Serg't, Ozias C. Sprague, Bushnell, Ill—wounded at Averysboro'
Serg't, Rowley Page, Galesburg, Ill.
" Hiram A. Drake, Galesburg, Ill.
" William A. Bell, Oneida, Ill.
Corporal Silas Area, Wataga, Ill—wounded at Resaca.
" Frank L. Barnhisel, Galesburg, Ill.
" William Dunlap, Woodhull, Ill.
" Augustus Sherman, Galesburg, Ill—wounded at New Hope Church—captured in North Carolina,—exchanged.
Corporal Edward A. Hulick, Virgil, Ill.
" Charles M. Castle, Knoxville, Ill.
" William M. Cone, Galesburg, Ill.
Benj. F. Hackett, Wagoner, Prairie City, Ill.

PRIVATES.

William Allen, Muscatine, Iowa.
Reuben B. Anderson, Galesburg, Ill.
William J. Bing, Galesburg, Ill.
Elisha Billings, Oxford, Ill—captured in South Carolina—exchanged.
Robert Billings, Oxford, Ill—captured in North Carolina—exchanged.
Philetus G. Burch, Knoxville, Ill.
Hiram Boon, Galesburg, Ill.
Thomas M. Bell, Galesburg, Ill.
Lewis C. Currier, Prairie City, Ill.
John Conley, Woodhull, Ill.
Ario W. Davison, Galesburg, Ill.
Charles Fast, Virgil, Ill.
Charles L. Groscup, Galesburg, Ill.
Frank Hilton, Galesburg, Ill.
Charles L. Huestis, " " captured in North Carolina—exchanged.
William Hills, " "
Sydney B. Henry, Bushnell, Ill.
Kindred Johnson, Galesburg, Ill.
John Kite, " "
Moses J. Keller, " "
John J. Kipp, Bushnell, Ill.
Franklin Letts, Woodhull, Ill.
Robert N. Lester, Galesburg, Ill.
Joseph E. Lester, " "
Frans Maul, " " wounded at Kenesaw Mountain.
Daniel T. Page, " " wounded at Resaca.
Edmund M. Pugh, " "
Erastus W. Rhykert, " "

Jos. H. Rhykert, Galesburg, Ill.
Albert M. Stoddard, Prairie City, Ill., captured near Goldsboro — exchanged.
Josiah P. Spencer, Hinckley, Ohio, wounded at Resaca.
Lewis G. Strong, Osceola, Ill.
James Strow, Knoxville, Ill.
John O. Smith, Bushnell, Ill.
Samuel Taylor, Prairie City, Ill.
George W. Turner, Woodhull, Ill.

ENLISTED SUBSEQUENT TO ORGANIZATION OF REGIMENT.

Albert B. Nixon, Musician, Woodhull, Ill.
Henry C. Castle, Knoxville, Ill.
Dennison Randall, " "
Dennison P. Randall, " "

RESIGNED.

Captain Horace H. Wilsie, April 8, 1863.

DIED.

James White, of disease, at Stewarts' Creek, Tennessee, Aug. 9th, 1863. Elias E. Champlin, killed at Resaca. John Barker, of disease, at Wauhatchie, Tenn., April, 1864. Jesse H. Marble, of disease, at Gallatin, Tenn., Jan. 20th, 1863. Eugene Corkins, of wounds received in action near Kenesaw Mountain, June 22d, 1864—died Aug. 4th, 1864.

DISCHARGED.*

Corporal James R. Randall, Corporal Joel E. Ragland, John D. Babcock, Wm. E. Canfield, Thomas Doyle, William Doyle, Jacob M. Grimes, Wm. B. Hunt (on account of wounds). John Kite, Sen. Timothy Page, Hosea Rounds, Isaiah Tompkins, Wm. Tribble, Lewis Tupper, Isaac D. Young.

TRANSFERRED.

Captain Hiland H. Clay, by promotion to position of Major. Lieut. J. B. Nixon, to 17th U. S. C. I. Serg't Coryden D. Hendryx, to 17th U. S. C. I. F. G. Daggett, to 107th U. S. C. I. Nicholas G. Chesebro, to Carr's Brigade. John W. Ames, to Non. Com. Staff. Geo. W. Chamberlain, to 1st Tenn. Artillery. Larkin B. Ellis, to V. V. Engineers. Wm. R. Hendryx, to Mississippi Marine Brigade. John H. Lippy, do. T. J. McClurg, to Veteran Reserve Corps.

DESERTED.

Geo. W. Doyle, Sept. 6th, 1862. Hugh Lavery, Sept. 16th, 1862.

*No date given.

ROLL OF COMPANY "E."

LIST OF ORIGINAL MEMBERS DISCHARGED WITH THE REGIMENT.

Brevet Major. Dan W. Sedwick, Pope Creek, Ill.
1st Lieut., Thomas G. Brown, "   "   "
1st Serg't, Jonathan E. Lafferty, North Henderson Ill.
Serg't, Thomas Simpson, "   "   "   lost left arm in battle of Averysboro'.
" John T. Morford, Ionia, Ill.
" Jno. Tidball, Pope Creek, Ill—wounded at New Hope Church.
" Allen Dunn, North Henderson, Ill.
Corporal, Henry W. Mauck, Pope Creek, Ill.
" Robert Godfrey, North Henderson, Ill.
" Cornelius Brown, Pope Creek, Ill.
" Simeon Rothrock, "   "   " lost right eye in action at New Hope Church.
" Thomas Barban, "   "   "
" James C. Middaugh "   "   " wounded at Averysboro'.
William H. Dickie, Musician, North Henderson, Ill.

PRIVATES.

William Artman, Pope Creek, Ill—wounded at Resaca.
Philip T. Bridger, "   "   "
Henry Banks, North Henderson, Ill—wounded at New Hope Church.
John H. Bentz, Sunbeam, Ill.
Abram J. Carmichael, North Henderson, Ill.
Edward Chilson, Pope Creek, Ill.
Geo. W. Edwards "   "   "
Elijah Gilbert "   "   "
Charles Hartsell "   "   "
John Laughhead, North Henderson, Ill.
James M. Lee "   "   "
James H. Lafferty "   "   "
Stephen D. Lethco, Pope Creek, Ill.
Francis M. Morford, "   "   "
Abner T. Morford, "   "   " captured at Vinings, Ga., Oct., 1864; exchanged, April, 1865.
Jonathan P. Morrison, North Henderson, Ill—wounded at Resaca.
Henry S. Middaugh, Pope Creek, Ill—wounded at New Hope Church.
Hiram T. Morford, "   "   " wounded near Atlanta.
William H. Morford, Ionia, Ill.
James H. McKnight, North Henderson, Ill.
Richard H. McGee, Sunbeam, Ill.
Henry McNeal, Pope Creek, Ill.
Leslie Patterson, Sunbeam, Ill.
Joseph Patterson, North Henderson, Ill.
Robert Ross, Sunbeam, Ill—wounded at Resaca.
Edward M. Shearer, North Henderson, Ill.

David R. Simpson, North Henderson, Ill.
William L. Stewart, "   "   "
William R. Simpson, "   "   "
Amos Wright, Pope Creek, Ill.
Richard Wright, "   "   "
John H. Wiley, North Henderson, Ill.
Reuben Wiley,   "   "   " wounded at Resaca.
Robert Wilson,   "   "   " wounded at Golgotha Church.
Gilbert Zend,   "   "   " wounded at Resaca.

ENLISTED SUBSEQUENT TO ORGANIZATION OF THE REGIMENT.

Matthew C. Boggs, North Henderson, Ill.

RESIGNED.

Capt. Thomas Likely, April 25th, 1863. 2d Lieut. John Allison, March 5th, 1864.

DIED.

Serg't Albert C. Bridger, of disease, at Gallatin, Tenn., Dec., 8th, 1862. Corporal W. T. Sevits, killed at Lawtonville, S. C., February 2d, 1865. Richard Brown, of disease, at Gallatin, Jan. 3d, 1863. Peter F. Cook, killed at Resaca. J. B. Carmichael, of wounds received in action at New Hope Church, at Chattanooga, June 4th, 1864. Seth Gravatt, of disease, at Gallatin, 1863. Michael Oswalt, of wounds received at Resaca, at Nashville, Tenn., June 29th, 1864. J. C. Simpson, of wounds received at Lawtonville, at Fayetteville, N. C., March 14th, 1865. Chauncey Royce, of disease, at Gallatin, Jan. 2d. 1864.

DISCHARGED.

1st Serg't, S. R. Moore, at Gallatin, Tenn. 1st Serg't, W. J. Abdill, July 1st, 1863, to accept commission in colored regiment. Corporal Henry M. Carmichael, at Gallatin. W. P. Morgan, at Stewart's Creek. D. T. Porter, at Camp Butler, Ill. William B. Cullison, at Quincy, Ill., Feb. 22d, 1865. H. T. Bridger, at Gallatin, Tenn., Andrew Boger, at Louisville, Ky. Isaac Carson, Keokuk, Iowa, Dec. 12th, 1864, lost right hand at New Hope Church. Thomas Godfrey, at Gallatin, Tenn. Orange Lucas, at Bowling Green, Ky., 1863. Samuel Lyon, at Jeffersonville, Ind., 1862. Nelson Morey, at Springfield, Ill., Dec. 9th, 1864. Geo. T. Nevius, at Gallatin, Tenn. Robert Neeley, at Gallatin, Tenn. Peter Peterson, Nashville, Tenn. F. T. Porter, Alexander Patterson and W. B. Torbet, at Gallatin, Tenn.

MISSING.

John A. McCutchen—was seen to fall at Resaca, but could not be found after the battle was over.

ROLL OF COMPANY "F."

LIST OF ORIGINAL MEMBERS DISCHARGED WITH THE REGIMENT.

Captain, Geo. W. Woolley, Oneida, Ill.
1st Lieut., Robert S. Peebles, "   "
1st Serg't, Geo. W. Plummer, Henderson, Ill., wounded at Kenesaw Mountain.
Serg't Myron Nelson,   "   "
" Stephen Levalley, Victoria, Ill.
" Isaac A. Hardenbrook, Centre Ridge, Ill.
" James K. Weir, Abingdon, Ill.
Corporal, Oscar F. Presson, Galesburg, Ill.
" John H. Champion, Henderson, Ill.
" Alfred B. Firkins, Wataga, Ill—wounded at Resaca.
" John S. Hall, Oxford, Ill.
" Joseph Inick, Henderson, Ill—captured near Averysboro, exchanged.
" Lorenzo L. Maxson, Oxford, Ill—wounded at Resaca.
" Joseph Smith, Henderson, Ill—wounded near Atlanta.
Eri Bennett, Musician, Henderson, Ill.

PRIVATES.

Alfred C. Briggs, Henderson, Ill.
Aaron B. Brooks,   "   "
Oliver Burton, Galesburg, Ill—wounded at Kenesaw Mountain.
David Bair, Oxford, Ill—wounded at New Hope Ch.
James Cubbage, Henderson, Ill—wounded at Resaca.
Isaac C. Durdan,   "   "   "   "
Joseph Driffle, Ionia, Ill.
Thomas Dean, Henderson, Ill—wounded at Kenesaw Mountain.
Daniel Dean,   "   "
George Dew,   "   "
William Epperson, Oxford, Ill.
Joseph Fulton,
Caleb J. Green, Oneida, Ill.
Caleb Green,   "   "
John G. Gulliher, Knoxville, Ill.
Martin V. Key, Henderson, Ill.
William Linn, Oxford, Ill—wounded at Savanah.
James H. Murphy, "   "
Matthew O'Brien, Henderson, Ill.
Thomas H. Pool,   "   "
Hiram Rusk, North Prairie, Ill.
Michael Rafferty, Henderson, Ill.
Enoch Rush, Oxford, Ill.
John Swancer,   "   "
Frederick Stegall, Henderson, Ill.
David Wilson,   "   "
Thomas Welch, Galesburg, Ill.
William Westerdale, Oneida, Ill.
Michael Young, Henderson, Ill.

XIV APPENDIX.

ENLISTED SUBSEQUENT TO ORGANIZATION OF THE REGIMENT.

Charles N. Bond, Galesburg, Ill—taken prisoner near Cheraw, S. C.
George Bennett, Henderson, Ill.
Hiram C. Dawson, Mount Sterling, Ill.
Joseph H. Dredge, North Prairie, Ill.
John Edleman, Henderson, Ill.
Swan Erickson,   "   " wounded at Resaca.
Samuel Holton,   "   "
James H. Hill,   "   "
Richard Maxwell,   "   " wounded at Resaca.
James F. Maxwell,   "   "
Peter McGuire,   "   "
William H. Shepherd, "   "
Geo. G. Sperry,   "   " wounded at Averysboro, N. C.
Hosea Wiley,   "   "

RESIGNED.

1st Lieut. Orlando J. Sullivan, at Gallatin. 2d Lieut. Ethan A. Cornwall, at Scottsville Ky.

DIED.

1st Serg't Thomas Merrick, of wounds received near Vinings, Ga. John B. Gorman, at Nashville Tenn. Vandorn Amy, of disease, at Gallatin. William Drury, of disease, at Frankfort, Ky. Nelson Gokey, of disease, at Mound City, Ill. Paul Hahn, of disease, at Nashville. Thomas McDermott, and Andrew Rose, of disease, at Gallatin Tenn.

DISCHARGED.

Chas. I. Epperson, Wm. Timberlake, at Gallatin. John W. Heare, Thomas P. Epperson, Martin Robertson, John A. Bueschel, Stroud Vanmetre, Levi Casson, Levi W. Fairbanks, Charles Meadows, Augustus Morse, John M. Morse, Pat. McDermott, John Rusk, Geo. A. Spence, Laland Salts, Ceylon Smith, and David Young, (time and place not given.) Asa H. Jones, at Lavergne, Tenn.

TRANSFERRED.

Capt. C. H. Jackson, by promotion, to position of Major. Amos K. Tullis, promoted to Chaplain.

DESERTED.

Asa H. Warner, Hosea Fuller, Joseph Kernell, William Nation and David Rusk, on the march from Frankfort to Bowling Green, Ky. William D. Roundtree and Stephen H. Waters, in front of Atlanta, Aug. 14th, 1864.

APPENDIX. XV

ROLL OF COMPANY "G."

LIST OF ORIGINAL MEMBERS DISCHARGED WITH THE REGIMENT.

Captain Isaac McManus, Keithsburg, Ill.,—Commissioned Lieut. Col., was wounded at Golgotha Church, near Pine Mountain.
William H. Bridgford, Millersburg, Ill.,—Commissioned as Captain.
1st Serg't Lemuel S. Guffey, Perryton, Ill.,—Commissioned 1st Lieut.
Serg't Elisha J. Grandstaff, " "
  " R. W. Kile, Keithsburg, Ill.
  " James H. McCommon, Millersburg, Ill.
  " John C. Cummins, Ohio Grove, Ill—wounded at Resaca.
Corporal Lewis Wilkinson, Abington, Ill.
  " Oliver M. Goldsbury, Keithsburg, Ill.
  " William M. Bunting, Millersburg, Ill—wounded at Resaca.
  " William F. Cochran, " "
  " Samuel McHard, Perryton, Ill.
  " Squire W. Butcher, Abington, Ill.
  " James H. Fox, " "
Joseph O. Calhoun, Musician, Keithsburg, Ill—wounded at the Kulp House.

PRIVATES.

Walter Brown, Suez, Ill—wounded at Resaca.
James B. Brewer, Keithsburg, Ill.
Charles P. Brock, " "
Roderick Cameron, Abington, Ill.
John A. Connolley, Keithsburg, Ill.
Peter Cameron, " " wounded at Resaca.
John Dunn, Ohio Grove, Ill—wounded at Resaca.
Martin V. Eckley, Keithsburg, Ill.
Frederick Friebele, Burlington, Iowa—wounded at Resaca and at Bentonville.
John B. Felton, Millersburg, Ill—wounded at Resaca.
Alexander Glasgow, Keithsburg, Ill.
William Gorman, Perryton, Ill—wounded at Resaca.
William P. Hardin, Keithsburg, Ill.
Wesley Hunt, Millersburg, Ill.
Jacob E. Hauck, Perryton, Ill.
John A. Hicks Edgington, Ill.
Alvah Jay, Abington, Ill.
William H. Johnston, Ohio Grove, Ill.
Dexter M. King, Millersburg, Ill.
Michael R. Murphy, Abington, Ill.
John Mingles, Keithsburg, Ill.
Geo. H. Mingles, " "
James R. Minor, Ohio Grove, Ill.
John J. McDonald, Keithsburg, Ill.
Otto Ott, " "
William S. Pearson, Abington, Ill.
Samuel S. Pearce, Keithsburg, Ill.

XVI   APPENDIX.

John A. Stevens, Abington, Ill.
Isaac N. Stevens,   "   "
Patrick Smith, Keithsburg, Ill.
Samuel Stearns, Abington, Ill.
Gabriel E. Shaw, Millersburg, Ill.
Thomas Spence, Perryton, Ill—wounded at Resaca.
Geo. W. Thomas, Abington, Ill.
William H. Turner, Keithsburg, Ill.
William H. Wilson, New Boston, Ill.
Charles B. Wakeland, Millersburg, Ill.
David Woliver, Perryton, Ill—wounded at Resaca.
Thomas Winters, Abington, Ill.
John C. Vance,   "   "
James M. Walker, Viola, Ill.

ENLISTED SUBSEQUENT TO ORGANIZATION OF THE REGIMENT.

Thomas C. Johnson, Millersburg, Ill.
Lucien Murphy, Keithsburg, Ill—wounded at Resaca.
William W. Wakeland, Millersburg, Ill.
Mordecai Terry,   "   "

RESIGNED.

Capt. Joseph P. Wycoff, at Gallatin, Tenn. 2d Lient. Luke P. Blackburn, Gallatin, Tenn.

DISMISSED.

2d Lieut. Aaron G. Henry—without proper cause and by an incompetent Court Martial—See "Supplementary."

DIED.

Serg't Richard H. Cabeen, killed at Resaca. Corporal John Gibson, killed at Resaca. Watson W. Hibbs, killed at Resaca. Samuel Harvey, killed near Cassville, May 19th, 1864. 1st Serg't John C. Reynolds, Aug. 8th, 1864, of wounds received at Peach Tree Creek. Serg't John McHard, July 25th, of wounds received at Peach Tree Creek. Corporal Jared Y. Harris, May 17th, of wounds received at Resaca. John Burnett, May 17th, of wounds received at Resaca. William T. Todd, July 17th, of wounds received at Resaca. William P. Irwin, wounded at Resaca and probably died in Hospital. Serg't Robert B. Seaton, of disease, at Nashville. Lloyd H. Casebolt, of disease, at Gallatin. Richard M. Hoy, of disease, at Gallatin. Alonzo T. Dopp, of disease, at Atlanta.

DISCHARGED.

Corporal Andrew J. Douglas and John G. Poague, at Gallatin. Corporal Andrew J. Campbell, at Lavergne. William Murphy and William S. Dilley, at Louisville, Ky. James O. Baker, at Nashville. Samuel H. Danner and Eolus Elrick, at Gallatin. Josephus Gray and Ebenezer Gray, at Louisville. Geo. W. Hoover, at Quincy, Ill. John Henry, Daniel C. Halsted, Frederick W. Johns, Martin V. Morgan and John O. Minor, at Gallatin. Samuel Parks, at Quincy, Ill.

Joseph A. Webster, at Davenport, Iowa. William Wilson, John Workman, Moses N. Warren, David Ritchie, William C. Hardin and Henry B. Worden, at Gallatin, Tenn.

TRANSFERRED.

Thomas M. Garrett, Duncan B. Seaton, Norman F. Wood, to Vet. Vol. Eng. Corps. Almyron Luce, to Miss. Marine Brigade.

XVIII   APPENDIX.

ROLL OF COMPANY "H."

LIST OF ORIGINAL MEMBERS DISCHARGED WITH THE REGIMENT.

Captain Hiram Elliott, Knoxville, Ill.
2d Lieut., Samuel Tucker, Eugene, Ill.
1st Serg't, Lucius A. Lawrence, Yates City, Ill.
Serg't Samuel S. Seward, Truro, Ill.
   " Albert Bullard, Knoxville, Ill.
   " Geo. W. German, Eugene, Ill.
   " John German,   "   "
Corporal Eber Parish,   "   "
   " Allen Millen, Truro, Ill.
   " Jerome Gearheart, Oneida, Ill.
   " Robert Bryson, Eugene, Ill.
   " Warren Elliott, Knoxville, Ill.
   " George Walker,   "   "
   " John W. Hogue, Eugene, Ill.
Tufva S. Johnson, Musician, Galesburg, Ill.
Winslow H. Bradford, Musician, Knoxville, Ill.

PRIVATES.

Matthew Ackerson, Galesburg, Ill.
Calvin Bullard, Eugene, Ill.
Egbert Bullard, Knoxville, Ill—wounded at Resaca.
Oloff Bankson, Galesburg, Ill.
Edgar Balch, Yates City, Ill.
James W. Collins, Truro, Ill.
Thomas Canny, Yates City, Ill.
James Daniels Victoria, Ill.
William Daniels, Knoxville, Ill.
Orange Daniels Elmwood, Ill.
Robert N. Freeborn, East Springfield, O.
Alfred Gardner, Knoxville, Ill.
Jonathan Hogue, Eugene, Ill.
Oloff A. Hunt, Galesburg, Ill.
Joseph Kimler, Eugene, Ill.
John F. Mire, Knoxville, Ill.
Francis McClellan, Galesburg, Ill.
George Owens, Yates City, Ill.
Cornelius Powell, Eugene, Ill.
Harrison Palmer, Knoxville, Ill.
Ira L. Parish, Eugene, Ill—wounded at New Hope Church.
Sidney Rowland, "   "
Charles Selstrom, Galesburg, Ill.
Silas Snider, Knoxville, Ill.
Fitch Shaw, Laharpe, Ill,
James B. Smpkins, Wataga, Ill.
Charles G. Smith, Knoxville, Ill—wounded at Resaca.
Jeremiah D. Shinn, Woodhull, Ill.
Wm. G. Sargeant, Knoxville, Ill—Accidentally wounded at Overall' Creek.

APPENDIX. XIX

Simeon Temple, Truro, Ill.
Thomas Tucker, Eugene, Ill.
Ira E. B. Mott, Prairie City, Ill.

ENLISTED SUBSEQUENT TO ORGANIZATION OF REGIMENT.

Richard F. Mire, Knoxville Ill.
Amos Snider, Galesburg, Ill.
Warren Wolf, Truro, Ill.
William Lemmon, "   "
Thomas Arie, Knoxville, Ill.
Henry Arie,   "   "

DIED.

Serg't Geo. P. Cumming, wounded near Atlanta and killed by R. R. accident, while going home. Serg't Harmon C. Shinn, killed at Peach Tree Creek. Corporal Demetrius H. Baird, killed at Resaca. Corporal Peter F. Dillon, May 27th, 1864, of wounds received at Resaca. Samuel Kight, killed near Peach Tree Creek, by falling tree, while Reg't was building breastworks. Francis Ralph, May 20th, 1864, of wounds received at Resaca. James Elliott, killed at Resaca. James L. Thomas, of disease, at Gallatin. Paul Vanwinkle, of disease, at Bowling Green, Ky. Augustus Johnson, of disease, at Gallatin. William P. Volk, of disease, at Bucyrus, Ohio, while at home on furlough.

DISCHARGED.

Serg't Geo. W. Parker, Corporal Joseph Kasiah, Corporal Stephen D. Cole, Isaac Wilhelm, Frank Barlow, Ira B. Belcher, Thomas B. Farquar, at Gallatin, Tenn. Charles R. Pratt, David M. Patten, Robert B. Cunningham and Joseph W. Gaston, at Lavergne, Tenn. George Miranda, Aug. 26th, 1864, and Nels Truelson, May 31st, 1865, at Quincy, Ill. Obed Brobest, at Jeffersonville, Ind. Harvey Owens, at Louisville, Ky. Charles H. Gordon, at Springfield, Ill., July 5th, 1864. Samuel H. Matthews, at N. Y. City, May 1865.

TRANSFERRED.

Capt. L. D. Shinn, by promotion, to position of Major. Lieut. John Thomas, to Vet. Vol. Eng. Corps. Corporal John B. Shaw, to Non. Com. Staff, as Hospital Steward. Andrew J. Bergquist, to Vet. Vol. Eng. Corps. James Catterton, to Vet. Reserve Corps.

DESERTED.

Richard F. Hammond, at Knoxville, Sept. 17th 1862. Nathan B. Coakley, Oct 28th, 1862, at Bardstown, Ky. Daniel J. Farster, Wm. W. Farster, Joseph A. Light, in 1863, while at home on furlough.

APPENDIX.

ROLL OF COMPANY "I."

LIST OF ORIGINAL MEMBERS DISCHARGD WITH THE REGIMENT.

Brevet Major, Edwin H. Conger, Galesburg, Ill.
1st Lieut. Daniel W. Sheahan, Galva, Ill.
1st Serg't Reuben F. Beals, Oneida, Ill—wounded at Golgotha Church.
Serg't Geo. W. Hall,
  " William H. Brown, " " wounded at Averysboro, March 16th.
  " Peter McCormack, " " wounded near Atlanta.
  " John W. Brinkerhoff, Hackensack, N. J.
Corporal Myrenn Loomis, Galesburg, Ill—wounded near Kenesaw Mountain.
  " Eli S. Ricker, Oneida, Ill.
  " John A. Bulkeley, " "
  " James H. Millen, Abingdon, Ill.
  " Silas A. Duntley, Oneida, Ill—wounded at Averysboro.
  " John Whannell, " " wounded at Resaca.
  " Edwin J. Calkins, " "
  " Amos H. Reynolds, " "
Rodney M. Willis, Musician, Galesburg, Ill.
John Doyle, Wagoner, Woodhull, Ill.

PRIVATES.

James F. Bunnell, Hannah Station, Ind.
David Billington, Oneida, Ill.
Taylor D. Blakley, Yates City, Ill.
James R. Chapman, Big Rock, Iowa.
Geo. F. Duntley, Oneida, Ill.
James H. Davie, Knoxville, Ill—wounded Aug. 8th, near Atlanta.
Thomas Y. Finley, Oneida, Ill.
John S. Fuller, " "
Nathan H. Gallant, " "
John Goodheart, " " wounded at Resaca.
Douglas Howey, Walnut Grove, Ill—wounded near Kenesaw Mountain.
Weymouth Hadley, Oneida, Ill.
Emery C. Humphrey, Wataga, Ill—wounded at Averysboro.
Oloff Hanson, Wataga, Ill—wounded at Resaca.
Wesley L. Kenney, Oneida, Ill.
Ezra Lee, Centre Point, Ill.
William D. Lee, " " wounded at Resaca, 14th.
William H. Merriatt, Virginia City, Cal—wounded at Golgotha Church.
James McKown, Walnut Grove, Ill.
James B. McConchie, Oneida, Ill.
William Mills, Abingdon, Ill.
William Main, Oneida, Ill.
Jesse McQuade, " " wounded in South Carolina, Feb. 28th, 1865.
Thomas Milsom, " "
Rufus H. Moore, Galesburg, Ill.
Lars Olson, " " wounded at Resaca.

APPENDIX. XXI

John H. Ostrom, Woodhull, Ill.
Plummer F. Pierce, Oneida, Ill.
James Powell, Woodhull, Ill.
Oliver F. Pierce, Walnut Grove, Ill—wounded at Resaca, 14th.
Charles H. Robertson, Oneida, Ill.
William I. Reed, " " captured near Louisville, Ga.
James M. Ralston, " "
Theodore M. Rikert, " "
Alfred D. Richards, Knoxville, Ill—wounded at Resaca.
Albert R. Riley, Galesburg, Ill—wounded at Resaca.
Simon Stone, Oneida, Ill.

ENLISTED SUBSEQUENT TO ORGANIZATION OF REGIMENT.

Joseph Kilpatrick, Oneida, Ill—wounded at Resaca.
Peter Olson, Oneida, Ill.

RESIGNED.

Capt. Geo. H. King, at Lavergne, Tenn. 2d Lieut. J. L. Bonnell, at Lavergne, Tenn.

DIED.

Robert Watson, Nov. 15th, 1862, at Frankfort, Ky., of disease. William Kenney, of disease, at Gallatin, Feb. 22d, 1863. John N. Ralston, of disease, at Gallatin, May 23d, 1863. Harvey L. Aiken, of disease, at Stewarts Creek, June 22d, 1863. Corporal William Reynolds, killed at Resaca. Corporal Edward A. Aiken, killed at Resaca. Corporal John Watson, killed at Resaca. Corporal Wm. Olson, of wounds received near Goldsboro, March 16th, 1865. Corporal Cornelius Lott, killed at Averysboro. Herman Swanson, June 20th, 1864, of wounds received at Resaca.

DISCHARGED.

Oliver E. Blossom, Chas. Moore, M. G. Waldron, Alex. M. Sweet, Samuel McConchie, St. Clair Powell and Rufus B. Harmon, at Gallatin, Tenn. Nels Olson, Oct. 1863. Geo. Murray, Oct. 1864, Serenus C. Amend, May 20th, 1865, James Reed and Phillip Humphrey, Jan. 22d, 1863. Andrew Brodine, Jan. 14th, 1865.

TRANSFERRED.

Serg't M. L. Courtney, by promotion to position of 2d Lieut. in Co. A. Serg't Ed. C. Courtney, to Non. Com. Staff. C. C. Fulton, to Co. A. Samuel W. Walker, to Vet. Vol. Eng. Corps. Wm. T. Brennan and Wm. Fuller, to Vet. Reserve Corps.

MISSING.

William O. Jones—disappeared May 16th, 1865, at Chancellersville battleground; was probably killed by guerrillas.

APPENDIX.

ROLL OF COMPANY "K"

LIST OF ORIGINAL MEMBERS DISCHARGED WITH THE REGIMENT.

Capt James Y. Merritt, New Boston, Ill—wounded at Averysboro, N. C.
1st Lieut. J. E. Harroun, Aledo, Ill.
1st Serg't William Winders, Aledo, Ill.
Serg't Alexander Carnahan, " "
" Aaron R. Purdam, New Boston, Ill.
" Leander Officer, Pre-emption, Ill.
" Ambrose H. Rowe, Millersburg, Ill—wounded at Resaca.
Corporal Peter Griffith, Pre-emption, Ill.
" Benj. F. H. Reynolds, Aledo, Ill.
" Reuben Shields, High Point, Ill.
" Jas. E. Gilmore, Aledo, Ill.
" Madison A. Retherford, Ferdinand, Ill—wounded at Resaca.
" Nelson Taylor, Millersburg, Ill.
" Jacob A. Reed, Eliza, Ill.
" James Kiddoo, Keithsburg, Ill.

PRIVATES.

Theophilus L. Ashbaugh, Aledo, Ill.
James L. Brewer, Eliza, Ill.
Thomas J. Beverlin, " "
James N. Barlett, " "
James Clark, Aledo, Ill—wounded near Atlanta.
William Carr, Eliza, Ill.
Eugene Davis, Aledo, Ill.
Henry F. Endicott, New Boston, Ill.
Ezra Fuller, Eliza, Ill—wounded at Resaca.
Harvey J. Fisher, Eliza, Ill—wounded at Averysboro.
Elijah Gardener, Duncan, Ill.
Edwin Gilmore, Aledo, Ill.
Alexander F. Graham, " "
Joel Hill, Oxford, Ill—wounded near Kenesaw Mountain.
John Haverfield, Millersburg, Ill.
Jacob W. Kelley, Aledo, Ill—wounded at New Hope, Church.
James Mays, Millersburg, Ill.
Oliver Mays, " "
David W. McKee, Aledo, Ill.
Geo. H. Mills, " "
Daniel McEowen, " " captured at Goldsboro—exchanged.
John A. Ramsey, " "
Joshua Spicher, Eliza, Ill.
John J. Swartz, Aledo, Ill—wounded at Resaca.
William Sabins, New Boston, Ill.
James M. Shingledecker, Millersburg, Ill.
Isaac Thompson, New Boston, Ill.
William Valentine, Aledo, Ill.
James R. Wood, Eliza, Ill.
Laughlin H. Woodward, New Boston, Ill.
Philip Walston, Duncan, Ill.

APPENDIX.   XXIII

William H. Woodward, Aledo, Ill.
Henry R. Wells,   "   " wounded at Resaca and again at Lawtonville, S. C.
Lewis Welty, New Boston, Ill.
Chester S. Willits, Duncan, Ill.

ENLISTED SUBSEQUENT TO ORGANIZATION OF REGIMENT.

Arthur R. Agy, New Boston, Ill—wounded at Averysboro.
Robert Boyle, Millersburg, Ill.
Melville Danford, New Boston, Ill.
William Danford,   "   "
Pyrrhus Glancy,   "   "
Sylvanus Hersom,   "   "
Isaac Spicher,   "   "
John C. Summers, Millersburg, Ill.
Perry Thompson, New Boston, Ill.

RESIGNED.

Capt. Sanderson H. Rodgers, at Gallatin, Tenn. Capt. Wm. A. Wilson, Oct. 26th, 1864. 2d Lieut., Van Willits, Nov. 17th, 1862. 2d Lieut. Samuel E. Willits, Jan. 21st 1865.

DIED.

Corporal Allen Wilson, of disease, March 3d, 1862. Corporal Waters P. Willit, killed at Resaca. Corporal Isaac N. Stevenson, killed at New Hope Church. Michael Bryant, of disease, Dec. 16th, 1862. Geo. W. Barlett, May 18th, 1864, of wounds received at Resaca. Abram Fuller, Feb. 8th, 1863. James P. Collier, of disease, Dec. 4th, 1862. Madison Dagger, Feb. 23d, 1863, of disease. Thomas H. Hand, of disease, March 12th, 1863. James P. Hampton, of disease, June 10th, 1863. Samuel D. Hutchinson, killed at Averysboro, N. C. William H. Hampton, March 23d, 1865, of wounds received near Bentonville. Albert Kiddoo, Nov. 10th, 1864, of wounds received July 20th, 1864, at Peach Tree Creek. Peter O. Pierce, May 17th, 1864, of wounds received at Resaca. Jacob Shields, of disease, Jan. 16th, 1863. Noah Spicher, of disease, Oct. 17th, 1863. Marvin R. Wright, of disease, Feb. 3d, 1863. Moses White, jr., killed at Resaca.

DISCHARGED.

Serg't John M. Miller, Jan. 15th, 1862. 1st Serg't John G. McGuffin, Oct. 1864. Serg't L. V. Willits, Feb. 20th, 1864, on account of wounds received near Chattanooga. Serg't Jesse E. Huston, Dec. 21st, 1862, to accept Com. as Chaplain. Corporal Eli Cook, Jan. 13th, 1863. Edwin R. Dulin, Jan. 13th, 1863. Otis Albee, March 29th, 1865, was wounded at Resaca, May 15th, 1864. Francis M. Beverlin, Jan. 15th, 1863. James H. Crane and John Downing, Jan. 1863. Robert H. Day, Jan. 13th, 1863. Joseph J. Delebar, Jan. 13th, 1863. Henry T. Davis, Jan. 1864. David H. Edgar, Andrew J. Foote, Robert N. Gilmore, Daniel Knapp, John Kiddoo, John H. Murfin, James McIntyre, during month of Jan. 1863. Franklin

APPENDIX.

Ferguson and Samuel M. Smith, March, 1863. Dewit C. Updike and James M. Wilson, Feb., 1863. John J. Meyers, [April, 1865, on account of wounds recieved near Keneraw Mountain. Levi Walston, March, 1864.

TRANSFERRED.

Walter Smethers, Geo. Braucht, Henry Smethers and Abraham Spicher, to Vet. Vol. Eng. Corps, Aug., 1864. Eli C. Crossley, to Miss. Marine Brigade, Jan., 1863.

NOTE :—When the Regiment was discharged the "Recruits" were transferred to the 16th Ill. Vet. Vol.

www.ingramcontent.com/pod-product-compliance
Lightning Source LLC
Chambersburg PA
CBHW020816230426
43666CB00007B/1035